The New Accountability:
Environmental Responsibility
Across Borders

The New Accountability:
Environmental Responsibility
Across Borders

Michael R Mason

London • Sterling, VA

First published by Earthscan in the UK and USA in 2005

ISBN: 1-84407-067 paperback
      1-84407-066-2 hardback

Typesetting by TW Typesetting, Plymouth, Devon
Printed and bound in the UK by Cromwell Press Ltd, Trowbridge
Cover design by Yvonne Booth

For a full list of publications please contact:

Earthscan
8–12 Camden High Street
London, NW1 0JH, UK
Tel: +44 (0)20 7387 8558
Fax: +44 (0)20 7387 8998
Email: earthinfo@earthscan.co.uk
Web: **www.earthscan.co.uk**

22883 Quicksilver Drive, Sterling, VA 20166-2012, USA

Earthscan is an imprint of James and James (Science Publishers) Ltd and publishes in association
with the International Institute for Environment and Development

A catalogue record for this book is available from the British Library

Library of Congress Cataloging-in-Publication Data

Mason, Michael, 1966–
    The New Accountability: environmental responsibility across borders. Michael R. Mason
      p. cm.
    Includes bibliographical references and index
    ISBN 1-84407-067-0 (pbk) – ISBN 1-84407-066-2 (hardback)
      1. Environmental protection–International cooperation. 2. Environmental
policy–International cooperation. 3. Environmental responsibility. I. Title.

    JZ1324.M37 2005
    333.7–dc22

                        2004024814

Printed on elemental chlorine-free paper

For Witchuda Damnoenyut

Contents

Preface

In contemporary debates about democratic governance, the concept of accountability is hard to avoid. At least from a European perspective, recent innovations in political and administrative decision-making have multiplied opportunities for citizens to hold to account those who exercise governmental authority. Or so we are told. Whether busy modernizing constitutional structures or realigning public services along market-led lines, our political representatives have proclaimed a new era of open and responsive government. Accountability, in these terms, denotes enhanced processes of public oversight and answerability for decision-making involving political authority. In practice it has seen the emergence of an audit culture in which administrative efficiency and service delivery targets are paramount – where citizens become clients and public officials become managers. Nevertheless, it has not been easy to shake off the core political dimension of accountability – that decisions made in our name can be discussed and challenged.

As I write this preface in London, as arguments persist about the legal basis on which my country went to war in Iraq, and as civilian and military casualties rise further, the UK Government mantra of policy transparency sounds particularly hollow. When the United Nations Secretary General Kofi Annan states that the invasion of Iraq was not in conformity with the United Nations Charter, I am expecting something more from my government than the giving of (shifting) reasons, something more than a series of quasi-judicial reviews blunted in their mandates and powers. Actions taking place in the name of the British people are profoundly altering the lives and living conditions of countless others. And these actions are claimed by the UK and US administrations to be motivated, as least in part, by their desire to introduce to Iraq a constitutional system subscribing to principles of democratic accountability. By ignoring international legal constraints on the use of military force and domestically curtailing civil liberties, these governments have exposed how fragile webs of accountability can be. Moreover, the intimate involvement of major transnational companies (such as Bechtel and Halliburton) in the decisions moulding the future of Iraq has also shown how arbitrary it is to exclude private corporations from issues of accountability to affected publics.

This book is preoccupied with overcoming the tendency to think about accountability as only taking place within state borders and only featuring governmental actors. Looking above all at transboundary flows of pollution, its central claim is that processes of public answerability for harm rest most justly on treating all victims (real or potential) with equal respect. That means that both state and non-state producers of significant harm have a moral obligation effectively to consider the interests of all affected parties, whether these parties are fellow co-nationals or foreigners. In the study I employ a non-territorial notion of the 'public' to break away from the idea that we need only worry about the harm we cause to those immediately around us (both in space and time). Environmental responsibility – that is, accountability claims entailing claims to redress as well as answerability – should be established in open public discussions about harm and risk, where affected publics become collectively aware of harm received as being attributable to particular decisions or policies. The question of redress, of effective regulatory controls, is crucial to realizing what I label this new (non-territorial) accountability. And in the book I try and show how new accountability norms are informing the campaigning of transnational activist networks and also starting to feature in international environmental regimes. These accountability norms feed into, and are bolstered by, transnational spaces of public communication. In mapping out shared pathways of social and ecological harm, transnational publics cannot avoid thinking about alternative futures.

I want to thank all those who have helped shape my thoughts on these issues, however much this book falls short of the understanding they would likely have forged tackling the same subject matter. At the London School of Economics I have learnt much from discussions and seminars with colleagues in the Department of Geography and Environment, notably my 'environment cluster' colleagues – Giles Atkinson, Andy Gouldson, David Jones, Eric Neumayer, Tim Rayner, Judith Rees and Yvonne Rydin. I am much indebted to the Earthscan referees who took time to offer careful, considered feedback on earlier versions of this manuscript. Various parts of the book have also benefited from the comments and suggestions of Andy Dobson, Andrew Linklater, Bryan Norton, Richard Perkins and Derek Wall: my thanks to them all. Chapter 4 features research funded by the British Academy under grant number SG-34522 (2002–3): I acknowledge their valued support. Several chapters have been reworked and revised from arguments first put forward in academic articles: for Chapter 1 this was a paper published in *Transactions of the Institute of British Geographers* (2001), Vol 26, No 4, pp407–29; for Chapter 4 this was a paper published in *Environmental Politics* (2004), Vol 13, No 3, pp566–89; and for Chapter 5 this was an article that appeared in *Marine Policy* (2003), Vol 21, No 2, pp77–98. I'm happy to acknowledge Blackwell Publications, Taylor & Francis and Pergamon Press as the publishers of these papers. Also, I thank Professor Roger Kasperson for allowing me to reproduce the transboundary risk classification figure in the Introduction: the work of

Jeanne and Roger Kasperson rightly holds a leading position in the field of environmental risk management. Lastly, and by no means least, I would like to thank Bill and Michelle Antrobus for so ably transforming my manuscript into this book.

Michael Mason, November 2004.

Figure and Tables

Figure

Tables

Acronyms and Abbreviations

BP	British Petroleum
CAFOD	Catholic Fund for Overseas Development
CERES	Coalition for Environmentally Responsible Economies
CITES	Convention on International Trade in Endangered Species of Wild Fauna and Flora
CLC	International Convention on Civil Liability for Oil Pollution Damage
CTE	Committee on Trade and Environment
DSB	Dispute Settlement Body
EC	European Community
ECE	Economic Commission for Europe
ECOSOC	Economic and Social Council
EEZ	exclusive economic zone
EMAS	Eco-Management and Audit Scheme
EMS	environmental management system
EU	European Union
FDI	foreign direct investment
FOEI	Friends of the Earth International
G7	Group of Seven
G8	Group of Eight
GATT	General Agreement on Tariffs and Trade
GRI	Global Reporting Initiative
ICC	Inter-continental Caravan for Solidarity and Resistance
ILC	International Law Commission
IMF	International Monetary Fund
IMO	International Maritime Organization
INGO	international nongovernmental organization
ISO	International Standards Organization
IOPC	International Oil Pollution Compensation Fund
ITOPF	International Tanker Owners Pollution Federation Limited
IUCN	World Conservation Union
LOS	Law of the Sea

MARPOL	International Convention for the Prevention of Pollution from Ships
MEA	multilateral environmental agreement
NATO	North Atlantic Treaty Organization
NGLS	Non-Governmental Liaison Service
NGO	nongovernmental organization
OECD	Organization for Economic Cooperation and Development
OPA	Oil Pollution Act
PGA	People's Global Action Against Free Trade
PSSA	Particularly Sensitive Sea Area
SPS	Agreement on the Application of Sanitary and Phytosanitary Measures
SRI	socially responsible investing
TBT	Agreement on Technical Barriers to Trade
TNC	transnational corporation
TRIPS	Trade-Related Aspects of Intellectual Property Rights
UK	United Kingdom
UN	United Nations
UNCED	United Nations Conference on Environment and Development
UNCTAD	United Nations Conference on Trade and Development
UNEP	United Nations Environment Programme
UNCTC	United Nations Centre on Transnational Corporations
US	United States
USSR	Union of Soviet Socialist Republics
WB	World Bank
WBCSD	World Business Council for Sustainable Development
WWF	Worldwide Fund for Nature
WTO	World Trade Organization

Introduction

One of the most influential frames of reference offered in recent years to capture the core challenges facing us in the twenty-first century is the notion of a world risk society. Associated above all with the work of the sociologists, Ulrich Beck (1992, 1999) and Anthony Giddens (2000), a central claim of this model is that contemporary societies across the globe are united in their exposure to (largely unintended) physical threats arising from the far-reaching transformation of material environments and organisms by industrial technologies. More precisely, they contend that these threats are not only unprecedented in their worldwide scope, they also present novel dangers due to the uncertainties of 'manufactured' environmental change. Obvious examples here include the extensive but locally indeterminate impact of rising anthropogenic greenhouse gas emissions, the depletion of global biodiversity, the (potential) use of biological, chemical or nuclear weapons, and the dissemination of genetically modified organisms.

Such threats test severely the traditional expectation within Western societies that we can, with some confidence, assess the possibility of injury and loss from anticipated dangers – the conjunction of impact and probability defining the very notion of risk. However, these dangers have historically been localized and tangible – flooding, fire-damage, smog-related ailments, and so on. The world risk society is instead crosscut by transnational and global threats separated in space–time from their sources, sometimes synergistically combining, and portending irreversible effects. Furthermore, heightened social awareness of global environmental risk is both dependent on experts to identify the often invisible parameters of danger, and also rendered insecure by dramatic examples of the limitations of that expertise. Beck and Giddens both emphasize how the active *construction* of global risk through scientific and technological knowledge has become politicized: which competing claims should we believe on risk? Which decision-making authorities can be trusted? To whom can we attribute responsibility for (potential) harm?

The question of responsibility to affected parties for actions generating transnational and global environmental threats is at the heart of this book. According to Beck, a governing logic of the world risk society is 'organized irresponsibility' (1999: pp54–8): the difficulties in attributing causes and consequences to actors for catastrophic risks overwhelm conventional risk-assessment capacities and regulatory systems. Political and legal rules of accountability demanding clear pathways of causation and damage founder on complex, collective dangers. Those affected by the incidence or threat of significant harm to human health and ecological sustainability commonly face, it is argued, an onerous burden of proof; first to identify a responsible agent and, second, to express their interests as a form of present or future economic loss understandable to decision-makers.

Like many of the bold generalizations informing the world risk society model, the idea of organized irresponsibility deserves systematic analysis. My contention in this work is that there is indeed an 'accountability deficit' in relation to growing transnational and global hazards. This is evident, above all, in the *spatial mismatch* between national territories of governmental responsi-bility and transboundary pathways of (potential) harm: the interests of those exposed to environmental dangers often do not correspond with state and corporate priorities. Nevertheless, I claim that there is an emerging set of norms and rules promoting democratic accountability for transnational harm. These transnational obligations constitute what I term a 'new accountability' – modes of moral and legal responsibility owed by state and non-state producers of significant transboundary risk effectively to consider the interests of non-national affected parties. It is, I will show, a responsibility both called for by various nongovernmental activist networks and one also acquiring legal weight within international regimes of harm prevention and liability. In this Introduction I set out briefly the global context of the question of transboundary environmental responsibility, indicating why this prompts us to recast established notions of democratic accountability and risk management.

Environmental globalization and democratic accountability norms

For the proponents of the world risk society notion, the hazards produced by advanced industrialization possess an inherent tendency toward globalization – they are physical impacts of an intensified transnational connectedness involving a range of social, political and ecological forces. Globalization of environmental risk is therefore seen as bound up with wider transformations of modern life, taking in the creation of a world capitalist economy, the changing role of nation-states, the global diffusion of military power, and the invasive reach of machine technologies. Needless to say, social scientists have argued at length about the significance of the various dimensions of globalization, including whether the term itself actually advances understand-ing of the contemporary world. There seems, at least, to be a widespread acknowledgement that information and communications technologies have facilitated the 'rescaling' of social relationships, such that transnational information networks influence increasingly the experience, value and scope of local events. Depending on access to, and involvement in, global networks of economic and political power, local activities are deemed profitable or loss-making, with or without authoritative force, culturally significant or irrelevant, and so on (Castells, 1996: pp376–418).

No dimension of globalization exhibits the physical consequences of this rescaling more vividly than the transformation of socio-ecological systems: the globalization of environmental degradation – through transboundary pollution, increasing ecological interdependence and the economic pressures on the global commons – has exposed the negative effects of actors displacing environmental costs across or beyond national borders and onto future generations. Above all, this 'globalization of side effects' (Mol, 2001: pp71–93) is linked to lengthening chains of capitalist production and consumption, with their substantial transboundary flows of matter and energy. The new pathways of actual and potential harm have, at least initially in Western societies, sparked regional institutional reforms and raised expectations that responsibility for the condition of the biosphere should become more of a focus for international governance regimes. The overarching moral obligation here, justifiable at minimum by a simple imperative of life support, is that producers of harm affecting vital human and ecological interests should be required to defer to those interests. Yet, production and consumption impacts are becoming spatially detached from national legal-regulatory activities – responsible actions may well be distant and diffuse in space–time. What challenges does this present to prevailing accountability norms in liberal democracies?

In the first place, the very notion of political accountability has become *unsettled by shifts in the nature of governance*. Accountability, as traditionally understood in liberal democratic societies, denotes modalities of oversight and constraint on the exercise of state power (Flinders, 2001: pp9–15). It refers to the capacity of citizens to keep in check those who possess public authority through mechanisms compelling these office-holders to give reasons for their actions and, when performance is deemed unsatisfactory, to sanction them by media-enabled protest, legal challenges or, more routinely, the withdrawal of electoral support for the governing party. Now, this dual function of political accountability – answerability and redress – has become clouded by the emergence of decision-making arenas where (sub)national political authorities are increasingly interacting with each other and a wide range of non-state actors. Cross-border environmental harm arising from economic transactions has prompted numerous regulatory efforts, but the sheer diversity and complexity of these (generally issue-specific) policy responses has often made it difficult to determine who is responsible for what to whom. As Newell and Bellour (2002) demonstrate in the development field, the growing role of corporations and nongovernmental organizations (NGOs) in delivering public goods in multiple and overlapping jurisdictions has heightened the indeterminacy of political accountability. Significant, often contested, changes in the relative power of state and non-state actors suggest the urgent need to map out anew the lines of responsibility between the authors and addressees of policy decisions.

Secondly, new environmental risks expose the *reactive scope* of political accountability as conventionally understood. In principle, accountability measures should allow citizens to monitor the exercise of public authority in all policy arenas. As John Dunn (1999) observes, though, such is the opacity of most governmental decision-making, that citizens face major informational obstacles in seeking accountability for specific actions. To uncover political complicity in the production of environmental (and other) hazards in particular, affected parties will struggle to identify culpability when the negative consequences arise from economic processes or activities routinely authorized by the state. Investigating expert-based systems of regulatory approval, including their risk-management procedures, presumes a technical competence beyond the ability of most citizens. Not surprisingly then, democratic political accountability becomes more an exercise in assessment and attribution of responsibility *after* damage has taken place, impacting on ordinary life experiences (for example, water or food contamination, the loss of a valued ecosystem). Only then is the policy perhaps altered, the bureaucracy realigned. Of course, as the world risk society theorists caution, we are faced with the possibilities of catastrophic and irreversible harm, which render even more problematic this backward-facing character of political accountability.

Informational obstacles are compounded when, as with many environmental hazards, the distance between responsible actions and threats stretches across national borders. Moreover, even assuming that sources can be pinpointed, those affected often lack the means directly to sanction the political office-holders in the source country. Given that democratic political accountability is tied to the sovereign authority of states, cross-border environmental degradation has, thirdly, triggered an *erosion of the legitimacy of state-based accountability*. Transnational and global ecological risks undermine the credibility of state authority: governments are often unable to prevent externally generated threats to the well-being of their populations, while their diplomatic efforts to hold responsible actors to account through international treaties often falter against competing geopolitical interests and disincentives to unilateral action for collective environmental problems. This 'protection failure' (Jones, 1999: pp217–22) should not be equated with an inexorable decline in state sovereignty: as the case studies in this book illustrate, emerging norms of transnational accountability for environmental harm include new state capacities and responsibilities. However, it does highlight the challenge to the traditional containment of political accountability within domestic borders when, in order to address cross-border threats, states now have to negotiate and share authority with international institutions.

The implication here is the need, fourthly, to *move beyond territorial norms of responsibility*. Democratic political accountability normally presumes a territorial congruence between producers of harm, affected parties and regulatory authorities. Indeed, this rests on the traditional association of political identity with membership of a community territorially defined by the state. For the liberal democracies this has historically been accomplished by the construction of national identities: to have been outside such a community – as a non-national or a distant stranger – is typically to have been accorded little if any legal standing, even as the recipient of harm generated by individuals from that nation-state. Increasing transnational environmental harm reveals the moral injustice of locating accountability duties only among co-nationals. Beck (1999: p16) suggests political responsibility for global risk as a cultural basis for the creation of 'non-territorial' communities of shared risk, but offers little elaboration. We can nevertheless identify the emergence of such cosmopolitan norms of accountability within the human rights field, where international duties of criminal and non-criminal responsibility for human rights abuses are designed to promote redress for victims whatever the nationality of the offender (Ratner, 2000). These are supplemented by informal norms of answerability provided by such transnational civil society actors as Amnesty International and Human Rights Watch. In this volume I argue that there is a necessary role for human rights duties in developing accountability norms for transnational environmental hazards.

Lastly, globalization of environmental risk exposes the shortcomings of *democratic accountability norms detached from economic institutions*. The global spread of capitalist market relationships attests to the dominance of organizational forms centred on private ownership of the means of production. Neoliberal arguments, evident in rule-making and arbitration for world trade and investment, maintain that the vigorous defence of private property rights and investment freedoms underpins the welfare gains of economic globalization. Yet although new trajectories of environmental harm are being produced, these claims uphold the traditional liberal democratic principle that business organizations should not routinely be required to account for the negative impacts of their activities on non-shareholder interests. The history of the company form in advanced capitalist countries indicates only limited progress made by unions, interest groups and others in breaching this corporate immunity to public scrutiny. Where regulation has been socially acceptable and politically feasible, this has tended to relate to the negative domestic impacts of businesses in their home countries, rather than the harmful consequences of their production, trade and investment activities overseas. Since the 1990s, pressure has mounted for companies to account for their social and environmental performance in all operating regions (Warren, 2000: pp94–109). So far, new norms of corporate environmental responsibility have been largely confined to voluntary reporting initiatives: however, as shown in Chapter 6, some political and legal inroads have been made by civil society actors in holding corporations to account for the consequences of their actions in other countries.

In so far as democratic accountability in liberal societies is ultimately addressed to a 'public', it is clear that the five points above unsettle the cardinal organizing principle that members of local and national communities suffering the incidence or threat of significant harm can effectively seek redress through – and against – their political representatives. It becomes apparent to individuals and groups exposed to transnational environmental hazards that these representatives frequently have difficulty even in identifying responsible agents across borders, let alone securing appropriate mitigation and/or compensation. This weakens the moral justification that a democratic government has authority to govern through its exclusive capacity to act in the public interest. Indeed, central to the concept of new accountability is the recognition of transnational publics, composed of individuals who may not necessarily be co-nationals or, indeed, have any contact with one another. Their collective bond arises from the joint exposure to current or threatened environmental harm as consequences caused by the activities of others across political borders, and their common interest is in regulating those activities.

Transboundary environmental risk: rescaling assessment and management

The capacity of affected publics to hold actors accountable for environmental hazards rests on their involvement in open risk communication and the effective incorporation of their interests by those with relevant decision-making authority. It has become widely acknowledged by environmental scientists, though, that this requires a shift from conventional risk assessment and management techniques, where expert-led technical appraisals on the probability of adverse impacts directly feed into top-down regulatory controls. Here, the inclusion of (sub)national publics has routinely consisted of no more that the provision of factual evidence and predictions, often leaving unresolved concerns about institutional performance or value disagreements (Renn and Klinke, 2001: pp247–9). For transnational and global environmental risk, such concerns may well be accentuated: the lack of effective governance regimes highlights the challenge of institutional competence (e.g. for addressing global climate change), while conflicting values and interests are particularly evident where affected parties reside in different jurisdictions from the beneficiaries of activities producing harm (e.g. transboundary air pollution). In these circumstances, it is not surprising that demands for the representation of affected publics are being heard in various arenas for transboundary risk management.

The categories of transboundary risk set out by Jeanne and Roger Kasperson (2001a) provide a valuable starting point for distinguishing transnational and global affected publics. Within the overarching class of cross-national risks 'that arise when human activities in one or more nation-states threaten current or future environmental quality, human health, or well-being in at least one other nation-state' (p 213), their fourfold classification (Figure 1) explicitly incorporates social and economic attributes of risk production and reception (pp 213–16):

- *Type 1, border-impact risks* involve economic and industrial activities in a border region that affect human populations or ecosystems in the border area on both sides of the political boundary. Typical of this type of risk, they claim, is the Gabcikovo-Nagymaros hydroelectric power scheme impacting a stretch of the Danube River from Slovakia into Hungary: here a protracted dispute between the two countries has centred on the Hungarian concerns about the negative economic and environmental consequences of decreased water supplies.
- *Type 2, point-source transboundary risks* involve one or several clear point sources of potential pollution and accident-related discharges threatening at least one adjoining country or region. Emissions of sulphur dioxide and nitrogen oxides travelling from industrial point sources in the UK and being received as acidifying rain in Scandinavian countries is a familiar example of such transboundary pollution, while the Chernobyl nuclear accident in 1986 exemplifies the incidence of a high-consequence or catastrophic risk event.
- *Type 3, structural/policy transboundary risks* comprise less identifiable and more diffuse pathways of harm *associated* with state policies or the structure of the economy. The pervasiveness of risks in this class is often concealed by their embeddedness in routine systems of transportation, energy use, food consumption and so on. As evident in transnational public anxiety about nuclear waste generation and genetically modified crops, the risks triggered by policy decisions can be challenged. However, the health and environmental ill-effects arising from entrenched policies and economic structures may not be evident in everyday choices even though their cumulative impact can be significant (e.g. respiratory problems aggravated by vehicle emissions, tropical deforestation advanced by land clearances, contaminated beef caused by industrialized agriculture).
- *Type 4, global environmental risks* involve human activities in any given region or country, or set of regions and countries, that register their effects on other areas through changes to globally functioning biogeochemical systems. As the core example of greenhouse gas emissions illustrates, this risk class presents particular difficulties in predicting environmental impacts and has raised strong international disagreements over apportioning responsibility for harm production.

The above classification moves beyond mainstream technical framings of transboundary risks, making conceptual space for the social and political

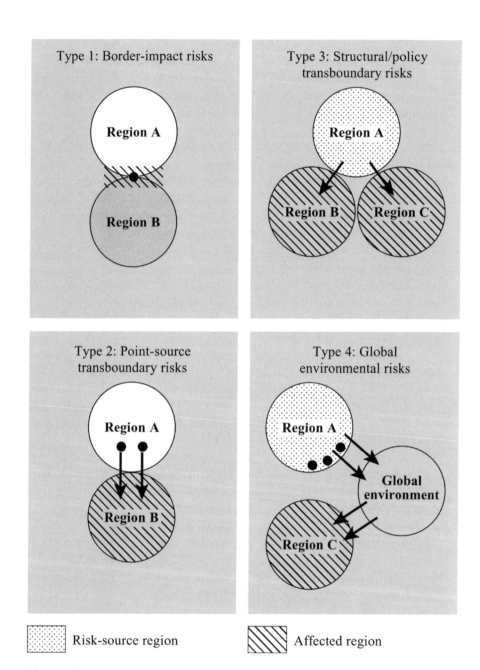

(*Source:* Kasperson and Kasperson 2001a: p214)

Figure 1 *A fourfold classification of transboundary risk*

analysis of risk assessment and management. A key thesis advanced by Kasperson and Kasperson is that risk events 'interact with psychological, social, institutional, and cultural processes in ways that can heighten or dampen perceptions of risk and shape the risk behaviour of institutions, groups, and individual people' (2001a: p217). In other words, the experience of biophysical threats of harm is always mediated by social contexts of communication. *Risk amplification* denotes the social intensification of risk signals, whereby various actors, facilitated by favourable cultural, organizational and institutional tendencies, escalate collective concern about potential harm, creating political pressure for risk reduction (e.g. the activities of environmental interest groups). On the other hand, there are also cultural and social propensities allowing certain actors (for whatever reasons) to dilute disquiet about apparent sources or pathways of biophysical harm – this *risk attenuation* serving politically to stall or block regulatory efforts (e.g. the efforts of the industry-led Global Climate Coalition in opposing the Kyoto Protocol on greenhouse gas emissions). For transboundary risks, the claim is that the potential for social amplification or attenuation is heightened by geographical divergences in interests and responsibilities. In a risk–source region, material benefits from productive and consumptive activities generating the threat or incidence of harm across borders are likely to favour social attenuation processes, while in the risk–consequence region(s), the involuntary receipt of risks, divorced from any benefits, is likely to promote social amplification. Kasperson and Kasperson caution that this geopolitical asymmetry in risk communication can be deepened further if the risk–source country and the recipient country share overlays of past conflicts, cultural difference and ongoing distrust (2001a: p211).

The spatio-temporal location of those persons directly affected by transboundary risk and risk events is a crucial determinant in the scope for social amplification and attenuation. A preliminary differentiation of affected publics may be mapped onto the fourfold classification of transboundary risk (2001a: pp234–9):

- Border-impact risks typically have near-term, biophysical impacts concentrated among border inhabitants, with more diffuse extra-regional consequences. Cultural and political differences across jurisdictional boundaries may be exploited in the recipient country by those linking the interests of the directly affected parties to national political agendas, amplifying the perception of threat.
- For point-source transboundary risks, normally it is possible to locate pathways of (potential) harm issuing from discrete sources, enabling at least the identification of proximate affected publics, with other effects rippling out less clearly. Assessment and management are aided by the pronounced risk profile here, although political disputes can still arise from divergent national perceptions of respective costs and benefits.

- The affected publics of structural/policy transboundary risks are widely dispersed within the risk-source country and surrounding border states, extending also through time to future generations for such long-term threats as those posed by nuclear energy and some genetically modified organisms. Construction of a transnational public interest in regulation of these risks faces a significant geopolitical hurdle in the attenuation practices of governments and corporate elites.
- Global environmental risks entail the most diffuse affected publics: the causal links between scattered risk sources and planetary-wide affected parties are remote in space and time. Given the scientific complexities involved in attempting to map pathways of present or future harm in this risk class, social amplification and attenuation processes feed on competing expert interpretations as well as more general differences in societal values.

The acknowledgment of these transnational affected publics requires risk assessment and management explicitly to address the multi-scale effects of human-induced environmental change. For transboundary risk assessment, already attuned to interdisciplinary work on planetary impacts (e.g. global climate change models), the lack of regional or local specificity on ecological and social consequences has been flagged up as a major deficiency for decision-makers (Cash and Moser, 2000: pp112–13). A number of scientific programmes have been established to tackle this shortcoming in environmental risk research: launched in 2001 by a partnership of intergovernmental and nongovernmental organizations, the Millennium Ecosystem Assessment represents perhaps the most ambitious recent programme globally to coordinate multi-scale studies on the consequences of environmental change on human well-being and ecosystem services (www.millenniumecosystem.org). An explicit objective is to establish interlinked assessments where local ways of knowing feed into, and are enriched by, non-local scientific appraisals. This participatory approach to knowledge – targeting in the first-phase (2001–2004) impacts of biodiversity loss, wetlands use and desertification – is in line with calls for a 'sustainability science' (Kates et al, 2001) aiming to integrate plural methodologies and understandings in the investigation of multi-scale nature–society interactions. Included here are, it is claimed, the needs interpretations of affected publics. Where the proponents of sustainability science press further, converging with the world risk society theorists, is for increased research on the social and political processes shaping human environmental transformations across the planet.

Rescaling risk assessment to meet the challenge of transboundary environmental problems necessarily implies that the information generated for decision-makers integrates the negative effects of socio-ecological processes on affected parties within and across jurisdictions. An emerging framework open to this task is adaptive environmental management, preoccupied with the participatory design and implementation of policy for environmental sustainability. The literature on adaptive management has employed the term 'panarchies' to represent the cross–scale effects of environmental degradation caused by human influences (Gunderson et al, 1995; Holling et al, 1998). Panarchical relationships suggest dynamic temporalities and spatialities of environmental change which, by no means absent from natural evolutionary cycles, are nevertheless scaled up by the socio–economic forces of globalization, extending and intensifying transboundary risks. The adaptive management perspective exposes in particular the adverse ecological consequences of technocentric resource extraction and management practices, which are predicated on short-term yield maximization and drastic biophysical simplification. Of crucial relevance for transboundary risk regulation, adaptive management recognizes numerous non–linear feedbacks in biophysical systems, such that the cross–scale effects of human interventions are often uncertain and unpredictable. Given these circumstances, adaptive management proponents advocate incorporating affected publics – and other stakeholders – in ongoing forms of policy experimentation. This is designed to elicit open communication on participants' values and preferences, rooting management proposals in a democratic problem-solving discourse.

In its implications for transboundary risk governance, the participatory ethos shared by sustainability science and adaptive management uncovers entrenched inequities of risk reception across the world – the question of *differential vulnerability* of affected publics; that is, the susceptibility of their lives and livelihoods to harm (Blaikie et al, 1994). For example, Kasperson et al (2001: pp263–71) note the various distributional burdens faced by impoverished, ecologically marginal populations as a consequence of past and present fossil fuel emissions by the advanced industrialized countries. From this perspective, the social and ecological conditions of risk bearers are as important as the physical threats they face in determining potential impacts on their well-being. Moreover, the environmental burdens on the most vulnerable are often compounded by wider, enduring inequities in development possibilities and life opportunities. As publics affected by particular transboundary threats, their interests are typically unrepresented or passed over in relevant political and economic decision-making. Democratic accountability for transboundary risk production is rendered more complex – and politically far-reaching – by these considerations: it points in principle beyond individual or group responsibility for discrete acts of (potential) harm production to encompass also the systemic accountability of public and private institutions for producing environmental change and conditions of vulnerability.

The new accountability: the structure of the book

Observing widespread and growing demands for citizen involvement in transboundary risk management, Renn and Klinke (2001: p271) nevertheless note that 'the general public as a nongovernmental actor in foreign policy-making has been rather neglected in theoretical studies on international policy-making as well as in practice'. The common coupling of publics to national political communities has prevented an appreciation of expressions of well-being not mediated by states. Nowhere is this more apparent than those instances in which a collective group shares an involuntary fate as recipients of transboundary exposure to current or potential environmental harm. Detached geographically from the territorial jurisdiction in which the material activities producing the risk arise, these affected parties are effectively disenfranchised, as non-nationals, from appealing to the relevant rules of responsibility within that state – rules that, were the harm to be received domestically, typically enable aggrieved citizens in liberal democracies to seek redress.

In this book I elaborate on, and employ, a non-national notion of the public in order to capture the distinctive domain of collective interest-formation constituted by those facing transnational environmental threats. As set out in Chapter 1, the 'public' encompasses all those affected by the indirect consequences of material transactions – consequences generated by activities that, having a significant impact on a group not immediately involved in them, are perceived by the latter as adversely affecting their interests and therefore in need of regulation. This concept of the public draws on the formulation of pragmatist philosopher John Dewey (1954): its orientation to joint problem-solving in a world of growing cross-border consequences accords with our central theme. Dewey's account makes clear that state institutions are responsible for the general regulation of indirect consequences, recognizing, however, that this presents a demanding challenge when the effects are transnational and inter-state regulation is needed. It falls to the respective publics associated with particular transboundary consequences to press for that international cooperation: relevant questions here, as articulated by Cochran (1998: pp267–71), include the conditions by which such affected publics will know themselves as publics, their relationships across issue areas, and of course the nature of their impact on international policy-making.

In Chapter 1 I argue that the notion of affected publics provides the basis for a new understanding of democratic accountability for transboundary harm production. The central claim is that there are no compelling moral reasons why the accountability norms of inclusiveness and equal consideration of interests commonly recognized within liberal democratic states should not be extended to non-national publics affected by cross-border environmental harm. If we accept that, at least in these cases, responsible agents should be answerable to more than co-nationals, then an equitable framework would pull in all affected parties. Rather than territorial (state-centred) terms of reference, the geographical scope of this responsibility is set in principle by open and inclusive public discourse on the perceived harm or risk. Democratic accountability is advanced in so far as producers of harm can be called upon to justify their actions to affected parties and can be sanctioned in some way for failing to prevent harm across borders received involuntarily. For reasons given in Chapter 1, where the interests of individuals or groups affected by transboundary harm are deemed to be vital (e.g. provision of clean air and water), there is a strong argument for buttressing accountability rules with human rights considerations.

Civil society actors are at the forefront of efforts across the world to redefine democratic accountability norms in favour of transboundary publics. Chapter 2 addresses these advocates for the new accountability, focusing on environmental NGOs and coalition movements. Whether as high-profile groups (e.g. Greenpeace International, Friends of the Earth International, World Wide Fund for Nature) or through advocacy networks (e.g. Third World Network, International Forum on Globalization, Rainforest Action Network), environmentalists have become increasingly adept at monitoring and scrutinizing the ecological footprint of state authorities and private companies, bearing dramatic witness to space–time pathways of environmental harm and seeking explanations from those responsible. Since the mid-1980s, transnational forms of environmentalist mobilization have taken advantage of growing constituent organizations, communications technologies and new channels of influence to enlarge also their repertoire of sanctions – political lobbying, direct action protests, consumer boycotts and so on. However, these activities are by no means uncontested: as I discuss, environmentalist networks face interrogation themselves about the legitimacy of their own claims to represent affected publics.

Norm promotion by transnational activist networks usually entails seeking the support of state actors and intergovernmental organizations to institutionalize the new norms in international rule-making. Chapter 3 finds evidence for transnational accountability norms receiving recognition in global environmental regimes. This is in large part due to the wide-ranging currency of the liberal no-harm principle in international law, reflected in what Andrew Linklater (2001) terms 'cosmopolitan harm conventions' – inter-state agreements to regulate injury and distress to others, regardless of nationality. If these are still, above all, associated internationally with human rights law (protecting the vital interests of the individual) and humanitarian law (protecting individuals during armed conflict), harm prevention is also a central tenet of the emerging body of international environmental law. I survey a number of environmental treaties to locate commitments between states to prevent transnational ecological harm. They demonstrate that rules to regulate environmental harm are starting to register, albeit gradually, the interests of transboundary affected publics (not denying of course the political propensity of many state and non-state actors to express national concerns in universal terms). International consensus may be lacking on the precise scope and nature of these transnational obligations, but their presence in numerous issue-specific conventions represents a significant extension of preventative norms to environmental risk and damage.

At the same time, transnational environmental obligations are entering a global geopolitical context in which neoliberal norms of economic globalization – the so-called Washington consensus – still hold substantial sway over the perceived interests of state and private actors. Nowhere is this more evident than in the area of international trade governance, where rules of cross-border market liberalization and access bind the 146 member states of the World Trade Organization (WTO). The consolidated legal force of WTO rule-making and enforcement not only contrasts with the fragmentary reach of multilateral environmental agreements, it also exists in tension with the trade obligations contained in some of these treaties. More generally, environmental NGOs and activist networks have challenged the WTO with neglecting the negative ecological (and social) effects on affected publics of its trade policy-making. Chapter 4 sets out the politically charged accountability questions raised here, which feature the claim that the WTO – and its constituent member states – should be obliged to answer for the extra-territorial environmental impacts of international trade. I outline recent moves by the WTO to become more transparent and increase its engagement with transnational civil society actors. A survey of NGOs participating in regular briefings on the WTO Committee on Trade and Environment identifies shared goals among these actors for institutionalizing modes of environmental accountability at the WTO, which centre on new and strengthened points of civil society access and representation. I argue that the political feasibility of these WTO reform recommendations largely rests on the ability of sympathetic European member states to convince developing-country members that they are not a front for green protectionism.

Ensuring that those responsible for transnational ecological harm are made liable for their actions is a widely accepted principle in international environmental treaties and declarations. However, the reluctance of states to specify liability rules in these legal instruments has called into question the ability of affected interests to seek financial redress from identifiable harm producers. In Chapter 5 I first summarize the protracted efforts of the International Law Commission to codify general rules of liability for activities involving the risk of significant transboundary harm, then turn to the major vehicle for the development of financial accountability for environmental damage – civil liability treaties. Examined in detail is the first civil liability regime to allow environmental damage claims from non-nationals – the international oil pollution liability regime. As discussed, the reliance on civil liability norms for cross-border environmental compensation encounters particular challenges concerning quantification of damage and coverage outside spaces of national jurisdiction – problems encountered in other civil liability regimes. Finally, I identify new trajectories of criminal liability for transnational environmental damage, which may well be the most appropriate instrument to seek redress for harm to extra-territorial spaces.

Legal liability rules for environmental compensation represent an accountability domain in which producers of transboundary harm face binding norms of answerability and redress. In recent years, a number of environment and development NGOs have campaigned to extend their reach from particular risk-bearing activities to routine corporate behaviour entailing cross-border social and ecological costs. Chapter 6 addresses the topic of corporate accountability for transnational environmental harm, contrasting the ambitious efforts of NGOs to advance civil regulation and foreign direct liability as effective tools of redress for corporate wrongdoing with the growing employment of environmental self-reporting and self-regulation by corporations. The voluntary mechanisms of corporate environmentalism are united by their framing of ecological responsibility in market liberal terms: they articulate ways in which corporate practices address cost-based environmental expectations; for example, in the cross-border greening of supply chains, production technologies and management systems. I examine corporate voluntarism, civil regulation and foreign direct liability as mechanisms of transnational environmental accountability, suggesting finally that there is a need to entrench corporate environmental obligations to affected publics in international law.

Transboundary and global flows of environmental harm, as perceived by affected publics, invoke space–time pathways of responsibility at odds with the territorial boundaries of state sovereignty. Being able to hold actors to account for such harm requires mechanisms for empowering those affected by it to organize themselves and engage politically. Following an overview of the trends toward a new accountability identified in the preceding chapters, the Conclusion pulls out some key pointers on conditions conducive to the formation of democratically organized transnational and global publics. It then considers the prospects for new accountability norms in an unsafe world where powerful states are preoccupied with security concerns. It is necessary, I argue, to consider the exceptional circumstances in which the threat by states to use force for humanitarian goals may need to encompass grave and systematic threats to environmental well-being.

Chapter 1

Transnational Accountability for Environmental Harm: A Framework

How is accountability for transboundary environmental harm to be determined? On what basis should activities that impose present and future costs outside national borders be regulated? And how should the producers of this harm be made answerable and responsible to affected groups? This chapter is concerned with providing a framework for understanding transnational environmental obligations, relating them to spaces of communication where actors are held to account by affected parties for the negative social and ecological consequences of their actions. Obligations denote legal and moral requirements: the chapter therefore combines an outline of the emergence of accountability duties within international environmental law with a normative justification for addressing the interests of transnational publics.

The governance implications of transnational environmental accountability are most obviously located in the field of planetary environmental management. Since the 1972 United Nations Conference on the Human Environment (the Stockholm Conference), the development of regional and international environmental conventions has become the major vehicle of global ecological governance, generating a complex of loosely connected regimes. Scholars have tended to explain this regime-building within a rational choice model of inter-state cooperation: environmental obligations serve to coordinate governments' responses to collective action problems; that is, situations where private claims on natural resources have generated uncompensated environmental costs across and beyond national borders. In an international arena without an authoritative rule-making body, multilateral environmental treaties bring order and agreement on how common ecological goals can be harmonized with the preferences of sovereign states. According to this preference-based (utilitarian) model of international cooperation, environmental duties are instrumental in reconciling state-centred objectives: the nature of the obligations themselves – and the norms they embody – is of secondary importance.

More recently, social scientists have paid increasing attention to the role and status of norms in global politics (Finnemore and Sikkink, 1998; Risse, 2000). As standards of appropriate behaviour, norms represent shared, evaluative assessments actively shaping actors' interests and identities. Communication on norms is central to the adoption (or rejection) of new obligations as justifiable rules for governing behaviour in a particular issue area. If it is to embrace claims to democratic deliberation, this communication cannot avoid appealing to reasoned arguments that attempt to persuade all affected by the obligation that it is acceptable as a legitimate constraint on their actions. That the legitimacy of social norms depends on meeting the expectation of actors that they can be rationally justified in public interest terms is central to the argument of this chapter. It roots a critical notion of accountability for environmental harm not in strategic bargaining between states, but in the open deliberation on appropriate norms by affected publics.

Of course environmental nongovernmental organizations (NGOs) and activist networks, pursuing ecological goals within and across state borders, are leading organizational platforms for promoting environmental norms. Environmentalism represents, with its life-centred, transgenerational values, perhaps the most important contemporary challenge to neoliberal prescriptions for economic globalization. Against the market expansionist ethos and privileging of private authority of neoliberalism, environmentalism counters with calls for ecologically adaptive, publicly accountably institutions and practices. At the same time, defenders of market-led development paths are questioning strongly the democratic accountability of NGOs and activist coalitions: what is their responsibility to constituent members and groups? How can they claim to represent the concerns of transnational publics? The divisions between private and public interests, between particular and universal constituencies, become part of the politically charged way in which the framing of environmental norms is contested.

Questions of democratic legitimacy thus apply to *all* actors making international or transnational political claims, although the concept of public accountability developed here is oriented towards those networks of power *producing* transboundary and global environmental harm. Following initial comments on transnational relations and state sovereignty, a theoretical formulation of affected publics is set out. Transnational accountability for environmental harm is directed as moral justification to those affected publics, as informed by principles of harm prevention, inclusiveness and impartiality. Moral obligations to protect environmental quality find legal currency in the developing principles of public international law: transnational relations are pulling non-state actors into that legal discourse and practice. At the level of state responsibility are, I claim, those ecological obligations that build on existing rules of harm prevention to promote environmental accountability. Furthermore, I argue that transboundary risks clearly threatening vital conditions of life suggest the need to invoke rights-based environmental obligations consistent with existing multilateral treaties and human rights law.

Transnational relations and state sovereignty

Within international relations theory, recent debate on transnational relations has taken as its conceptual focus the creation of a cross-boundary political space, diverging from traditional state-centred notions of sovereign territory. *Transnational* relations denote 'regular interactions across national boundaries where at least one actor is a non-state agent or does not operate on behalf of a national government or an intergovernmental organization' (Risse-Kappen, 1995: p3). Their contemporary salience attests to the dramatic growth in nongovernmental actors undertaking transnational practices, notably activist coalitions and transnational corporations whose political influence derives respectively from communicative expertise and economic power. Transnational interactions encompass social, cultural and economic practices as much as political exchanges *per se*: while international relations theorists have fixed onto shifting spatio-temporal contours of governance (Risse-Kappen, 1995; Rosenau, 1997), other social scientists have opened up wider conceptual discussions on transnational flows (e.g. Sklair, 1994; Shapiro and Alker, 1996). As a result, the core political categories at the heart of international relations research in this area have been challenged and deconstructed from many theoretical angles. A full survey of this literature is outside the scope of this chapter: in this section, instead, I address the central concept of state sovereignty, outlining the relationship between territorial conditions of authority and transboundary environmental responsibility.

The most important source of environmental obligations created to limit transboundary ecological harm is public international law. Through the development of legal principles and rules, international environmental law imposes binding obligations on state and non-state actors to conform to specified norms of behaviour. In their *ad hoc* development over the past couple of decades, international legal obligations to protect the environment have, like international law generally, drawn their authority from treaties, customary practice, general legal principles and so-called subsidiary sources, such as court or tribunal decisions and jurisprudence. Furthermore, international environmental obligations also arise from a more diffuse body of 'soft law' comprising legally non-binding, but influential, conference resolutions, declarations and action plans. These soft obligations are an important vehicle for establishing new environmental norms on the world stage, which is why many environmental NGOs are active in lobbying for, and/or participating in, international environmental conferences. By definition, international law recognizes that, in order to become legally binding, environmental norms must be accepted by, and between, states as the only subjects with 'sovereign rights' to decision-making authority within the global political arena – that authority resting on their claim to political autonomy over populations within their territories and the recognition of the equality and independence of other states. States have the legal responsibility to represent their respective jurisdictions in international environmental negotiations and to implement agreed treaties, as signatories, through their own domestic political and administrative systems (Economy and Schreurs, 1997; Brown Weiss and Jacobson, 1998). They are thus the primary holders of rights and obligations under international law.

If state sovereignty is formally recognized as a core principle of public international law, there is less agreement about the practical currency of this notion in global politics. Stephen Krasner (1999; 2000) claims that breaches of the sovereign state model have long been an enduring characteristic of the international system, whether through voluntary agreements (e.g. human rights accords), contractual arrangements (e.g. conditionality attached to international loans), or straightforward coercion (e.g. economic sanctions) and imposition (e.g. military intervention). In these circumstances, the notion of exclusive state authority and territorial control informs norms and practices which may or may not be adhered to depending on the strategic interests of the states involved: the sovereign state model is a cognitive framework of 'organized hypocrisy' where there is little consistency between the employment of sovereign norms and state actions. Notwithstanding this necessary reminder that state sovereignty is a principle regularly compromised by instrumental motives and actions, it remains a fundamental constitutional parameter of international relations. For global environmental governance, where transnational risk profiles highlight the need for states to agree new obligations on harm prevention, sovereign powers are the only indisputable juridical basis of national and international regulation. However, we can accept that they are being recast or qualified in a more interdependent global community (French, 2001).

The continuation of the state as the principal domain of authoritative law-making and regulation clashes with the farewell to the state in neoliberal representations of globalization (Ohmae, 1995), but is in keeping with a more contextualized understanding of the reconfiguration of political and economic authority in response to transnational economic, socio-cultural and environmental practices (Sassen, 1996; Yeung, 1998). A largely reactive pattern of state responses to transboundary ecological risks has led to numerous regimes of international environmental governance, generating new state obligations. Nevertheless, as Rosenau (1997: pp189–213) observes, these new state responsibilities coexist with a redistribution of authority upwards (to supranational and international bodies), sideways (to transnational activist coalitions and corporations) and downwards (to subnational public authorities and non-state actors). Rosenau employs the term 'frontier' to capture the relational field of political action generated when transnational practices dissolve domestic-foreign boundaries of state authority, pulling in non-state actors (Rosenau, 1997: pp3–11).

Identifying frontiers is a methodological question: one general thesis already informing such empirical work, and already with evidential support from across a range of policy domains, is that the governance impact of transnational coalitions and actors varies according to domestic state forms and the institutionalization of international cooperation:

> *the more cooperative international institutions regulate the inter-state relationship in the particular issue-area, the more channels should transnational coalitions have available to penetrate the political systems and the more should they be able to use international norms to legitimate their demands* (Risse-Kappen, 1995: p3).

For environmental issues, where various regional and international organizations have become the favoured foci for the creation and implementation of governance regimes, environmental NGOs have become increasingly adept at shaping these regimes. Environmentalists have influenced international environmental agreements through international lobbying and the mobilization of public opinion; for example, the key role of a transnational conservation network in creating and monitoring the 1973 Convention on International Trade in Endangered Species of Wild Fauna and Flora (CITES) (Princen, 1995); similarly, the environmental NGO campaigns leading to a moratorium on commercial whaling under the 1946 International Whaling Convention and also the 1985 ban on the dumping at sea of radioactive waste under the 1972 Convention on the Prevention of Marine Pollution by Dumping of Wastes and Other Matter (Vogler, 2000). Aided in part by the active encouragement of the United Nations Environment Programme, environmental NGOs also played a significant role in developing parts of the climate and biodiversity conventions agreed at the 1992 United Nations Conference on Environment and Development (UNCED) (Arts, 1998). There are, in addition, emerging opportunities for non-state actors to play an enforcement role in law relating to transnational environmental harm, although their limited legal standing restricts a more proactive compliance role for environmental NGOs in international environmental law.

The transnational accountability of producers of environmental harm demanded by NGOs accumulates evidential support as global environmental monitoring enables the increasingly precise attribution of ecological degradation to particular emission sources. To take transboundary air pollution as an example: in Europe the Cooperative Programme for Monitoring and Evaluating of Long-Range Transboundary Air Pollution is building up consensual knowledge on the emission flows and effects of sulphur dioxide, nitrogen oxides and volatile organic compounds. The critical loads methodology informing this programme gauges harmful environmental effects by integrating emission sources, transport mechanism and receptor exposure conditions (Wettestad, 2000; Albin, 2001: pp82–5). The increasing sophistication of air transport modelling has in recent years enabled the first continent-wide study of dioxin space–time pathways, tracking the long-range air transport of dioxins from geographical sources in the US, Canada and Mexico to deposition at eight receptor locations in the eastern Canadian Arctic (Commoner et al, 2000). It has also facilitated the mapping of the transnational movement of anthropogenic aerosols over South Asia, offering preliminary findings on how this air pollution is impacting on climate, agriculture and human health (United Nations Environment Programme and Center for Clouds, Chemistry and Climate, 2002).

Of course, it remains necessary to interrogate the theoretical constructs and empirical predictions of such modelling including, as the sociologists of science would insist, the social processes by which the researchers determine their knowledge claims. The scientific framing of regional and global environmental pollution links into the political arena not just at the downstream stage of policy choices shaped by scientific findings, but also at the upstream stage of research question formulation, selection of methods and standards of proof, etc. (Demeritt, 2001). We need to be aware, therefore, of the influence of sovereign state preferences (as well as those of private actors) on the study of transnational environmental flows; for example, national science policy priorities, public and corporate funding criteria, opportunities for interdisciplinary research, and relationships with user groups and citizens. What is clear, as the analysis of transboundary source–receptor relationships for environmental pollution develops, is that territorial alignments of state authority and responsibility have not prevented the transmission across national borders of substantial pollution, and that these pollution loads with their chemical products are having far-reaching impacts on biophysical systems and human health.

Affected publics: a critical pragmatist conception

The adaptive management perspective (see Introduction) exposes the stubborn ecological mismatch between spatial pathways of environmental degradation and the fixed cartography of sovereign nation-states. While regional and international environmental agreements indicate the possibility of limiting or pooling state sovereign powers, they consistently face the difficulty of reconciling transboundary ecological goals with territorial boundaries of authority. Adaptive management proponents recommend 'de-linking' environmental decision-making authority from territorial rules of responsibility. As Ward (1998: p83) remarks: 'ecosystem management, applicable to designated ecological entities, which themselves may cross existing state boundaries, may well require that affected parties share the right to establish rules of conduct to govern behaviour within the ecosystem'.

In the merging of adaptive management with an open process of rule deliberation among all those significantly affected by material practices, there is a clear debt acknowledged to American pragmatism, notably the ideas of Charles Sanders Pierce and John Dewey (Norton, 1999; Minteer and Manning, 1999). The moral responsibility to protect ecological life-support processes here relates to the pragmatist notion of inclusive discourse on the consequences of human action as they unfold across multiple scales (Norton, 1996: p133).

For Dewey the perception of enduring, harmful consequences arising from human activities determines the scope of the public as an associative space of joint problem-solving: 'the public consists of those who are affected by the indirect consequences of transactions to such an extent that it is deemed necessary to have these consequences systematically cared for' (Dewey, 1954: pp15–16). Indirect consequences are those impacting on third parties not directly engaged in the material transactions in question. These might seem to correspond to the economic notion of external costs, which are uncompensated welfare losses to third parties generated by private market transactions (the focus of 'market failure' research in environmental economics). However, there is a crucial theoretical distinction here: Dewey locates the public in the *collective exercise of practical judgment* in any instance where a perceived cluster of indirect consequences is seen to require regulation. In contrast, the economic model, as evident in rational choice formulations of the public interest (e.g. Downs, 1998: pp48–83), identifies the public as that *aggregated set of individual preferences informed* by third-party concerns. While uncompensated economic costs might be one significant valuation of indirect consequences perceived to be harmful by an affected public, the Deweyan process of reasoning about these negative effects is more than a monetary calculus of subjective preferences. It features cooperative communication on why and how these consequences should be controlled.

Daniel Deudney (1998) employs John Dewey's conception of the public in order to counterpoint a 'green sovereignty' to the sovereign state framework. As the adaptive management approach has demonstrated, the cross-scale environmental effects of dominant productive and consumptive practices impact both across state boundaries and extend temporally into the future. For Deudney there is now a transgenerational public to which political and economic institutions should be made ecologically accountable. What he labels *terrapolitan sovereignty* constrains state authority according to the ecological sustainability rules of a mutually agreed planetary constitution, but there is little elaboration on how these norms are operationalized. In an international system unlikely in the foreseeable future to embrace such a radical rewriting of state responsibility rules, I argue that the pragmatist recasting of sovereignty can build on existing norms of democratic governance and accountability. This implies an understanding of the generation of transnational environmental obligations that differs both from the dominant academic perspective on global environmental governance, regime analysis, and 'dissident' postmodern perspectives.

First, regime analysis has indeed centred on the specific principles, norms and decision-making procedures informing actors' interactions in various environmental issue areas, but its institutionalist framework has neglected the intersubjective development of new environmental norms, tending to treat actor preferences as predefined (Hansenclever et al, 1997: pp23–7; Hovden, 1999). International obligations are the outcome of strategic calculations between states, where to cooperate in the creation of new rules is judged to be mutually beneficial for advancing material and symbolic gains. New international rules have been shown by regime theorists to contribute significantly to resolving transboundary environmental problems in certain circumstances, yet the content of these rules escapes critical examination. To be sure, there exists a 'cognitivist' strand of regime theory attuned to how environmental regimes actively shape preferences and identities (Kratochwil, 1989; Hansenclever et al, 1997: pp136–210), although this more sociological take on global environmental cooperation restricts itself largely to the constitution of state-centred interests. There is little sense both of how norms emerge from the dynamic interactions of state and non-state actors, and of how obligations agreed as international legal duties hold at least a claim to legitimacy not solely reducible to instrumental motives.

Second, the pragmatist argument that those responsible for transboundary ecological harm should ultimately be held accountable to all those possibly affected, would seem to find support in the critique of state sovereignty offered by postmodern commentators (Kuehls, 1996, 1998; Luke, 1997, 1999). What Tuathail (1996: pp168–78) labels 'dissident international relations theory' has interrogated modern representations of state sovereignty, notably that inside/outside axis which conventionally separates an uncontested domestic arena of political jurisdiction and citizen identity from anarchic relations between states. Following Walker's (1993) suggestive work in this area, as well as the philosophical thought of Deleuze and Guattari (1987), Thom Kuehls (1996, 38–55; 1998) identifies a *rhizomatic space* of global ecological politics, exemplified by environmental NGOs bringing attention to the trajectories of pollutants across political borders. These activists, he claims, offer a nomadic mode of political representation, vigilantly tracking and witnessing the space–time pathways of environmental harm on behalf of a planetary community of environmental citizens. The postmodern deconstruction of state sovereignty finds geopolitical borders insecure as containers of legitimate power: permeated by transnational social, economic and ecological flows, the territorial coordinates of state authority correspond neither with the multiple scales nor with the complexity of environmental risk. Transnational environmental activists express and expose that spatial disjuncture.

Notwithstanding the valuable interrogation of sovereign norms provided by the above, the postmodern approach falls short of what we need in order to progress political accountability for environmental harm. Its cultural preoccupation with the expression of environmental values has tended to neglect how affected publics facing threats to their ecological well-being can jointly make claims against responsible parties. These claims for accountability may not be recognized in national or international law, but they have a socially integrative force in so far as they are publicly intelligible to all the relevant parties or, more strongly, actually attract general agreement on causes of harm and forms of redress. The philosophical touchstone for this communicative understanding of environmental accountability is formal pragmatics, which employs ideas about ordinary language use to develop pragmatist ideas on public discourse (Habermas, 1999a). Formal pragmatics identifies a rational potential inherent in everyday communication to the extent that speakers are able to justify their utterances reflexively on the basis of reasons recognized as legitimate by the other parties involved. This 'rational force' of ordinary language use rests on the presupposition of communicative accountability adopted by actors when attempting to reach a mutual understanding about something – accountability in the sense that what they say and do is answerable to others in terms of an appeal to reasons which would be deemed justifiable in free, uncoerced dialogue. Habermas (1999a: pp310–11) argues that such reflexive communi-cation (which he labels 'discourse') strengthens social bonds by promoting an understanding of the needs and values of others. For socio-environmental relationships, this means an orientation to open, inclusive communication on the nature and scope of the physical interventions we make in the biosphere.

Communicative accountability locates responsibility for actions in a public discourse where, following the pragmatist tradition, participants have a moral obligation to consider the perspectives of all others. Environmental norms, like any others, are justified only when they meet (or could meet) with the approval of all those affected by them, or their representatives, after rationally considering their consequences. This *discourse principle* of public justification (Habermas, 1990: p66; 1996: p459) entails a non-territorial understanding of democratic accountability. The legitimacy of collective decisions with signifi-cant transboundary ill-effects rests on their harmonization with the interests of those affected beyond state borders; as would, firstly, be communicated to the decision-makers were these affected publics given the opportunity openly to represent their collective concerns and, secondly, also be fairly and reasonably taken into account in the decision-making. In the next section I argue that it is possible to isolate three moral precepts here – harm prevention, inclusion and impartiality – which serve to delineate communicative spaces of environmental accountability.

State and non-state actors involved in producing transboundary harm face from the notion of communicative accountability a moral challenge to justify their actions according to the interests of affected publics, while activist networks claiming to represent the latter also face interrogation concerning their motivations and capabilities for doing so. For Habermas accountability as a discursive construct is *counterfactual*: it provides a standard of democratic justification with which the rightness of actions can be assessed. While any

communication is embedded in specific social relationships with the participants involved filling out the relevant content, the discourse principle invokes
(from the linguistic pragmatics of Pierce) the regulative idea of unconditional-
ity – that further and future voices with better arguments could in principle
refute any agreement reached in a particular situation (Habermas, 1987:
pp92–96; 1996: pp14–16). In other words, an extended conversation is
anticipated by the discourse principle and, within real-world contexts of
occluded and unequal communication, serves as a critical benchmark to help
identify the opportunities for, and constraints to, the equal participation of all
relevant interests. This challenges the modern geopolitical assumption that
territorial sovereignty precludes accountability for extra-territorial harm
produced by nationals. In order to remain democratically legitimate, (inter)state decision-making authority must facilitate, and engage with, the
interest representation of non-national affected publics (Habermas, 1996:
pp486–90; 2001: p20).

Given the multiplicity of relevant actors, mapping out the discursive spaces
of transnational accountability for environmental harm is by no means precise,
addressing contested identifications of affected interests and diverse communicative practices. Cross-territorial information flows, accelerated by electronic
communications media, can very quickly ascribe 'global' significance to the
concerns of affected publics – a state of affairs not lost on environmental
NGOs, who actively construct key issues through a variety of rhetorical
strategies (Macnaghten and Urry, 1998: pp97–101). Their descriptions of
environmental harm as 'transboundary' or 'global' are often disputed, not only
by those alleged to be responsible but also by other self-defined representatives
of affected publics (for example, media outlets, NGOs and politicians in the
global South). However, communicative accountability does not require
unanimity among relevant parties in the attribution of environmental
responsibility. As a space for open discourse, transnational environmental
accountability is less oriented in practice to universal agreement than to
affording more respect to the claims of extra-territorial environmental victims.
To accomplish this of course is to recognize the role of power relations in
shaping communication. There is little guidance in Habermas's work as to
how affected publics can be empowered and how authorities can be forced to
take their interests into account (Kohn, 2000: p425): this question of power
is addressed below and, more substantively, in subsequent chapters.

The focus of communicative accountability on open dialogue also invites
criticism that key affected parties unable to contribute discursively are unfairly
excluded, notably future generations and non-human entities: this violates, it
is argued, the commitment to inclusive moral consideration (Skirbekk, 1997;
Eckersley, 1999). However, these objections conflate moral discussants with
subjects or objects of moral concern. Moral (human) discussants are necessarily
the locus for assigning responsibility, but the pragmatist notion of affected
interests still leaves the determination of moral standing and concern to the

participants themselves, who are likely to introduce diverse sources of value into the discussion (these may well include the notion that ecological entities have an independent moral worth). Like any other terms these discussants put forward to support or reject transnational environmental obligations, claims about criteria for moral consideration would, in order to seek reasoned support among all those affected by environmental harm or risk, need to demonstrate that they embody and protect common interests. And if consensus is not possible on which interests deserve most protection, recourse is made to fair compromises in line with preserving minimal standards of social and ecological well-being for all (see below on environmental rights). This procedure seems to fall short of a secure ecological rationale for these obligations, but is consistent with a pragmatist focus on multiple forms of valuation in specific problem-solving contexts where ecologically adaptive, democratic development paths are sought (Norton and Steinemann, 2001).

Transnational environmental obligations

Within international law the sovereign right of states to exploit their own resources is constrained by a core principle of environmental responsibility: that states have a general obligation to ensure that activities within their territorial jurisdiction or control do not cause environmental damage to other states or to areas beyond state jurisdiction. This key norm was first set out in a declarative manner as Principle 21 of the Stockholm Declaration on the Human Environment (1972) and restated at the United Nations Conference on Environment and Development by Principle 2 of the Rio Declaration on Environment and Development. Prior to these declarations, the obligation on all states not to cause serious environmental harm to other states already constituted a principle of customary international law (Pisillio-Mazzeschi, 1991). However, the obligation on all states not to cause damage to areas beyond the limits of state jurisdiction and control was only formally confirmed as a general norm in customary international law by the International Court of Justice in 1996 in an advisory opinion on the legality of the threat of use of nuclear weapons (Brown Weiss, 1999). As an obligation *erga omnes* (to the international community as a whole), it arguably empowers states to act on behalf of the international community in holding other states to account for serious extra-territorial environmental harm, regardless of whether specific treaty obligations are applicable or not. While Sands (1995: p154) cautions that states historically have proven unwilling to adopt such a tutelary role, this development nevertheless points to an emerging recognition in international law of environmental protection as a shared obligation deriving from notions of common responsibility.

The overarching obligation on states not to cause transboundary environmental harm nevertheless lacks the commanding authority that would follow from its universal acceptance by states as entailing a peremptory norm (*jus cogens*) of international law – one that could invalidate treaty rules in conflict with it (Fitzmaurice, 1996: p307). *Jus cogens* norms, such as those prohibiting genocide, torture, forced labour and crimes against humanity, represent the highest international standards by which state and non-state actors can be held legally culpable. Principles generated by international environmental law – including specific norms embedded in multilateral treaties – have not accumulated the global legal authority and currency to qualify as peremptory norms. Furthermore, the continuing concern of many states that the expansion of peremptory norms risks destabilizing treaty relations means that there are significant geopolitical hurdles to such legal promotion for environmental norms (International Law Commission, 1999: para 311). Short of widespread state support in this area, and outside treaty commitments, attempts to consolidate and extend the spatial reach of international environ-mental principles and rules rest or fall in the short term on the *voluntary* willingness of states to recognize a general obligation not to cause significant transboundary harm wherever in the world that harm takes place (Crawford, 1999: p62; Pevato, 1999: p318).

In the longer term, the gradual erosion of the rule of unanimous consent (i.e. new multilateral rules bind only those states consenting to their application) in international environmental governance may allow norm-making and enforcement binding even on states not in agreement with this general obligation. A significant precedent for non-unanimous but binding changes to environmental treaty rules was set by a majority voting mechanism under the 1987 Montreal Protocol (to the Vienna Convention for the Protection of the Ozone Layer), although member states unhappy with new rules may, after due notice, withdraw from the treaty system altogether. Further progress in non-unanimous changes in international environmental rules may be promoted by the consolidation of multilateral environmental agreements and new, more coordinated, structures of global environmental governance. These changes would enable international rule-making to be more ambitious in setting standards of accountability for transnational environmental harm (see Conclusion).

Whatever the future trajectories of institutional reform in international environmental governance, the concept of transnational environmental ac-countability presented here already implies a moral space of public discourse, expanding or contracting according to the open identification of affected third parties. With the potential for, and growing incidence of, transboundary environmental harm, that non-territorial space is increasingly cosmopolitan. As Linklater (1998: p84) observes more generally:

> At the very least, causing transnational harm requires a commitment to
> regard insiders and outsiders as moral equals and it may involve placing
> the interests of the vulnerable members of other communities before the

interests of co-nationals on the grounds of common humanity. Transna-
tional harm provides one of the strongest reasons for widening the
boundaries of moral and political communities to engage outsiders in
dialogue about matters which affect their vital interests.

Linklater acknowledges a theoretical debt to Habermas in his formulation of transboundary dialogic communities, and there is also a strong affinity with Cochran's (1999) pragmatist notion of international public spheres. Both understand democratic accountability for harmful transnational practices in terms of answerability to, and involvement of, affected parties. However, these suggestive approaches largely leave open the question of their application to substantive issue areas. It is possible, I argue, to *locate* transnational environmental obligations by identifying – within international rule development – three moral principles that constitute necessary markers for the environmental discourse of affected publics – (i) harm prevention, (ii) inclusiveness and (iii) impartiality. These principles emerge from shared norms of democratic governance recognized as legitimate across the world, but are here cut loose from their traditional containment within territorial spaces of state sovereignty.

Harm prevention

At the heart of the liberal understanding of democratic authority is the principle that individuals may legitimately be subject to coercive legal controls only when the purpose of that regulation is to prevent harm – harm being that which interferes with or prevents persons from freely determining their own life opportunities and capabilities. Contemporary liberal democracies generally acknowledge that the state not only has a duty to protect individuals from activities depriving them of this autonomy, but also has a responsibility positively to promote the conditions for autonomous action (e.g. public education, preventive healthcare, affordable housing, employment opportunities). Beyond injury to basic physiological and biological needs, what constitutes harm entails of course an appeal to societal values and norms: in line with the perspective developed here, I argue that harm is defined in relation to publicly justifiable needs (cf. Miller, 1999: pp206–13). And as the growth of environmental regulation in many countries illustrates, national governments (for a variety of motives) regard ecological sustainability as an appropriate policy domain for harm prevention.

The high priority in international environmental law afforded to the general obligation not to cause environmental damage reflects acceptance of a liberal no-harm principle (*neminem laedere*) in global governance (Kratochwil, 1989: pp9–10). Various state obligations for internal and external action derive from this principle, but that most central to transboundary ecological harm is the obligation of conduct on states requiring the *prevention of damage to the environment*. Many international environmental treaties endorse a preventive approach, including the Climate Change Convention and the Biodiversity Convention, while in 2001 the International Law Commission, after many years of deliberation, agreed on a draft international convention codifying state obligations of prevention for transboundary environmental damage (International Law Commission, 2001: pp366–436). Moving away from the individualistic focus of political liberalism, our pragmatist formulation of environmental accountability recasts the no-harm principle in transnational terms, offering a wider principle of rejecting transboundary injury to ecological (and social) conditions of existence, and including non-state actors in the class of obligatory agents as well as addressees. O'Neill (1996: pp174–8) formulates a notion of environmental justice along these lines, whereby just institutions and practices are those that prevent or limit systematic (large-scale) or gratuitous (small-scale) damage to reproductive and regenerative ecological processes.

Scientific uncertainty regarding the precise environmental impacts of many human activities makes a precautionary approach a necessary condition for efforts to limit or prevent serious harm. Indeed, the precautionary approach is argued by some legal commentators to have become a universally accepted norm of customary international law: it is endorsed in the UNCED Rio Declaration and Conventions as well as other recent environmental treaties (Cameron and Abouchar, 1996; McIntyre and Mosedale, 1997). As an international norm, the *precautionary principle* obliges states to address threats of serious environmental damage even if there is a lack of full scientific certainty regarding causal pathways. Its implementation entails ancillary obligations of conduct on states including, depending on the agreement in question, the application of: clean production standards (e.g. 1991 Bamako Convention on transboundary movement and management of hazardous wastes within Africa); transboundary environmental impact assessment (e.g. 1991 Espoo Convention on environmental impact assessment and the 1992 Helsinki Convention on transboundary watercourses); and the collection and sharing of relevant research information (e.g. 1995 Fish Stocks Agreement) (McIntyre and Mosedale, 1997: pp236–40). To be sure, there are different formulations of the precautionary principle and these sometimes rein in its preventative momentum with the caveat of 'cost-effective' action (e.g. Principle 15 of the 1992 Rio Declaration). Nevertheless, environmental scientists, lawyers and NGOs have widened the scope of the no-harm principle through their support of precautionary norms. The precautionary principle increases the communicative burden on those who generate environmental harm (whether intentional or not) to demonstrate that they have at least minimized (potential) effects on affected publics.

Inclusiveness

Since the end of the Cold War, the collective right of peoples to democratic governance has acquired increasing legal currency across the world. As evident in the extensive involvement of international organizations in monitoring multi-party elections and, more exceptionally, the use of (United Nations-endorsed) military intervention to restore freely elected governments deposed by military coups (e.g. Haiti in 1994 and Sierra Leone in 1998), the external legitimacy of domestic systems of government is increasingly wedded to democratic criteria. The customary behaviour between states and their mutual interpretation of treaties (e.g. through rules of voluntary consent, transparency and domestic legislative ratification) is also entrenching democratic norms in international law, informing of course multilateral environmental agreements. This wave of democratization has invited both celebration and skepticism from commentators, one side invoking a generally positive spiral of self-determination and associated human rights, the other citing the selective, instrumental endorsement of democracy by powerful Western states (see Fox and Roth, 2000). Without entering into this debate, we can nonetheless acknowledge the widespread recognition accorded to the principle of democratic inclusion. Moreover, the global spread of the right of citizens to elect and hold accountable representative governments has created the expectation, for transboundary problems, that the concerns of affected publics will be incorporated in international rule-making.

Representation of the interests of transnational affected publics is most often located in the growing recognition of consultation rights for NGOs in global environmental governance, raising the prospect of more formal rights of participation in decision-making (Sands, 1998). Progress has been made in strengthening the consultative status of NGOs in intergovernmental decision-making fora. UNCED in 1992 is often cited as a catalyst in this respect, where 1400 NGOs attended the conference as UN-recognized participants, and Chapter 27 of Agenda 21 – the (soft law) programme of sustainable development agreed at the conference – endorsed an enhanced role for NGOs in developing and implementing policy actions at all scales. Since the Rio meeting, NGO input in intergovernmental implementation of sustainability actions has been formalized through the NGO steering committee of the United Nations Commission on Sustainable Development. Formal consultative status for transnational NGOs has been available since 1968 through accreditation to the United Nations Economic and Social Council, but this mechanism has not been widely employed until recently. United Nations consultative status is accorded to those NGOs of 'international standing' who are representatives of relevant fields of competence and are democratically constituted (Willetts, 1996). This has raised questions about representative parity in the United Nations system between Northern NGOs and those resource-poor groups from the global South often struggling to survive in hostile domestic political contexts. Regional criteria for NGO representation, such as those developed by the Commission on Sustainable Development, present one way of guaranteeing Southern NGO input into intergovernmental fora. However, more effective representation of the interests of affected publics in the global South requires NGO capacity-building there and, in particular, non-token access to powerful intergovernmental bodies outside the United Nations system (e.g. the World Trade Organization: see Chapter 5).

Inclusion of the interests of *transgenerational* affected publics also finds support in international law. The obligation to take into account and protect the developmental and environmental needs of future generations has in recent years been increasingly invoked in a wide range of multilateral agreements and treaties, including the UNCED climate change and biodiversity conventions (Sands, 1998; Malhotra, 1998). Despite uncertainties surrounding the definition of future generations, this notion entails a widely acknowledged legal subjectivity autonomous from state actors; indeed, most transnational environmental norms have a strong transgenerational character, reflecting an appreciation of the combined temporal and spatial cross-scale effects of ecological processes. The central future-oriented obligation here, often denoted under the rubric of 'sustainable development', implies an equal opportunity across generations; that is, a universal obligation to future generations to maintain specific social and ecological attributes into the indefinite future (World Commission on Environment and Development, 1987; Barry, 1999). There are competing theoretical accounts on the responsibilities suggested by this broad norm of intergenerational equity (e.g. Dobson, 1998; Wissenburg, 1999; Carter, 2001). The pragmatist approach adopted here invests this task not to philosophical debates but to the public discourse in which actors, discussing human activities with significant, long-lasting environmental effects, are required reasonably to justify their own assumptions about future generations and potential future claims. As environment and development-oriented NGOs have a proven record in building public awareness of obligations to the future generations, the transnational development of intergenerational equity would seem to be encouraged by extending participation rights to NGOs in the formulation and implementation of international environmental laws and standards. However, as discussed in Chapter 2, NGOs cannot themselves escape questions of representativeness with respect to deciding how future interests are formulated.

Impartiality

Expanding the discourses of justification for transboundary risks in order to include non-state representatives of affected publics moves towards the principle of equal inclusion implied by our formulation of accountability for environmental harm. However, the anticipation of that participation, whether used as a regulative idea or concretely to inform new institutional designs for environmental decision-making, must be accompanied by the corollary principle of impartiality – that just actions or norms are those that can reasonably be accepted by the participants. As Cohen (1998: p194) explains, the communicative expectations of participants:

are reasonable in that they aim to defend and criticize institutions and programs in terms of considerations that others, as free and equal, have reason to accept, *given the fact of reasonable pluralism and on the assumption that those others are themselves concerned to provide suitable justifications.*

Impartiality means that different perspectives are treated in an even-handed manner, so that the gains from including (the representatives of) affected publics in deliberative processes are not undermined by giving undue weight to private considerations (e.g. the monetary gains to corporate executives from pursuing the risk-bearing activities). This gives critical weight to the liberal democratic norm that decisions in the *public interest* should not unfairly ignore the concerns of any significantly affected parties, in terms of both decision-making procedures and distributive outcomes. For global environmental governance, this means, at least in part, that the balancing of interests in international policy-making owes affected parties not only opportunities for representation but also equal respect for their concerns, extending geographically the liberal norm of equal consideration for all interests.

In the fragmented policy arenas of international bargaining, the impartiality of such reasoning is impaired not only by the prevalence of strategic motives but also the lack of consensus concerning how equality norms should impinge on state responsibility for environmental harm. Within international environmental negotiations, impartiality is promoted by the presence of procedural and distributive fairness in norm development, particularly recognizing the special claims of poorer countries. Despite the pervasive presence of strategic motives, there is clear evidence of fairness dialogue in the environmental regimes governing ozone depletion, climate change, transboundary air pollution, the high seas and Antarctica: relevant shared provisions directed at poorer countries include third-party dispute resolution, differentiated responsibilities, technological and financial transfers from the global North, and the idea of 'equitable sharing' of common resources (Franck, 1995: pp380–412; Albin, 2001: pp54–99). Some of these substantive examples are addressed in Chapter 3.

Yet fair treatment between states, which may well increase their consent to new environmental obligations, is oriented of course to *territorial* spaces of interest aggregation. Communicative accountability for transnational degradation rescales impartiality to denote which assessments and actions non-territorial affected publics could reasonably accept as participants in an agreement addressing their exposure to (potential) harm. Methodologically, this directs our attention to the assumptions and modes of reasoning employed by state and non-state actors, evaluating the extent to which there are free and equal discursive spaces making impartial judgment possible. Once again, the claims of environmental NGOs to represent vulnerable or affected publics should not be uncritically accepted: Kellow (1999: pp99–132), for example, argues that the 1989 Basel Convention regulating transboundary movements of hazardous wastes has been undermined by the moralistic campaigning of environmental NGOs and supportive European states, resulting in a ban on waste trading with counterproductive environmental effects (e.g. prevention of transnational waste recycling and disincentives to environmental invest-ments). This position bypasses too neatly the question of legal and moral responsibility for hazardous waste production. Nevertheless, in any discourse on transboundary and global environmental harm, neither the spatial identifi-cation of affected publics nor the articulation of their interests can be taken as given.

Transnational environmental rights

The convergence of the general principles of harm prevention, inclusiveness and impartiality, as outlined above, represents the democratic space marked out by a deliberative notion of environmental accountability. Building on the general obligations on, and between, states to prevent transboundary environ-mental harm, a pragmatist perspective widens out this space to include obligations to extra-territorial publics. State responsibility to these affected publics legally derives in the main from national regulatory controls imple-menting the provisions of multilateral environmental agreements – controls that are typically designed to prevent or limit harm arising from the domestic activities of nationals or foreign nationals. Chapter 3 enlarges on the geographical reach of these international environmental obligations, ident-ifying ways in which they are advancing accountability norms across territorial boundaries. Broadening out from these inter-state relations, there is a distinct class of transnational environmental obligations potentially more empowering of affected publics; that is, those obligations tied to the environmental rights of individuals and groups.

The strongest expression of environmental obligations that are cosmopolitan in scope would seem to be as human rights-based requirements, tying environmental norms to international human rights law. Human rights as core expressions of personal integrity and autonomy are, in principle, available and applicable to everyone, regardless of legal practice within individual states at any particular time. This universality underlies their relevance to a range of transnational relations involving both state and non-state actors: 'the doctrine of human rights is a statement of standards to guide the structures and conduct of global political life insofar as these bear on the conditions of life for individuals in their societies' (Beitz, 2001: p277). Such standards are now widely accepted as reasonable grounds for holding actors to account, as evident most clearly in the customary authority attached to the Universal Declaration of Human Rights (1948) and the binding treaty provisions of the 1966 United

Nations covenants on civil and political rights (in force March 1976) and economic, social and cultural rights (in force January 1976). Along with other international human rights agreements, these core instruments have not only deepened the accountability of states to their populations, they have also invited the prospect that the cross-border effects of state-led or approved activities (e.g. trade, development assistance, security policies) are creating new transnational human rights obligations (Skogly and Gibney, 2001).

Could these new state responsibilities include transnational obligations owed to members of affected publics on the basis of human environmental rights? While lacking an unambiguous expression in international law, proposals for a substantive human right to a clean, healthy or viable environment have come from many sources, including environmental NGOs, intellectuals, several state constitutions and the United Nations Human Rights Commission – notably the 1994 report on human rights and the environment by its Subcommission on the Prevention of Discrimination and Protection of Minorities (the Ksentini Report). A draft declaration of principles on human rights and the environment presented by this body includes a universal right to a secure, healthy and ecologically sound environment. This declaration failed to find favour in the international community, reflecting significant state opposition and uncertainties regarding legal application (Pevato, 1999). It remains unclear, above all, how an autonomous class of human environmental rights would relate to existing categories of rights, which themselves have different governance implications (e.g. the realization of economic, social and cultural rights is perhaps more susceptible to transnational influences than state-centred civil and political freedoms). Furthermore, a new human right to a healthy and ecologically secure environment could be seen as redundant given the emergence of multilateral legal instruments and institutions promoting environmental protection (Boyle, 1996: pp53–7). Such misgivings have dissipated the initial momentum created by the Ksentini Report, at least in terms of state sponsorship of the draft declaration.

However, as argued by two leading legal scholars, environmental rights are acquiring force in international law as green interpretations and applications of existing human rights (Birnie and Boyle, 2002: pp259–67). In the first place, they note how the rights to life, private home life and property contained in the United Nations Covenant on Civil and Political Rights, the 1950 European Convention on Human Rights and the 1969 American Convention on Human Rights have been successfully invoked for environ-mental purposes in a number of cases. For example, in the *Lopez* v. *Spain* (1994) and the *Guerra* v. *Italy* (1998) rulings, the European Court of Human Rights found that states had violated the applicants' right to respect for private and home life (Article 8 of the 1950 European Convention) as a result of illegal pollution emissions (this illegality, in particular, undermining the sovereign states' defence of fair treatment of affected parties). And in 1985, in another important ruling, *Yanomani Indians* v. *Brazil*, the Inter-American Commission on Human Rights found that the social and environmental consequences of the construction of a road through the traditional lands of an aboriginal group had violated their rights to life and health. While confined to the domestic human rights effects of governmental decision-making, these cases attest to the ability of affected individuals and groups to seek transnational legal remedies against state authorities for what external courts interpret to be serious, unreasonable harm. They also leave open the further possibility that states may face responsibility for the harmful effects of domestic activities on private life and property in neighbouring countries (Birnie and Boyle, 2002: p265).

Secondly, existing civil and political rights provide mechanisms for pursuing environmental protection through procedural rights, including access to environmental information, participation in relevant decision-making, freedom of association for ecological campaigning, and access to effective administrative and judicial remedies for environmental harm. The Ksentini Report identified such a list of participatory rights which stand on firmer legal ground than substantive human environmental rights: they find expression in Principle 10 of the Rio Declaration as well as a range of international environmental agreements surveyed by Birnie and Boyle – for example, Articles 2(6) and 3(8) of the 1991 Convention on Environmental Impact Assessment in a Transboundary Context, Article 14 of the 1992 Biological Diversity Convention, and Articles 14–16 of the 1993 Council of Europe Convention on Civil Liability for Damage Resulting from Activities Dangerous to the Environment. More, ambitiously, such rights are the regional focus of the 1998 (Aarhus) Convention on Access to Information, Public Participation in Decision-making and Access to Justice in Environmental Matters (United Nations Economic Commission for Europe, 1999). This far-reaching treaty is forecast to shape legislation and policies across Europe: its key significance for widening transnational accountability for environmental harm turns on the explicit recognition of participatory rights in environmental governance (see Chapter 3).

Given that most progress in enabling non-state parties to seek redress for transboundary environmental harm has come from their increasing access to the national legal systems of responsible actors, a third area in which human environmental rights are being facilitated, according to Birnie and Boyle (2002: pp267–82), is the use of private law remedies. The opportunity for affected individuals and groups directly to pursue transnational civil litigation against particular polluters bypasses the more elevated realm of inter-state claims, where state responsibility for cross-border environmental damage may be difficult to establish. Transboundary environmental rights for civil claimants are realized by mechanisms allowing them legal equality of consideration regardless of nationality or residence. Under the non-discrimination principle of international law, states are obliged to provide equal treatment for non-national affected parties on a par with nationals in respect of access to judicial remedies. As noted by Birnie and Boyle, there remain significant procedural and jurisdictional obstacles to securing such equality of access, exacerbated by divergent legal systems. Inter-state harmonization of national civil liability systems, whether through multilateral treaties or the erosion within states of legal grounds for dismissing claimants from other countries, nevertheless provides evidence for the development of private law instruments promoting transnational environmental accountability. Substantive discussion of this area is provided in Chapter 5.

The three domains of rights application outlined here indicate distinctive trajectories for transnational environmental rights, none of which seems likely to recede in the foreseeable future. Yet to discard also any prospect for further elaboration of a universal human right to a clean, healthy or viable environment ignores the vocal arguments of environmental activists, taking as politically settled what is actually strongly contested (see Chapter 2). More pertinently in this chapter, it also accepts as legitimate for transnational publics what has emerged from an international legal framework crafted above all by states upholding national interests. The non-territorial notion of democratic accountability is certainly consistent with the global aspirations of core civil and political human rights: indeed, such rights are a necessary precondition for promoting the reciprocal recognition and open identification of individuals as members of affected publics. But I wish to press beyond this point: transnational environmental obligations may be owed by responsible state and non-state actors to members of affected publics not only as participatory entitlements or health, home life and property rights, they may also be owed because of (potential) damage to wider social and ecological conditions of life. In other words, whatever the current legal ambiguities, there is a clear moral case that transnational publics affected by the threat or incidence of serious environmental harm have human rights-based reasons for prioritizing their socio-ecological interests. As I have argued elsewhere, a compelling rationale for recognizing basic environmental rights to socially and ecologically secure conditions of life is that they are necessary for the effective exercise of civil, political and other freedoms (Mason, 1999: pp58–63).

This justification highlights the parallel between this aspect of environmental rights and existing social and economic human rights (e.g. rights to essential health services, social welfare, free choice of employment and trade union representation), which are designed to promote adequate conditions of life. It is generally recognized that (trans)national obligations generated by these rights in public international law (i.e. those falling upon states) are less obvious in their application than for civil and political rights. Discretion is afforded to governments to pursue appropriate policies, cooperating across national borders where appropriate with other states and NGOs to help ensure transnational fulfillment of social and economic rights (Skogly and Gibney, 2001). Extending this category of rights to selected environmental entitlements faces the same challenge to apportion obligations among relevant actors. To recall the schema of transboundary publics presented in the Introduction, it is reasonable to anticipate increasing difficulty in locating accountable actors as the move is made away from border-impact and point-source risks to the more diffuse pathways of (potential) harm associated with entrenched systems of political and economic decision-making. At all scales, furthermore, transnational obligations on responsible actors to deliver necessary levels of environmental protection or remediation will necessarily entail context-sensitive institutional designs and regulatory instruments.

Yet even allowing for such contingency in meeting human rights-based obligations for transnational environmental accountability (which applies also to the green application of existing rights), their moral and political thrust is clear. The environmental interests of individuals or groups affected by transboundary harm invite human rights consideration when they are associated with *vital* conditions of existence (e.g. clean air and water, ecologically sustainable land use). Charles Jones (1999) demonstrates in this way how the provision of secure social and ecological living conditions underpins basic human rights: 'it follows from the commitment to protect rights to subsistence and security that one should be directly concerned with large-scale environmental degradation whose likely long-term consequences threaten the interests those rights are designed to protect' (p219). In so far as the legitimacy of states is tied to rights protection, he adds, then this is questioned not only if governments struggle to provide vital living conditions for their own national citizens, but also if they disregard any concern for the human rights of others – particularly when domestic-based activities may have undesirable human rights impacts on non-nationals. Of course, as far as transnational publics are concerned, environmental rights may be invoked *against* the state – as well as private agents – for activities violating their vital interests.

Furthermore, it should not be assumed that harm is received uniformly between or within affected publics – even given the same physical exposure. Individuals and groups have varied capacities to respond to environmental hazards (which themselves are more or less mediated by technological processes). As Blaikie et al (1994) suggest in their comparative analysis of 'natural' hazards in the global South, the differential *vulnerability* of populations to disastrous events must be related to the socio-economic patterns of access of affected parties to life and livelihood opportunities, including their capabilities to take advantage of these opportunities. The social production of vulnerability by networks of economic and political power systematically restricts the life and livelihood opportunities of certain individuals, groups and even populations. Threats to vital interests are obviously felt most acutely by those already constrained in their capacities to act, who may therefore be less able and/or willing to challenge them. What is crucial for the communicative framework of transnational accountability developed here is that its critical principle of public justification – resting on the shared approval of all affected by harm – reflects the needs of vulnerable agents. Here we can draw on Onora

O'Neill's (2000: pp162–3) notion of possible consent to reject oppressive situations in which vulnerable people, weighed down by low expectations, may 'accept' circumstances harmful to their basic interests. Possible consent, as legitimate consent, highlights the extent to which a set of arrangements affecting vulnerable lives can effectively be refused or renegotiated by those whom they constrain in practice. In effect this reveals that environmental (ecological and social) obligations fall on those actor groups producing not only particular environmental changes but also systemic conditions of vulnerability (e.g. trade-related ecological harm; see Chapter 4).

Both obligations to environmental integrity and obligations to the vulnerable are not exhausted by human rights claims (or their anthropocentric valuation framework). Where risks to affected publics clearly do not entail threats to vital interests, it is still possible to justify general obligations of environmental virtue related to the rejection of indifference to environmental protection (O'Neill, 1996: pp203–5). Such care for the environment, expressed transnationally, typically reflects diverse ethical and aesthetic motivations for valuing perceived non-human nature. It may also, on a more direct human level, promote actions by sympathetic parties designed to reduce or mitigate the environmental vulnerability of distant strangers. To be sure, these obligations – deriving from membership of a shared planet and species – are imperfect, in that they cannot be claimed as a moral (human) right by their addressees in the way that obligations to prevent significant transboundary harm can: the difference expresses the asymmetry between, on the one hand, strong moral obligations to refrain from injuring vital ecological interests and, on the other, less binding obligations to promote environmental care (O'Neill, 1996: p191; 2000: p107). As with transnational humanitarian obligations, it is wrong never to undertake virtuous acts on behalf of the less fortunate, but permissible not always to be behaving in this way. The onus to act increases the more non-national affected parties reasonably identify the consequences of indifferent behaviour as potentially causing them significant harm.

Conclusion

Transnational accountability for environmental harm concerns cross-border obligations owed to negatively affected publics by relevant state and non-state producers of ecological change. The moral justification for these obligations arises from recognized liberal democratic entitlements to harm prevention, inclusiveness and impartiality, but extends these outwards from national spaces of self-determination. As transnational *moral requirements*, they presuppose non-territorial communicative spaces where affected parties are afforded the opportunity to question the justification of harmful activities; in particular, whether these activities have effectively taken into account their interests. This notion of accountability inherits from pragmatist arguments both the commitment to social inquiry among those actors most directly affected by the indirect consequences of material transactions (John Dewey's formulation of the public) and the interest in institutionalizing such transnational democratic discourse. Its critical function is to evaluate the democratic legitimacy of harm production (including its unequal effects between and within publics) issuing from specific networks of political and economic power.

Transnational environmental obligations as *political or legal requirements* refer to mechanisms designed to realize accountability norms in practice. What rules can be formulated and implemented in order to enable the democratic determination of collective interests by affected publics, and then to endow these concerns with some form of authority? Domestically, liberal democratic states are vested with the legal power and financial resources to address the demands of their (sub)national publics for common goods and services, retaining also the core capacity to sanction those causing unacceptable social and ecological damage. Globally, in an era of volatile transboundary risks, the 'return of the public domain' (Drache, 2001) signals efforts by many states to reassert collective regulatory control, including the protection of common ecological assets. As noted above, international accountability rules allow some redress for publics receiving cross-border harm, whether this is mediated through state-centred norms of environmental responsibility or drawing more directly (and tentatively) on human environmental rights. That many environmental NGOs and activist networks still find both areas lacking the necessary force to change behavioural incentives for offending actors explains in part their continued reliance on other forms of pressure (e.g. political lobbying, public shaming, consumer pressure, direct action protests) to bring to account those they hold responsible for causing social and ecological harm to others.

Of course representations of concerns as 'public' cannot themselves escape critical examination: there are political struggles over which interests can be justified as generalizable. Different actors bring different experiences and motivations to bear on claims for public policy consideration: their capacities to do so reflect wider inequalities in economic and social power. Governments in particular have substantial resources and obvious political motivations for wanting to monopolize claims featuring public-interest norms, reinforcing the universal pretensions of state authority. But these considerations should not lead us to identify the presence only of strategic or instrumental forces in debates on the common good, dismissing the 'fantasy of a public' as an ideological fiction imposed on social discourse by dominant groups (Dean, 2001). A critical pragmatist notion of the public, as presented in this chapter, pushes to the foreground the conditions of democratic communication for transnational problem-solving. It retains the idea of a 'rational force' of deliberation on the effects of transboundary harm production, such that the formation of self-aware publics can be promoted, and the needs of their constituent individuals and groups can be collectively directed at responsible agents. The other chapters in this book bring this framework of accountability to bear on a range of actor groups and issue areas.

Chapter 2

Advocates for Environmental Accountability: Activist Groups, Networks and Movements

It has become increasingly difficult for democratic states and corporations to ignore public questioning when activities they are engaged in are seen to be generating the possibility or incidence of significant ecological harm. Since the rise of modern environmentalism in the 1970s, concerned individuals and interest groups have tirelessly pressed those in authority to address the negative ecological impacts of various material practices. And the growth of environmental regulation – nationally and internationally – attests to the recognition by many governments that this is now a legitimate area for action, even if the content and scope of this rule-making have often been constrained by other – typically economic – policy priorities. At any one time, in any one place, the political influence of environmentalist claims rises or falls according to a host of dynamic, interrelated factors, including the nature of perceived risks, shifting social values, political systems of interest representation and technological-economic changes. What is noteworthy, therefore, is the recent growth of transnational forms of environmentalist association and action converging on demands for greater accountability of state and market actors for behaviour producing ecological damage. This political networking is even more striking if considered a constituent part of a broader expression of disquiet with current paths of economic integration, as relayed by numerous transnational activist groupings – both reformist and radical.

It is possible to identify here the workings of a transnational or global civil society; that is, a 'sphere of ideas, values, organisations, networks and individuals located primarily outside the institutional complexes of family, market and the state, and beyond the confines of national societies, polities, and economies' (Kaldor et al, 2003: p4). Growing civic engagement across borders is by no means restricted to political activism: it entails a rich variety of associational forms, such as inter-faith dialogue, nongovernmental organization (NGO) delivery of development programmes, scientific communities, charity work, cultural events and amateur recreation. In this chapter, though, I examine transnational activist groups and networks motivated, above all, by environmental protection goals. What they share politically with other 'global justice' groupings (e.g. human rights, development activists) is the concern that processes of global economic integration – driven by hyper-mobile capital and information flows – are undermining the ability of communities and governments to support non-market aspects of well-being. For environment-alist activists, of course, the focus is on transboundary ecological damage associated with the global scale and rising intensity of economic transactions, rather than, say, income inequality or public health impacts. Nevertheless, there is a common diagnosis of a global accountability deficit – an absence of organized, effective control of economic globalization and its effects (Paehlke, 2003).

Transnational civil society activists routinely advocate greater public accountability from those who exercise economic or political power across borders. They claim to represent legitimately the interests of affected publics by scrutinizing the behaviour of power-holders and assigning moral responsi-bility for harm production, whether or not this attribution fits with existing territorial or privates rules of accountability. The accelerating spatial reach and falling costs of electronic communications networks have, since the 1980s, technically enabled these global accountability challenges. Indeed, what Dryzek (1999: p45) labels the *communicative power* of transnational civil society – questioning, criticizing and publicizing abuses of authority – has arguably become its key political resource (see also Risse, 2000; Keane, 2001). Furthermore, this capability of civil society organizations accords with the communicative notion of public accountability advanced in this book. To restate briefly, accountability for environmental harm across borders involves answerability and redress to those (potentially) affected by that harm, invoking the principle of equal respect for all individuals. The more the public interests at stake can be demonstrated to be vital to the ecological well-being of the affected parties, the greater their moral entitlement to strict protection rather than mitigation or compensation.

The accountability-driven structure of much transnational civic activism represents empirical support for my general assertion that new (non-territorial) responsibility norms have political currency, although the validity of these norms is of course contested. After outlining the broader civil society context of the growth of transnational advocacy for the environment, I consider the major organizational forms of this activism – NGOs, advocacy networks and global justice movements – in order to set out their distinctive accountability claims. As civil society activism has mushroomed in recent years, its own presumption to democratic legitimacy has been increasingly questioned, and not only by neoliberal and conservative opponents. Here I discuss what public accountability means applied to civil society organizations, and how this poses particular challenges for environmental groups and networks.

Environmental activism within global civil society

In the past few decades, civil society groups committed to environmental protection have been at the forefront of efforts to publicize transboundary and global pathways of ecological harm. The adoption of transnational advocacy structures presented a logical organizational response not only to a rising incidence of cross-border environmental impacts, but also to a perceived failing of states to respond with effective international regulation. Given the profusion of transnational environmental activism in the 1990s, it is not surprising that this type of civic action provided evidence for early sightings of a global civil society, notably by American political scholars Ronnie Lipschutz and Paul Wapner.

Both authors recognize that cross-border environmental activism goes beyond engagement with state actors, seeking to advance ecological protection goals through wider attitudinal and behaviour changes. Its broader contribution to global environmental governance is to redirect social choices voluntarily, appealing directly to individuals through particular knowledge claims, norms and actions. Lipschutz is sensitive to the new forms of political solidarity possible when groups of people affected by environmental injury are able to identify themselves as implicated adversely in specific chains of production or consumption (Lipschutz with Mayer, 1996: pp217–33). Although the accountability implications are not developed, this constitution of political community in relational rather than territorial terms overlaps neatly with the notion of affected publics put forward in this study. Wapner's elaboration of the civic political influence of transnational environmental activist groups highlights their interaction in economic, social and cultural realms of life. Leading environmental groups serve as exemplars for the distinctive types of civic intervention possible: the witnessing and campaigning of Greenpeace serves globally to disseminate an ecological sensibility; the concrete project interventions of WWF in socially and ecologically vulnerable communities strive to realize sustainable development as a vehicle for local empowerment; while the strategic fixation of Friends of the Earth on pinpointing ecologically damaging investment and commodity cycles raises responsibility claims not acknowledged or enforced by state authorities. This rich tapestry of associative action seeks, in short, to alter social behaviour outside the arena of inter-state regulation (Wapner, 1996).

As measured by membership and income, the three groups studied by Wapner remain the key triumvirate of transnational environmental NGOs. WWF operates in more than 90 countries, claims 5 million members and received US$332 million in income in 2002 – almost half of that coming from individual subscriptions and donations, with other major revenue streams from governments and aid agencies (22 per cent), legacies (13 per cent), trusts and foundations (6 per cent) and corporate donations (5 per cent) (WWF, 2003).

Over the past decade WWF membership has risen five-fold and income six-fold. Worldwide, Greenpeace has 38 national offices, over 2.8 million subscribing supporters and maintains impressive income growth, with a total revenue in 2002 of Euro165.4 million (US$209 million): membership and income have doubled since the early 1990s. The great bulk of Greenpeace's income comes from individual donations and grants from independent foundations: the NGO continues to refuse funding from corporations and governmental bodies (Greenpeace International, 2003). As a global federation of 5,000 local activist groups in 68 countries, Friends of the Earth International (FOEI) claims over a million individual members. While the NGO releases financial records only of its international secretariat in Amsterdam – which recorded a 2002 income of Euro1.52 million (US$1.86 million), the aggregate income across the whole network is estimated to be approximately US$200 million. Like Greenpeace, the vast majority of this income comes from membership fees and foundation grants, although FOEI also receives non-campaign funding from selected government agencies (Friends of the Earth International, 2003).

The continued prominence of these three NGOs runs alongside a sharp rise of environmental and other NGOs operating transnationally. The *World Directory of Environmental Organizations* records 317 active 'international environmental NGOs' (Trzyna and Didion, 2001: pp69–120). As recorded by the Union of International Associations, the number of 'international NGOs' (INGOs) – not-for-profit, non-state organizations with cross-national structure and/or purpose – increased from 13,309 in 1981 to 47,098 in 2001. Most of these are not politically active. Environmental INGOs make up 2.9 per cent of the latter total (over 1,350), reflecting a broader definition than the *World Directory*. Interestingly, environmental INGOs still lag behind education, research and economic development INGOs in terms of numbers, but are significant in comparison with other value-based or advocacy INGOs (e.g. politics, religion). Analysis of these figures by London School of Economics researchers indicates that the traditional concentration of INGOs and their membership support in Europe and North America is being weakened by high INGO expansion rates in the new democracies of central and eastern Europe, as well as in Asia (facilitated by new associative freedoms). This recent growth includes the creation of many new environmental INGOs (e.g. in the Russian Federation, Malaysia, Philippines and Thailand). Furthermore, world value surveys demonstrate that the motivational support helping drive new environmental INGO formation – that is, the willingness of individuals to become members of, or volunteer for, environmental voluntary activities – jumped up during the 1990s in democratic states (Kaldor et al, 2003: pp10–19, 346–50).

Explanations for the spread of environmental INGOs and advocacy networks fall into three broad perspectives. First, a *liberal institutionalist* approach cautions against understanding transnational activism as a separate sphere of political activity cut loose from state structures and interests. Here, the creation of international institutions reflects the desire of states to cooperate in the resolution of collective problems. This regime-building generates incentives for transnational activism, which in turn serves the interests of international institutions and their supporting states: NGOs and advocacy networks may provide technical assistance (e.g. research, monitoring of states' behaviour) and/or political support (e.g. pressuring member states over treaty implementation commitments and encouraging non-members to sign up) (Raustiala, 1997). The increase in the reach and complexity of international environmental rule-making opens up ever more opportunities for ecological activists to meet these regulatory needs, although whether they do or not rests on their own organizational beliefs, skills and resources. From this perspective, a key factor behind the flourishing of transnational environmental activism since the 1980s was the pressing need of a weak United Nations Environment Programme (UNEP) to elicit NGO participation in the agenda-setting for, and formulation of, international ecological regimes (Kellow, 2000: pp3–7). External incentives to NGO activism are bound up also with domestic political contexts, and these need not be favourable; for example, environmentalists may be attracted to transnational advocacy because they are politically weak in their home state relative to economic development proponents.

A counter-argument to this preoccupation with material interests is offered, secondly, by a *constructivist* perspective maintaining that ideas and norms have a significant causal role in accounting for the rise and characteristics of cross-border environmental activism. Both transnational NGOs and advocacy networks share a principled commitment to secure changes in social understanding and action, which derives in large part from the identification of their members with environmentalist values. Already we have noted Paul Wapner's stress on what he labels the 'cultural agency' of environmental NGOs, framing issues in a way that seeks to alter the normative context within which citizens, states and corporations operate (see also Wapner, 2002). It has also been argued that the rise of transnational activist networks, in which NGOs play a central role, is encouraged by their organizational stress on this cultural agency – creating flexible, horizontal patterns of communication effectively to promote value-based claims (Keck and Sikkink, 1998). The constructivist position also posits, though, that the larger cultural and institutional context for this communication is crucial: proposed environment-alist (and other) norms, as new standards of appropriate behaviour, are more likely to succeed if they 'fit' or resonate with established social norms. For some authors, this serves as a moderating influence, which may well compromise environmentalist goals. An obvious example is the wide currency accorded in global environmental governance to sustainable development principles, which arguably dilute ecological protection goals by fusing them with mainstream market norms promoting economic growth (Bernstein, 2001). However, as stated below, norm resonance can also enable activists to extend existing democratic accountability norms in innovative, challenging ways.

Third, the interplay of transnational civil society groupings with the forces of economic globalization, as structured by capitalist modes of production, is the central focus of a *critical political economy* perspective. Both liberal institutional and constructivist approaches are viewed as downplaying the power relations deeply embedded in global capitalism. For example, Alejandra Colás identifies 'international civil society' as 'an area of antagonistic class relations where conflicting socio-economic interests and rival political programmes contend for power' (2002: p167). The emergence and growth of NGOs is thus explained by their legitimating value to dominant state and class interests: they take over regulatory and welfare services abandoned by governments. From this position, reformist NGOs campaigning for environmental protection tend to be reproached for their complicity in apolitical notions of global governance, representing the incidence of ecological harm as a technical, problem-solving exercise rather than a question of justice for victims. In contrast, the rise of 'anti-globalization' or 'anti-capitalist' movements attests to the possibility of more oppositional civil society responses to the global political and economic order. Their vocal demonstrations and other protests, informed by independent spaces of interest formation (e.g. alternative forums and summits, internet bulletin boards) generate uncompromising accountability demands, particularly of international economic institutions (Chandhoke, 2002; Ford, 2003).

Not surprisingly, given this last point, the three explanatory models carry distinctive political policy agendas: the contrast is clearest between the self-professed radicalism of critical political economy and the managerial problem-solving of liberal institutionalism. In so far as the constructivist position is arguably more open to understanding public expressions of environmentalist interests in and of themselves – as shared realms of experience bound up with, but not wholly reducible to, territorial or class-centred identities – it could be seen as contributing more effectively to political mappings of environmental accountability. Yet both the liberal institutionalist and critical political economy approaches home in on particular forms of transnational advocacy and their associated accountability demands. There are good analytical reasons, therefore, to consider all three perspectives when looking at the major organizational types of this activism – NGOs, advocacy networks and social movements – and their respective accountability politics.

Transnational environmental NGOs

NGOs remain the preferred mode for cross-border environmentalist advocacy. In spite of the preference of the Union of International Associations for the term 'international' to designate this reaching out beyond domestic political systems, I shall refer to 'transnational' NGOs in order signal their basic autonomy *vis-à-vis* inter-state relations. To be sure, the Union treats the non-state, not-for-profit characteristics of NGOs as their key identifying trait but, as already noted, additional qualifications are necessary to capture the value-based, advocacy stance of environmental NGOs. Again, Wapner (2000: pp89–92; 2002: pp39–40) distils most adeptly the nature of those preoccupied with cross-border activism: *transnational* environmental NGOs are groups formed on a voluntary basis with the aim of protecting some dimension of the 'non-human world'. They utilize multiple means of political engagement but focus on regional or global dimensions of environmental harm. As Wapner notes, organizationally they may not actually have many members in other countries (e.g. US Sierra Club, Centre for Science and Development in India) but they articulate transnational and global issues of concern: 'these groups are able to project extra-territorial relevance because the campaigns in which they are involved often relate to broader struggles in other countries or because communication technologies advertise their efforts and relate them to the sensibilities of citizens outside their domestic context' (2000: p90).

The fluid spatial imagination of environmental NGOs is central to their construction of public accountability claims against states, international organizations and corporations. NGOs assert that they are accurately conveying the full scope of negative biophysical impacts arising from the behaviour of certain actors; in other words, that their representation of harmed ecological interests captures the geographical scale of the problem. Where transnational risk or harm is invoked, this political representation presumes moral authority on behalf of affected publics because these communities of shared fate are, NGOs contend, routinely ignored or neglected by state-centred (territorial) and market-based (contractual) rules of responsibility. Thomas Princen (1994) was one of the first commentators to recognize this type of transnational positioning as a core political asset for environmental NGOs. It entails the mobilization of information and media attention to highlight dramatically pathways of ecological harm, tracking back from damaged ecosystems to particular human choices. And supported by this environmental communication, it then involves engagement with centres of decision-making authority, demanding answers and redress. Several types of political advocacy typically feature here – provision of policy-relevant information, participation in United Nations (UN) global environmental conferences, lobbying state and economic actors and monitoring of multilateral environmental agreements. I shall address each in turn.

Provision of policy-relevant information

From a liberal institutionalist perspective, the most tangible benefit to states arising from their engagement with environmental NGOs is the provision of policy-relevant information. The existence of complex ecological interdependencies means that, for any one issue, it is often not clear to governments if their national interests are served by committing to international rule-making. Uncertainty and the costs of policy research oriented to transboundary ecological issues (which includes, of course, not only applied environmental science but also work on the feasibility of regulatory options) create an information deficit inviting to NGOs claiming to possess relevant expertise. Given that environmental NGOs are usually prepared to provide such information to governmental actors at little or no cost, states can draw from a substantial pool of civil society analysis to maximize policy intelligence in a cost-effective manner (Raustiala, 1997: pp726–8). It is not surprising, therefore, that NGOs are attuned to these opportunities for policy research and agenda-setting, though the preference of states for fact-based analysis serving their own territorial priorities militates against the acceptance of value-based accountability claims encompassing the social and ecological needs of foreigners. This presents a dilemma for NGOs, as favoured access to policy-makers may well compromise their own advocacy goals.

One response is for NGOs to separate out their information-exchange role. For example, over 750 NGOs belong – alongside numerous states, government agencies and knowledge-based experts – to IUCN, the World Conservation Union, which is a well-established information clearing house for nature conservation, with a global reputation for credible, authoritative research (both scientific and policy-oriented). Other transnational environmental NGOs have been set up with a research and/or policy development focus. This is most evident in the US, where the availability of substantial foundation funding means that their income sources are not reliant on advocacy-led membership drives – for example, the World Resources Institute and the Worldwatch Institute (both located in Washington).

Participation in UN global environmental conferences

As high-profile forums setting out, for ecological protection and human development, international policy agendas and political commitments to institutional capacity-building, UN global environmental conferences have attracted substantial NGO involvement. To follow environmental NGO input into the landmark events – from the Stockholm Conference on the Human Environment (1972), through the Rio Conference on Environment and Development (1992) to the Johannesburg World Summit on Sustainable Development (2002) – is to notice their growing participation, albeit one conceded by states on condition that NGOs have no negotiating (rule-making) rights. While NGO interaction with the UN system covers more than participation in international conferences, encompassing interactions with general or specialist bodies and service-delivery funding, opportunities for political influence have historically been very limited. In particular, the routine access of environmental NGOs to UNEP must be set against the relatively weak status of that body within the UN system. In UN conferences, however, more open agendas and procedures have allowed environmental NGOs to adopt more influential methods of participation, such as dialogue with the conference secretariat, input into the deliberations of national delegations, networking with other NGOs in parallel meetings and producing unofficial conference bulletins (Willetts, 1996; Clark et al, 1998).

Environmental NGO success in building support for conference declarations and action plans has encouraged the UN to extend NGO accreditation and conference participation rights to more environmental groups. Accreditation of NGOs by the Economic and Social Council (ECOSOC) is enabled by Article 71 of the UN Charter, as elaborated on by ECOSOC Resolution 1996/31. In August 2003, of 134 'international NGOs' with the highest ECOSOC consultative status ('general consultative'), six were environmental advocacy groups (Environmental Development Action in the Third World, Global 2000, Green Cross International, Greenpeace International, International Council for Environmental Law and World Wide Fund for Nature International). More importantly, some 60 environmental advocacy groups possessed lower 'special consultative' status – a more feasible designation given the issue- and sector-specific concerns of these NGOs, but one which still accords them significant consultative entitlements at ECOSOC. An ECOSOC subsidiary body, the Commission on Sustainable Development (a product of the Rio Conference), has institutionalized an expanded role for NGOs through its NGO Steering Committee, which annually elects caucuses of civil society representatives to coordinate the communication of NGO concerns to states.

To qualify for UN accreditation, NGOs must demonstrate at least an independence from governments, no ambitions for political office, a non-profit-making status, a commitment to non-violence and clear support for the work of the UN. These criteria have served as the benchmark for inviting NGOs not accredited with ECOSOC nevertheless to attend UN environmental conferences as registered participants. Maurice Strong, Secretary-General of both the Stockholm and Rio meetings, was instrumental in facilitating this wider NGO involvement, particularly at the latter conference: over 250 NGOs were registered for the Stockholm Conference, while 1450 were accredited to the Rio Conference. For Strong the parallel NGO event at Rio – the Global Forum (attended by an estimated 18,000 people) – was one of the most important successes of the 1992 gathering, coordinating NGO positions and feeding these into the official intergovernmental meeting (Strong, 2001: pp196–7, 223). Ten years later, the parallel civil society event at the Johannesburg Summit attracted some 40,000 people while some 4,500 NGOs were registered for the conference.

Lobbying state and economic actors

The efforts of environmental NGOs to influence state behaviour in international rule-making and enforcement constitute their core political advocacy in relation to global governance. While often the first to draw attention to the modest ambitions of most multilateral environmental agreements (MEAs), NGOs nevertheless recognize their capacity legitimately to constrain the acts of harm producers. As already noted, states themselves find value in the skills, resources and potential support of NGOs in global environmental governance. Even at the negotiations stage of proposed MEAs, environmental NGOs can assist treaty-sponsoring states by, for example, relaying intelligence on other state actors and lobbying recalcitrant ones. Recent research suggests that the political influence of environmental advocacy on MEA formulation and implementation is very much context-dependent. Studies of environmental NGO lobbying targeted at international rule-making on biodiversity, climate change and desertification (Arts, 1998; Corell and Betsill, 2001; Arts and Mack, 2003) acknowledge the significance of their internal organizational resources and choices in exercising pressure, but that successful outcomes vary according to the nature and framing of the issue, as well as the relative openness of the negotiations (generally, NGO influence is most likely at the agenda-setting stage). The next chapter shows how the gradual emergence of new procedural entitlements for NGOs in MEAs is facilitating their limited input in treaty implementation.

Advocacy-based environmental NGOs are proving more adept at directly targeting corporate actors as key harm producers. This activism derives in part from a perception that governmental authorities are compromised in their efforts to regulate transnational trade and investment flows, unwilling to upset powerful business interests and unable, anyway, to subordinate them to non-market environmental norms. Peter Newell (2001) labels as 'civil regulation' the broad range of strategies employed by NGOs in order to hold corporations to account for their transnational environmental performance; for example, consumer pressure, codes of conduct, environmental stewardship regimes and shareholder activism. Chapter 6 examines the accountability gains claimed for these modes of civil regulation, which are discussed alongside other methods for making corporations answerable to affected publics. Transnational environmental NGOs are popularly associated with particular stances in relation to major corporations, typically the confrontation style of Greenpeace (e.g. with its consumer boycotts of Shell and Exxon Mobil) as against the partnership style of WWF International (e.g. its work with building-aggregates firm Lafarge to reduce its energy consumption and waste generation). But even Greenpeace has discovered positive corporate engagement, as in its promotion of 'ozone-friendly' refrigerators. Friends of the Earth maintains the most far-reaching advocacy in this area, spearheading lobbying for an international convention on corporate environmental and social accountability.

Monitoring of multilateral environmental agreements (MEAs)

NGO monitoring of state behaviour within MEAs is necessary to their effective functioning as political agents, generating information on the progress of selected arenas of international environmental regulation. Overwhelmingly, this monitoring of treaty implementation is informal, as states are obviously reluctant to cede any oversight authority to non-state actors, preferring to compile their own compliance records. The role of WWF staff members, through the TRAFFIC network, in providing research and surveillance services for the Convention on International Trade in Endangered Species is a well-known example of a formal monitoring responsibility delegated to a transnational NGO; and the next chapter identifies some other examples of new participation entitlements for NGOs in MEA implementation (notably access to compliance mechanisms within the 1998 Aarhus Convention). Such official involvement remains rare in international environmental treaties, but informal monitoring by NGOs often provides valuable information to member states on alleged cases of non-compliance: this information may be relayed directly to the relevant treaty secretariat and/or the media. And there are cases where environmental NGO scrutiny has led to compliance reforms following the exposure of weaknesses in implementation practices – for example, the new control measures adopted in 1997 under the Montreal Protocol on Substances that Deplete the Ozone Layer (1987) as a result of the London-based transnational NGO, the Environmental Investigation Agency, uncovering illegal trade in ozone-depleting substances (Andersen and Sarma, 2002: pp343–4).

Raustiala (1997: p729) cautions that this type of NGO monitoring remains imperfect, as environmental NGOs are often less concerned with legal compliance than with their own approval or disapproval of particular actions, even if these actions are not treaty violations (e.g. Greenpeace's opprobrium against states engaged in 'research whaling' under the International Whaling Convention, however much some of this hunting violates the spirit of the relevant treaty provision). However, this observation comes from a state-centred (liberal institutionalist) perspective: NGOs claim that they can properly have regard to broader issues of treaty effectiveness and environmental accountability.

Environmental advocacy networks

Since the mid-1980s, there has been a growing tendency for NGOs to participate, alongside other non-state actors and sympathetic (inter)governmental representatives, in strategic transnational alliances in pursuit of shared political goals. Normally coalescing around a particular issue, these 'transnational advocacy networks' are organized to promote causes, ideas and norms that entail changes in the behaviour of targeted political and economic institutions. The general preference of civil society actors for the network form (e.g. coalitions) reflects its organizational facility for dense information exchange at minimal costs, as enabled by modern communications technologies. Moreover, a decentralized structure provides flexibility for constituent groups to respond quickly to external events. In their seminal study of cross-border activists, Margaret Keck and Kathryn Sikkink (1998: p2) pinpoint the innovative ability of advocacy networks 'to mobilize information strategically and to help create new issue and categories and to persuade, pressure, and gain leverage over much more powerful organizations and governments' (see also Anheier and Themudo, 2002: pp199–202).

Networks tend to arise in response to what are alleged to be serious (potential) violations of human or ecological well-being; thus, as well as campaigning on environmental issues (e.g. transportation of hazardous wastes, tropical deforestation, biotechnology, climate change) disparate activists have worked together to address human rights, humanitarian and development-oriented concerns. Keck and Sikkink state that environmental advocacy networks differ in some respects from these other advocacy networks in being preoccupied more with addressing ecologically harmful property and resource use entitlements than with invoking violations of universally agreed rights (1998: pp121–2). Given the propensity of ecological activists to locate their claims within a transnational justice framework, this purported contrast now seems overstated. For example, the Climate Action Network – which draws together NGOs from over 80 countries – finds ideological unity in a commitment to the principle of international equity applied to actions both to reduce greenhouse gas emissions and to meet human development needs in poorer countries (Duwe, 2001). Furthermore, the accountability politics of advocacy networks shares common characteristics across issue areas.

In the first place, the structure of accountability challenges delivered by these networks is centred on their communicative capabilities, not only generating and disseminating information on harmful practices, but also using this publicity to seek answerability and redress from those held to be responsible. Transnational political advocacy need not relate solely to transboundary or global flows of harm: it can involve as well a cross-border convergence of activist pressure on particular governmental policies or the practices of private actors with negative domestic impacts. Keck and Sikkink (1998: pp12–13) identify a recurrent 'boomerang pattern' of activist pressure designed to overcome situations where domestic NGOs are blocked in their efforts to press home states to change policies or behaviour injuring the interests of local publics. With little internal political influence, these NGOs search out foreign activist allies to lobby their own governments and relevant third-party organizations (e.g. international financial institutions) to pressure the recalcitrant states.

Keck and Sikkink mainly discuss this type of flanking move against states in relation to Southern regimes who block or undermine the political campaigning of domestic activists (e.g. human rights networks targeting repressive governments in Myanmar and Zimbabwe). However, it can also include transnational advocacy networks coordinating pressure on Northern states where domestic political systems have not effectively registered the interests of affected publics (national or non-national) on a particular issue. The transnational campaign to ban anti-personnel landmines is often cited as a model example, where a media-literate advocacy network aligned with like-minded 'middle-power' governments (e.g. Austria, Canada, New Zealand, Norway, South Africa) to pressure militarily powerful states (e.g. US, Russia, China, UK, France) to abandon their landmines through international regulation (Rutherford, 2000; Cameron, 2002). Similarly, transnational environmental advocacy against commercial sea shipments of irradiated nuclear fuel between Britain, France and Japan has, since 1999, pulled in support from many countries with vulnerable coastlines (e.g. Chile, South Africa, South Korea and New Zealand). Indeed, close initial cooperation between Greenpeace – the lead environmental NGO involved – and Caribbean states forced the re-routing of planned shipments away from Caribbean waters (Singh, 1999; Townsend, 2002).

These examples reveal, second, that the content of accountability claims put forward by transnational advocacy networks is rendered more persuasive by invoking core international norms. Central to the effectiveness of the NGO coalition campaigning to ban landmines, it is argued, was the reframing of the issue away from a state-centred military security right to a breach of widely recognized humanitarian norms; in particular, those rejecting the indiscriminate harming of civilians during acts of war (Price, 1998: pp627–31; Cameron, 2002: pp71–2). In the case of irradiated nuclear fuel transportation, the shipping countries were charged with violating international legal norms governing the movement of ultra-hazardous materials, notably obligations to potentially affected states of harm prevention, prior notification, consultation and liability (Van Dyke, 2002: pp82–7).

The argument that claims on behalf of affected publics are more likely to strike a chord transnationally if they fit with existing accountability norms expresses a constructivist position noted earlier in the chapter. Cross-border advocacy networks have organized most effectively, Keck and Sikkink contend, where the issues of moral concern involve: (a) the exposure of vulnerable individuals to physical harm from obvious sources, and (b) breaches of legal equality of opportunity (1998: pp27–8). Of course, these normative properties reflect the wide transcultural acknowledgment of human rights norms as well as increasing adherence across the world to norms of democratic participation. Clearly there are parallels here with the framework of environmental accountability advanced in this book, which sets up harm prevention, inclusiveness and impartiality as necessary moral principles for marking out the obligations owed to affected publics by harm producers (see Chapter 1). Keck and Sikkink's findings offer empirical support that non-territorial 'horizontal'

(Cameron, 2002: p72) patterns of public accountability are emerging, liberating established responsibility norms from their territorial containment within national societies.

This is evident from Keck and Sikkink's discussion of environmental advocacy networks, specifically late twentieth-century activism targeting tropical deforestation. The general claim remains that the prevention or mitigation of physical harm was a central component of this transnational advocacy, but that Northern environmental campaigners judged that they could make more political headway by dwelling on the severe social impacts affecting indigenous peoples by industrial logging practices, rather than highlighting only threats to biological diversity. Of course, this by no means implies that the lead environmental activists from the US (Environmental Defense Fund, Natural Resources Defense Council, Sierra Club) or western Europe (Friends of the Earth International, WWF) were not convinced themselves by the human rights case; it is rather to locate a strategic rationale designed to maximize political influence across borders. Looking at transnational campaigns against deforestation policies in northwestern Brazil and the Malaysian state of Sarawak, Keck and Sikkink (1998: pp133–63) register the crucial switch made by the advocacy networks away from a scientifically informed preoccupation with conservation to a social justice concern with protecting ways of life, alternative livelihoods and cultural identities. Moreover, the public accountability thrust became much more direct; from trying to get states to realize forest management practices in line with conservation policy commitments to confronting these same governments with the testimony from those directly injured by their decisions. These recorded experiences of the negative consequences of state decisions created the locally affected publics from which activists gathered information about injuries and local preferences for alternative development paths.

In both the Brazilian and Malaysian cases, Keck and Sikkink note use of a 'boomerang' strategy, as transnational networking enabled domestic NGOs in the two countries to find outside activist allies and sympathetic states in order to build up pressure for change. For comparable regions of frontier development, though, there were marked divergences in outcomes, with some movement in Brazil towards more effective social and ecological regulation of economic development, but negligible change in Sarawak. To explain this, Keck and Sikkink (1998: pp162–3) stress key differences in the domestic governing systems, such as the more robust political dominance of Sarawak by elites profiting (legally and illegally) by the runaway timber extraction, and the lack of an outside material leverage on the Malaysian government, with no relevant multilateral loans for activists to target and an unwillingness of Northern states to sanction blanket import prohibitions of Malaysian timber. In contrast, in the Brazilian case, the reliance on a World Bank loan offered Northern members of the advocacy network an effective pressure point – above all, in terms of US and European campaigners lobbying legislative representatives to influence their respective national executive directors on the Bank's governing board. Indeed, the temporary suspension of the loan in 1985 triggered significant moves within the World Bank not only to monitor more carefully its funding in northwestern Brazil, but to begin a path of institutional reform towards making it more responsive to the complaints of those people directly affected by Bank projects (Udall, 1998).

The accountability politics of environmental advocacy networks thus seeks out opportunities to change policies as well as secure answerability and redress for the incidence or threat of specific harm production. Given the core capacity of the network form for mobilizing information and facilitating rapid communication between dispersed constituent groups, it is not surprising that substantial energy is devoted by activists to exposing publicly gaps between principled commitments and actual practices from those in authority (Keck and Sikkink, 1998: pp24–5; Dryzek, 1999: pp46–8). Less predictable is the means by which advocacy networks can go beyond persuasion, bringing into play legal challenges or material deprivations against the alleged wrongdoer. An important rationale for reforming governance institutions to allow more civil society participation is that this may well create additional regulatory possibilities for identifying and protecting public concerns. For example, a key governance demand of many environmental and consumer groups campaigning on plant biotechnology issues is that decision-making in this area – including risk assessments – is opened up to effective citizen and NGO input (Osgood, 2001: pp96–101). Yet this call has run alongside moves by other activists to mobilize transnational consumer pressure and direct action protests to reject biotechnology. The term 'social movement' is usually employed to grasp the oppositional character of these networks, which involve a more confrontational type of accountability politics. It is to these activist groupings that I now turn.

Transnational social movements

The rejectionist response of numerous groups and individuals across the world to genetically modified foods has encompassed types of actions which often take place within broad-based advocacy networks but which reflect a preference for resistance to, rather than communicative engagement with, biotechnology proponents. Examples include legal challenges to the patenting of genetically modified crops, globally coordinated demonstrations against the biotechnology company Monsanto, orchestrated consumer pressure on food companies to boycott products derived from biotechnology, and the physical destruction of field tests or commercial plantations of genetically modified crops (Osgood, 2001). There is a great diversity of actors involved in such opposition, driven by a variety of motives (with environmental concerns prominent – e.g. fears over potential impacts on biodiversity and soil fertility). What justifies the characterization of their collective mobilization as an 'anti-biotech movement' is a transnational commitment to take on powerful political and economic interests in order to defend certain ideas of human development and ecological well-being. Sidney Tarrow (2001: p11) neatly captures the generic property of transnational social movements as 'socially mobilized groups with constituents in at least two states, engaged in sustained contentious interaction with powerholders in at least one state other than their own, or against an international institution, or a multinational economic actor'.

In the case of the anti-biotech movement, this mobilization has fed into, and been informed by, wider protest networks rejecting the neoliberal project of economic globalization. Whether labelled as an anti-capitalist movement or, more positively, as a global justice movement, its central preoccupation is with challenging the transnational dominance of market liberalization as the arbiter of favoured development paths. Blocking or rolling back regulations seen as impeding free flows of capital, neoliberal policies continue to be championed by powerful Western states (notably the G7), transnational corporations, private financial actors and international economic institutions (e.g. International Monetary Fund (IMF), World Bank, World Trade Organization (WTO)). The global justice movement reacts to massive ecological and social dislocations associated with the expanding reach of market forces. From the critical political economy perspective, this transnational activism is directly provoked by the harmful consequences of neoliberal globalization. For example, Harvey (2003) observes an anti-capitalist movement railing against the systematic dispossession and privatization of communal environmental resources. Other like-minded commentators point to protests over the negative social and ecological impacts of foreign direct investment and IMF-imposed structural adjustment programmes in developing countries. Furthermore, the global justice movement is increasingly targeting global financial markets, highlighting their crisis propensity (e.g. the 1997–98 Asian private lending collapse) and a seemingly endemic cronyism spilling over repeatedly into corruption (e.g. recent corporate accountancy scandals in the US and Europe) (Desai and Said, 2001; Patomäki, 2001).

Not surprisingly, then, the public accountability concerns of this movement are *structural* – they relate to the social and ecological effects systemically produced by capitalist market relations and supported by sympathetic state policies. Neoliberal globalization accelerates environmental change in so far as it unleashes fully the growth dynamics of capital investment across borders, intensifying material/energy throughput, and scaling up the production and consumption of new commodities. Without denying the real welfare gains enjoyed by many from rising incomes, the dominance of economic development choices by profit-seeking market actors routinely socializes environmental risks; that is, ecological costs are displaced onto current and future publics. These costs entail not only the negative externalities arising from production processes, but also the harm rendered by financial crises, where the livelihoods and life quality of millions are blighted by collapses in personal savings and state tax revenues (Underhill, 2001). The most vulnerable are usually hit the hardest.

The global justice movement highlights the unfair distributional outcomes arising from economic development paths following a neoliberal trajectory. Environmental activists galvanized by ecological injury attributed to private investment and production processes have traditionally directed criticism at major corporations with poor pollution records or targeted particularly damaging commodity chains (e.g. tropical timber products). However, the oppositional politics of anti-capitalist campaigners has thrown up a broader, more demanding accountability challenge – 'holding those with power in the global economy, and/or in states to account, making them legitimise their actions, democratising them, transforming their effects' (Paterson, 2000: p149): in other words, to press them to take full responsibility for the social and ecological consequences of their decisions. Evidence that environmental concerns are informing such a radical accountability politics is apparent from global civil society summits and transnational spaces of resistance.

Global civil society summits

A notable innovation in the organized expression of the global justice movement is the convening of independent civil society summits. The early twenty-first century has seen a rapid growth of regional and global civil society gatherings, with increasing numbers of participants and new spaces for political deliberation on planetary futures. Their forerunners were the so-called parallel summits organized by activists and NGOs during the 1990s as shadow events to the official meetings of governments and international economic institutions. The more radical alternative summits combined street protests with the principled rejection of neoliberal policy-making, culminating at the turn of the century with high-profile demonstrations at the 1999 WTO ministerial conference in Seattle, the 2000 meeting of the IMF–World Bank in Prague and the 2001 G8 meeting in Genoa (Pianta, 2001). These parallel gatherings also served to assist the self-organization of global justice activists through policy discussions, information dissemination and networking. The first World Social Forum, held in January 2001 in Pôrto Alegre (Brazil) as a counter-summit to the World Economic Forum in Davos (Switzerland), heralded a shift to more autonomous gatherings of the global justice movement. By 2003, according to Pianta and Silva (2003: p387), the majority of transnational civil society summits had no corresponding intergovernmental meeting.

Environment-oriented NGOs are actively involved in these alternative gatherings: approximately a third of the civil society organizations attending recent summits recorded themselves as working on environmental themes (Pianta and Silva, 2003: p390). At the deliberative heart of the global justice movement, the World Social Forum process has, alongside economic and social development issues, engaged with questions of ecological sustainability. While, in deference to its diverse constituency of participant organizations, the forum does not adopt formal declarations, discussions at annual meetings have produced position statements on, for example, protecting common genetic resources (Pôrto Alegre, 2002), opposing water privatization (Pôrto Alegre, 2003) and the protection of forests and forests people's rights (Mumbai, 2004). At the same time, sharp divisions have emerged within the forum process over environmental questions, which track back to a basic cleavage between radical anti-capitalist activists and reformist groups (Schönleitner, 2003: pp138–9). Issue-based statements, as with the Mumbai Forest Initiative, have allowed participating environmental groups (e.g. World Rainforest Movement, Friends of the Earth International) to sidestep interrogation of their political philosophies by intervening with specific advocacy initiatives rather than general ideological commitments to global justice.

Transnational spaces of resistance

Transnational resistance to neoliberal economic policy-making has found popular support around the world by challenging trade liberalization head on. Arguably the first transnational network designed to bring together prominent Northern and Southern activists in order to address the systemic environmental impacts of neoliberal economic integration, the International Forum on Globalization was started in 1994 by campaigners who had been fighting the North American Free Trade Agreement. Since then, it has utilized electronic communication, as well as face-to-face meetings and teach-ins, to pursue its educational and advocacy goals for a more socially just, ecologically sustainable economic order (Roberts, 1998; www.ifg.org). Of greater political significance, however, is People's Global Action Against Free Trade (PGA) – a transnational network created to facilitate information exchange between anti-neoliberal movements, strongly influenced by the ideas and internet-based mobilization of the Zapatista insurgents in Chiapas, Mexico (Routledge, 2003; www.agp.org). The PGA network is uncompromising in its rejection of neoliberal globalization and commits supporters to undertake direct action and non-violent civil disobedience in support of its aims. Its constituent groups include Southern movements – for example, a federation representing landless peasants in Brazil and the Karnataka State Farmers' Association of India – as well as an assortment of green and social justice activist networks in North America and Europe. In addition, the bulk of organization and financial support for the PGA comes from support groups in Europe.

David Featherstone (2003) sets out clearly the radical accountability challenge constructed by the PGA in its transnational campaigning, dwelling on its organization of an Inter-Continental Caravan for Solidarity and Resistance (ICC) as an emblematic vehicle of political mobilization. The 1999 ICC brought 400 members of the Karnataka farmers' union to Europe, along with about 50 other Southern activists, to protest against biotechnology companies (e.g. Monsanto, Bayer) and state-centred institutions deemed to be at the heart of neoliberal rule-making (e.g. European Union and G8 summits, both in Cologne in that year, and the WTO headquarters in Geneva). Aligning with western European green and other 'anti-globalization' activists, the ICC physically traversed Europe in summer 1999, combining demonstrations, protests and activist networking. The selection, as sites of protest, of key centres of private and public authority promoting genetically modified agriculture and, more generally, market liberalization aimed to create conspicuous spaces of resistance – a political agency 'constituted through spatial practices that attempted to make visible and contestable key relations of power' (Featherstone, 2003: p411). In other words, locating sources rather than effects of ecological harm production; that is, core institutions exerting power without full environmental responsibility to (present or future) affected publics.

The political claims in play here are explicitly informed by social-justice norms. They portray, and contest, a systemic discrimination against weaker groups caused by enduring inequalities in the allocation of economic and political power. Environmental injustices relate both to the effective exclusion of resource-poor communities from taking part in governance processes affecting their basic living conditions, and also to their disproportionate exposure to significant environmental harm. Activists in many countries have fused ecological concerns with rights-based claims, yet most transnational environmental NGOs, being reformist in their political positioning, have resisted any radicalization of their message (Martinez–Alier, 2002; Ford, 2003). Indeed, such a step is unlikely for most as it would entail abandoning organizational certainties and potentially alienate the bulk of their passive supporters. As Featherstone (2003) argues, the accountability politics of the global justice movement entails active engagement with contentious action and the creative crafting of collective identities against centres of power. The shared concerns of vulnerable communities are expressed as emotionally charged grievances as opposed to 'environment' or 'development' interests mapped out objectively by NGO expertise. Not surprisingly, then, global justice activists have often proved hostile to mainstream environmental NGOs. In a situation where different environmental advocacy actors are making divergent political claims on behalf of affected publics, it becomes difficult to avoid questions about the accountability and representiveness of these activists themselves, as will now be discussed.

Accountability of transnational civil society actors

Whether reformist or radical in their goals, transnational civil society actors animated by environmental protection issues can no longer presume that their identification with affected publics will go unchallenged. Of course, civil society advocacy includes claims for regulatory actions involving the (re)allocation of scarce resources which potentially impact widely on societies. In so far as other parties see themselves as losing out, they will likely contest proposed reforms, and in the case of environmental regulation, this often means powerful sectoral lobbies (e.g. natural resource extraction and manufacturing interests) pitted against NGOs trying to mobilize on behalf of diffuse ecological interests. So it is arguably a symptom of the growing presence of transnational civil society advocates for environmental accountability that their legitimacy is being questioned from many quarters – governments, corporations, anti-environmental civil society groupings (e.g. free-market think tanks). It also reveals the dissatisfaction of defenders of neoliberal globalization that cross-border public interest claims are being projected which reject the association of market outcomes with global welfare gains. All in all, increasing calls for civil society advocates to demonstrate that they truly represent the concerns of non-territorial publics have pushed to the political foreground their own accountability (Kaldor, 2003; SustainAbility, 2003). What is their moral authority for speaking on behalf of the intended beneficiaries of their actions?

In the first place, there is the question as to whether civil society organizations have *internal accountability*; that is, credible management systems responsive to their immediate stakeholders – staff, supporters, trustees, donors and other resource providers (which may include governments and corporations). For transnational NGOs in particular, a significant source of recent criticism, both from the political right (e.g. www.ngowatch.org) and left (e.g. Chandhoke, 2002: pp48–9), is that their own functioning is not transparent enough: their funding sources, expenditures and decision-making procedures are argued to be resistant to independent scrutiny. With regard to revenue and spending, for the leading transnational environmental NGOs – WWF, Greenpeace International, Friends of the Earth International – this criticism is misplaced, as it is now common practice for them publicly to release annual accounts over and above the legal requirements in the countries in which they are headquartered, while internal financial systems are professionally organized and externally audited. Furthermore, transnational environmental NGOs also routinely incorporate their summary accounts in annual reports on their activities.

What often remains less clear is the governance structure of these bodies, which varies greatly between groups. The well-known contrast is between, on the one hand, the centralized decision-making favoured by Greenpeace, which relegates supporters to passive (financial) membership and, on the other, the more democratic federal structure of Friends of the Earth International, where local and national branches are constituted with voting powers for members. Less familiar, perhaps, is the internal constitution of WWF where supporting members have voting entitlements and the governing body strives, through regional groupings, to be geographically representative of the whole membership (Kovach et al, 2003: pp27–8). Whatever the differences in internal governance between the big three, their enduring capacity to maintain substantial membership bases suggests that, at least to their supporters (who always have the exit option of withdrawing subscriptions should they so wish), there is no significant anxiety about the fairness of internal management systems.

Of course the policy goals of advocacy NGOs, if realized, typically impact on non-members, so it is also crucial to their political integrity that they are *seen* to be free of unethical internal practices. The constitutions of transnational environmental NGOs rest on legal personalities recognized in states. Appropriate legal standards of behaviour for their (sub)national branches and international secretariats may therefore diverge between countries, threatening to produce organizational fragmentation. There is also the ever-present risk, even in liberal democracies, that state regulations may unnecessarily encroach on NGO autonomy. Several leading observers of transnational civil society action have recently recommended, therefore, that internal NGO accountability is most effectively served by self-regulation – 'the more standards of governance, management, and financial controls are developed internally, the less need there is for [external] regulation' (Fries, 2003: p236). John Clark (2003: pp175–6) finds evidence of such self-regulatory behaviour on the part of NGOs in the US and the Philippines, and voluntary codes of conduct have also been developed transnationally by the International Council of Voluntary Agencies (Schweitz, 2001). While such examples are rare, the interrogation of NGO practices by critics is likely to encourage their further development.

Criticisms have also been levelled at the lack of transparency of activist networks within the global justice movement; for example, against the Brazilian NGO organizing committee of the World Social Forum, which has maintained a tight control over forum decision-making (Schönleitner, 2003: pp130–5). Yet there is no separate legal identity of the forum, in line with the loose, often anarchic, networks of association favoured by global justice campaigners. Efforts have been undertaken by the Brazilian organizers of the World Social Forum to open it up procedurally, inviting the participation of other regional and global protest networks. Ultimately, though, as Kaldor (2003: p20) stresses, the internal accountability of social movement activism is necessarily rough and ready. Largely free of the management duties falling on environmental NGOs, the global movement for social and ecological justice has as its central organizational responsibility the capacity to mobilize. As long as the disparate collection of individuals and groups engaged by the movement is willing to continue participating in its contentious political action, its internal vitality is maintained.

At the heart of the transnational advocacy undertaken by environmentalists (reformist and radical) is, more often than not, a claim on behalf of parties threatened or injured with significant physical harm. The second source of their moral authority is thus their *external accountability* towards these affected communities – accountability in the sense of representing accurately and effectively the interests of those harmed. Traditionally, NGOs and NGO networks have not solicited the direct involvement of intended beneficiaries in their decision-making, at least for cross-border advocacy. This contrasts with the routine obligation for such participation when NGOs deliver local or regional services on behalf of funding bodies. For transnational environmental advocacy, where communities of ecological damage are dynamic in space–time and imprecisely defined, the moral case for formal stakeholder input has been seen as less of a priority. Moreover, as discussed in Chapter 1, assigning responsibility for ecological harm may well include future generations and non-human entities within affected communities, precluding direct testimonies from victims. The external accountability of environmental advocates rests on their persuasive communication of the common ecological concerns of affected publics. We can differentiate here between their claims to embody harm prevention norms and their claims objectively to represent ecological conditions.

Harm prevention claims

In harmony with their cross-border campaigning reach, transnational environmental activist groups and networks commonly justify their harm prevention goals as cosmopolitan – all those damaged or rendered vulnerable by significant levels of ecological harm are entitled to have their concerns effectively addressed by responsible state and private actors. Within the NGO community there is, to be sure, a distinction between organizations articulating this cosmopolitanism in broad-based human welfare terms (e.g. WWF, Conservation International) or in a more ecocentric manner (e.g. Greenpeace, Friends of the Earth). However, cosmopolitan values tend to be presumed rather than justified, as arguments are framed to meet immediate campaign goals and appeal to as many as possible. This tactical 'apolitical' stance is understandable in the context of issue-specific advocacy, yet it contrasts with the searching, justice-based manifesto of the movement against neoliberal globalization. And in so far as environmental NGOs are being asked to assume formal governance roles, such as consultation and monitoring responsibilities, critics see interrogation of their ethical positioning as necessary to judging the credibility of their public interest claims.

For example, Kellow (2000) questions the moral cosmopolitanism of Greenpeace International, arguing that the concentration of funding support and executive influence in four countries (Germany, the Netherlands, Switzerland and the United Kingdom) inevitably shapes a campaign agenda advancing northern European values. This is apparent, he maintains, for the issue of 'global' climate change, where European gains in energy efficiency and the emergence of a strong environmental services sector created a convergence between Greenpeace's policy position and the stances of northern European states in the international climate-change negotiations. Taking a liberal institutionalist perspective, Kellow accepts that the normative arguments of environmental NGOs have autonomous force and cannot simply be read off national interests, but insists, nevertheless, that state actors in international rule-making selectively support or constrain environmentalist norms in multiple ways. If Kellow's general case against Greenpeace is open to challenge (Greenpeace has not hesitated to challenge the national policies of countries where it has substantial membership support – e.g. the UK's shipments of irradiated nuclear fuel), he is correct to highlight the often unacknowledged interplay of state and NGO actions in the evolution of environmentalist norms.

Indeed, the interests of powerful states – expressed individually or through international organizations – can be seen as setting parameters for civil society agency. Even UN accreditation processes for NGOs, while putatively neutral, have reinforced the dominance of Northern-based environmental NGOs in international conferences and policy-making. Of course, this is in part the consequence of their superior resource endowments and networking competences relative to NGOs from developing countries. Hence, the unintentional result of the 1996 UN ECOSOC resolution (1996/31) relaxing NGO accreditation criteria: designed to encourage registration applications from Southern civil society actors by extending consultation rights to 'national' NGOs, it actually opened the door to numerous accreditation requests from NGOs located in North America and Europe. The asymmetry of participation here also reflects the more subtle political effects of a liberal governance understanding of NGO representativeness, to the detriment of Southern groups with more overt political goals (Colás, 2002: pp151–7). By framing the contribution of civil society organizations in functional terms, it has tended to sideline the direct participation of affected publics by focusing on top-down policy solutions. And it has led to a 'backlash from below' (Clark, 2003: pp178–83) in circumstances when, for example, Northern environmental NGOs advocate regulatory actions which may have negative welfare effects on Southern communities or, alternatively, sensationally portray 'environmental victims' without finding out their own self-professed needs.

Scientific claims about ecological conditions

In speaking 'on behalf of' publics facing the threat or incidence of transboundary harm, environmental activists may also be held answerable for their claims accurately to describe a state of affairs – that the ecological conditions they portray actually obtain. In other words, that the sources, pathways and reception of biophysical change identified as being of public concern accord with objective observations and explanations. More than any other movement for social change, environmentalism relies on the mobilization of scientific knowledge in support of its key aims. Demonstrating that an actor is responsible for certain environmental effects requires the collation, interpretation and dissemination of relevant scientific information. Transnational environmental NGOs, in particular, devote much effort to building up robust science-based arguments, often in association with politically sympathetic experts. At the same time, the inherent fallibility of environmental science – all too evident for complex transboundary ecological changes – invites deep questioning by critics of the scientific validity of environmentalist claims, including the procedures of environmental research from which these claims are drawn.

Such questioning is evident in contentions that environmentalist assessments of cross-border ecological problems routinely project 'global' representations of risk, presupposing planetary publics affected by uniform threats. At its most disapproving, transnational green networks are chided for pursuing governance goals set up to deliver selective material benefits to themselves or their host countries. Boehmer-Christiansen (2002), for example, claims that a small managerial clique of environmental experts more or less monopolized climate change policy development at the World Bank. Working closely with environmental NGOs, academics and sympathetic bureaucrats, their identification of 'global environmental benefits' from the decarbonization of energy production and consumption is argued to have masked the desired imposition of economic development paths favourable to Northern expertise, technology and investment. This conspiratorial take on green networking is overstated. But there have certainly been instances where scientific assessments of global environmental problems produced by NGOs have misrepresented or ignored vital social and ecological conditions within developing countries – for example, criticisms levelled at the World Resources Institute over reports published in the 1990s on climate change and the ecological vulnerability of major watersheds around the world (see Forsyth, 2003: pp174–7).

Moreover, aside from the environmental assessments generated by environmental activists, there is a cogent argument that, by virtue of their constitution as top-down technical appraisals, even transnational scientific assessments with no apparent political agenda can lack legitimacy in regard to affected publics in poorer countries. In part, this is an issue of the lack of involvement of Southern scientists, alongside a neglect of other Southern viewpoints – including those expressed by civil society groupings. Biermann (2001) identifies such participation deficits in the early scientific assessment work convened by the Intergovernmental Panel on Climate Change and the Global Biodiversity Assessment. And Forsyth (2003: pp191–200) points out that the constitution of some global assessments in terms of impacts received from biophysical changes renders vulnerable publics as passive recipients of risk rather than as active agents in defining their own social and ecological needs. The experience of environmental effects as problematic by individuals and groups in a particular region or locality is a necessary step to identifying themselves as affected publics. This means that civil society actors claiming to represent accurately the environmental interests of affected publics cannot presume moral authority simply by relaying projections of harm derived from global scientific assessments: they are obliged to ensure that the negative effects attributed to communities correspond with their living conditions and concerns. The Millennium Ecosystem Assessment mentioned in the Introduction to this book is one recent example of transnational knowledge production making efforts in this direction.

Conclusion

In this chapter I have argued that public accountability challenges are at the heart of environmentalist campaigning undertaken across national borders by NGOs, advocacy networks and social movements. Accountability demands are being levelled at centres of governmental and private authority for actions allegedly causing involuntary physical harm to individuals and communities. Furthermore, the moral norms invoked here comprise a 'new accountability' by registering political claims unshackled from territorial notions of responsibility. Civil society activists, that is to say, seek answerability and redress on behalf of affected publics identified, above all, by shared environmental impacts rather than joint citizenship ties or property rights. Accountability obligations to these publics are seen to arise from basic moral entitlements of their members to have their environmental well-being protected and their interests effectively incorporated in decisions significantly affecting them.

These accountability norms, as put forward by environmental activists, are thus routinely framed as cosmopolitan – they recognize the equal rights of all individuals, regardless of nationality, to have their basic conditions of life respected. Chapter 1 set out my reasons for suggesting that, at the transnational level at least, environmental accountability to affected publics is advanced by free and open communication (or discourse). Civil society advocates for accountability have indeed mobilized information and communications technologies as their main means of publicizing the threat or incidence of transboundary ecological risks. The discussion above noted, with examples, the emergence of 'horizontal' accountability claims in the activities of environmental NGOs and advocacy networks, where targeted state or private actors are exposed to multiple responsibility claims from beyond their home territories. Constructivist arguments help explain why environmental accountability claims resonating with existing transnational norms of harm prevention and equality of treatment have made most ground. This has consolidated the influence of reformist (liberal) environmentalism, but as an accountability politics is declared to be inadequate by the global justice movement. Not surprisingly, as elaborated above with reference to alternative civil society summits and global protests, social movement activists offer a radical accountability challenge to institutions supportive of neoliberal globalization. Here the focus is less on publicizing particular flows of physical harm or pressing for opportunities to participate in international environmental governance, than opposing what are seen to be systemic ecological and social injustices.

This chapter finished with an appraisal of the legitimacy of civil society actors as bearers of the concerns of publics affected by ecological risk or harm. Critics have argued that these actors are short on the transparency that they demand of states and corporations, while their moral cosmopolitanism is bogus, masking the sectional interests of Northern elites. For the leading transnational environmental NGOs, ever more professional in their internal management standards, the transparency charge has little bite. In contrast, there *are* pressing issues for Northern-based civil society organizations to address regarding their actions 'on behalf of' affected publics outside their home countries: necessary questions here include the selectivity of their chosen harm-prevention goals and the accuracy of their knowledge-based claims about ecological conditions. However, such interrogation demonstrates that advocates for environmental accountability are already well established as voices within global civil society. As Clark (2003: p176) notes, the legitimacy of civil society organizations ultimately derives from their honest communication about, and support of, their chosen constituencies. Efforts to represent environmental interests are unlikely to be effective if there is no correspondence with the ecological experiences and needs of relevant publics.

Chapter 3

Citizenship Beyond National Borders? Affected Publics and International Environmental Regimes

Citizenship has traditionally been understood to denote shared membership of a political community defined by national identity and the geographical borders of the state. Of course, national communities and state membership rarely overlap neatly: it is the historic achievement of modern liberal democracies to have assigned citizenship status on the basis of equal rights of political participation and communication, rather than common ethnic ties or national beliefs. The crucial move here was the conferral of a set of rights and obligations on all members of the state who, in democratic political systems, are assumed to have consented to this form of association. As free and equal individuals, they have access to processes of political representation and communication which accord legitimacy to their governments (and, at least in principle, hold them to account). As citizens, that is to say, their membership of − and identity with − the political community is formally bound up with its democratic construction. To be sure, their formal affiliation is still to a territorial state, which, under the enduring principle of sovereignty, is afforded both supreme domestic authority and legal recognition in the international arena. But in democratic states this ruling authority is understood to derive from the popular self-determination of the citizens.

In so far as these states have addressed fairly and (reasonably) effectively the general concerns of their constituent populations, there has been little need to question their exclusive determination of citizenship rights, for democratic entitlements and obligations have aligned comfortably with state membership. But this happy correspondence of citizen self-determination with a national government has been upset by the increasing willingness of states to share sovereignty in order to address new economic, environmental and security interdependencies. The 'unbundling' of functional governance from fixed territories has seen citizens give up their formal approval of key policy decisions in exchange for a more remote, indirect say in supra- or international decision-making bodies (Hilson, 2001: p336). Efforts to address growing transnational flows of ecological harm are at the forefront of these governance transformations, as is evident in the proliferation of multilateral environmental agreements (MEAs) over the past three or four decades. For citizens in countries facing transboundary ecological risks, the incapacity of their home states unilaterally to reduce these threats represents a potential breach of a core citizenship entitlement – the right to protection from injury caused by activities taking place beyond the territorial borders of their home country. Both the authority of a state over its citizens and their identification with it as citizens are deeply unsettled by such a *protection failure*: their state is exposed as incapable of preventing damage to their lives and vital interests (Jones, 1999: pp217–22). The pooling of sovereignty within MEAs may be the only realistic way for states to seek to prevent an ecological protection failure, yet the indeterminacy of international rule-making processes and outcomes clouds further the traditionally clear lines of political accountability running between citizens and their governing representatives.

If we accept that freedom of self-determination – founded on equal opportunities for participation – is at the heart of democratic citizenship, then the need to regulate transboundary (and global) environmental risks creates realms of public concern across and beyond nation-state borders. These public communities of shared fate are multiple and dynamic: they expose the political shortfall of the entitlement of citizens to have an influence on decisions significantly affecting their interests, as many such decisions are now taken outside the reach of their home states. Transnational notions of citizenship invoke the right of democratic governance for individuals affected by extra-territorial institutional orders and actors. In the first place this is a moral appeal that holds all persons to be entitled to equal standing with regard to the defence of their vital interests. Not surprisingly, the most obvious source of such universal moral regard is human rights protection, for violations of basic rights commonly elicit feelings of indignation among distant onlookers as well as co-nationals (Habermas, 2001: pp107–8). Some accounts of cosmopolitan obligations have emphasized the central role of human rights in determining participation rights in decision-making, as well as principles of distributive justice. From this cosmopolitan perspective, safeguarding individual well-being is paramount, and there has been some recognition that this protection may well extend beyond personal integrity and autonomy to encompass vital ecological conditions of existence (Jones, 1999: pp229–30; Mason, 1999: pp58–63).

The subject of this chapter is less the moral justification of a cosmopolitan citizenship than the identification of legal norms supporting perhaps its most relevant duty for environmental protection – the *prevention of significant harm to non-national affected publics*. There is an emerging body of international law which, although state-centred in its formulation and implementation, is attuned both to safeguarding collective ecological interests and to allowing at least some input from public actors in administering its constituent environmental obligations. The cosmopolitan scrutiny of sovereign state relations according to democratic criteria of interest representation and communication has, not so far, examined the existing regulation of sources of transnational environmental harm (e.g. Held, 1995; Linklater, 1998). Yet it is the intersection of individual rights and responsibilities with (inter)state obligations that offers concrete possibilities for citizen participation in global decision-making. In this chapter I begin by surveying customary and treaty-based law in order to highlight general obligations to prevent cross-border environmental harm, and show that these are not exclusively owed by and to states. This is followed by consideration, first, of those procedural public entitlements which support substantive environmental protection rules and, second, of nascent methods of public compliance and enforcement in international environmental law. Albeit slow, the emergence of access opportunities for individuals and nongovernmental organizations (NGOs) in these regulatory domains raises the question, addressed in the concluding discussion, of what type of cosmopolitan responsibilities falls on individuals and groups as the counterpart of new environmental entitlements.

Environmental harm prevention

As already noted in Chapter 1, the prevention of harm is a core justification for the exercise of political authority in liberal democratic states and, in a more arbitrary or selective way, in illiberal states. Domestically, states first developed harm-protection rules to regulate the behaviour of their citizens, while the experience of war prompted the emergence of international harm conventions to protect vulnerable groups (e.g. prisoners of war, civilians) from injury. Andrew Linklater (2001) observes behind the growth of 'cosmopolitan harm conventions' not just the mutual interest of states in regulating force but also the accumulating influence of transnational norms that attach moral consideration to individuals and groups whatever their national citizenship status. The international military tribunals hosted in Nuremberg (1945) and Tokyo (1946) are commonly recognized as the historic watershed marking the onset of new cosmopolitan obligations on governments towards all persons within and outside their borders – moral requirements to protect human dignity which have, over time, become legally embedded in, for example, international conventions on genocide (1948), apartheid (1973), torture (1984) and terrorist bombings (1997) (Ratner and Abrams, 2001). Of course, the preoccupation of humanitarian and human rights rules is with safeguarding the bodily integrity of human beings, and some commentators (e.g. Barry, 1995) have noted that the liberal no-harm principle has been deeply anthropocentric from the start, blocking its application to non-human nature. However, state practice indicates otherwise: the growth of environmental regulation within and between countries attests to the widespread extension of harm-prevention rules to non-human species and, more recently, the broader policy objective of ecological sustainability.

What merits attention here is the challenge to democratic frameworks of accountability arising from the nature of transnational environmental harm. Linklater (2001: pp269–71) contrasts the abstract forms of harm associated with environmental damage with the concrete injuries inflicted on fellow human beings by violators of human rights. Not only is the former type of harm often more diffuse in its generation and impacts, often making the determination of responsibility problematic, it typically entails the unforeseen consequence of routine market freedoms – liberties to produce and consume – being fostered by economic globalization. Growing market interdependencies and material transactions across state borders generate numerous environmental effects, rendering impractical and politically unfeasible any blanket prohibition of ecological harm. The international preference, instead, has been for states collectively to agree to prevent or restrict activities generating effects likely to exceed a set threshold level of environmental harm. Difficulties in disaggregating individual culpability for much transboundary harm has reinforced the existing propensity in international law to apportion responsibility for extra-territorial injury to states, so the duty to prevent harm to non-nationals has primarily been imposed on governments. States are deemed to be legally responsible if they have breached relevant treaty rule or customary obligations: whether there is a *cosmopolitan* citizen entitlement to the prevention of abstract environmental harm rests on the scope of its embodiment in international rule protecting general ecological interests (i.e. for everyone).

The International Law Commission (ILC) – the United Nations (UN) body charged with the codification and development of international law – has, in its work on state responsibility, concluded that there are indeed duties on states to cease and make reparations for wrongful injury ('material or moral damage') to collective interests. To be sure, these duties are attributed solely to states, but they entail remedying damage that may extend beyond injured states and the national publics represented by them. In its draft articles on state responsibility recommended to the UN General Assembly for development as an international convention, the ILC proposes, under Article 48(1), that any state other than an injured state is entitled to invoke the responsibility of another state if:

(a)   The obligation breached is owed to a group of States including that State, and is established for the protection of a collective interest of the group; or

(b)   The obligation breached is owed to the international community as a whole (International Law Commission, 2001: p56).

Applied to state environmental responsibility, the first type of breach might typically refer to an action of a treaty state that undermined a collective ecological interest protected by a MEA that it had ratified (e.g. a biodiversity conservation convention or a transboundary pollution convention); while the second type of breach would entail damage to vital ecological interests at such a level of seriousness that all states have a legal interest in preventing this happening. Such universal obligations to the international community (termed obligations *erga omnes*) are widely acknowledged in the human rights domain (e.g. prohibitions against acts of aggression, genocide and racial discrimination). A few environmental obligations have arguably received such recognition: these include deliberate massive pollution of the marine environment and atmospheric nuclear testing (Ragazzi, 1997: pp154–62; Peel, 2001).

This shortfall in significance compared with human rights obligations reflects in part the historical novelty of international environmental rule-making beyond established relations of good neighbourliness between states. The seminal international statement on extra-territorial environmental harm prevention is commonly taken to be Principle 21 of the 1972 Stockholm Declaration on the Human Environment, where it serves as a limit to the exercise of state sovereignty over natural resources:

> *States have, in accordance with the Charter of the United Nations and the principles of international law, the sovereign right to exploit their own resources pursuant to their own environmental policies, and the responsibility to ensure that activities within their jurisdiction or control do not cause damage to the environment of other States or of areas beyond the limits of national jurisdiction.*

As a declarative principle expressed in general terms, its legal force is by no means clear-cut; indeed, it has been argued to constitute a foundational 'myth' of international environmental responsibility at odds with state practice (Knox, 2002). Yet the sustained influence of Principle 21 on UN General Assembly Resolutions and numerous MEAs suggests that this criticism is overstated. Significantly, the international community chose to embrace it again at the 1992 UN Conference on Environment and Development, where it became, slightly amended, Principle 2 of the Rio Declaration.

Principle 21 is also clearly reflected in paragraph 29 of the advisory opinion on the legality of the threat or use of nuclear weapons issued in 1996 by the International Court of Justice at the request of the UN General Assembly:

> *The Court recognizes that the environment is under daily threat and that the use of nuclear weapons could constitute a catastrophe for the environment. The Court also recognizes that the environment is not an abstraction but represents the living space, the quality of life and the very*

*health of human beings, including generations unborn. The existence of
the general obligation of states to ensure that activities within their
jurisdiction and control respect the environment of other states or of areas
beyond national control is now part of the corpus of international law
relating to the environment.*

There is some restraint here on the force and geographical scope of Principle
21: the term 'respect' is weaker than the requirement not to cause damage,
while the application of the obligation to activities within the jurisdiction *and*
control of states (instead of 'jurisdiction or control') limits its extra-territorial
reach. Nevertheless, as Brown Weiss (1999) asserts, the advisory opinion
represents an authoritative recognition that general environmental obligations
exist in international law. Moreover, the cosmopolitan value of the obligation
in question is reinforced by the court: not only does it have a global purchase
across space, the mention of 'generations unborn' admits of a universal
application into the future.

Substantive endorsement of a general obligation on states to prevent damage
to the environment is evident in a wide array of MEAs, including ones
addressing air and marine pollution, climate change, biodiversity conservation,
the spread of pests and diseases, radioactive contamination and hostile
environmental modification techniques (Sands, 1995: pp194–7). Alongside its
proposed state responsibility rules, the ILC has also recommended a draft
convention on the prevention of transboundary harm from hazardous
activities, which encompasses environmental degradation (International Law
Commission, 2001: pp370–7). From this progressive development of international law, is it plausible to claim that, as inhabitants of a shared, vulnerable
planet, we are all equal addressees – as cosmopolitan citizens – of the
obligation on states of preventive action? Formally of course, states are the
legal addressees as centres of sovereign authority, so that our cosmopolitan
entitlement to ecological well-being is mediated through national political
representatives: it is a right and responsibility, in other words, of state
citizenship. However, this exclusive inter-state understanding is certainly
disrupted by notions of common environmental responsibility. In its conservative form, this denotes the 'common concern of mankind' affirmed, for
example, in the preambles to the 1992 Biological Diversity and Climate
Change Conventions; but there is also the more radical principle of 'common
heritage' first advanced at the UN in 1967 in relation to use of the deep
seabed. As eventually embodied in Articles 136 and 137 of the 1982 Law of
the Sea Convention, the common heritage principle suggests an obligation of
common trusteeship for which the addressees are not just states but 'mankind
as a whole', and while this legal framing of shared ownership has faced political
opposition (notably from the United States), claims that it also applies to such
spaces as Antarctica and the global atmosphere are morally justifiable in
cosmopolitan terms (Franck, 1995: pp393–405; Taylor, 1998: pp258–97).

The general obligation of preventive action is one of conduct rather than result: states are not required to be guarantors against *any* environmental harm, only 'to take all necessary measure as may be expected of a reasonable government in all circumstances' (Okowa, 2000: p81). What is known as the requirement of 'due diligence' enables an appreciation of context in the application of harm-prevention rules, encompassing the likelihood and seriousness of the damage, the determination of causation, the governmental capacity of the source state and the cost-effectiveness of relevant regulatory measures. In allowing for differentiated responsibility, it can result in separate as well as diluted legal obligations; for example, in the implementation allowances and technical assistance targeted at developing countries under the ozone protection and climate change regimes. Given diverse circumstances and needs, the notion of 'common but differentiated responsibility' is of course consistent with cosmopolitan environmental duties; although the typical focus on the special situation of poorer countries has sometimes deflected attention from the reverse side of this differentiation – that affluent states, with their far-reaching complicity in economic institutions producing systemic environmental injury, have a responsibility to meet more onerous obligations of harm prevention.

Where there is a threat of serious or irreversible damage, precautionary norms are increasingly invoked in international environmental law to shape what is expected of states under due diligence. As expressed by Principle 15 of the Rio Declaration on Environment and Development, the lack of full scientific certainty about potential effects should not be used as a reason for postponing cost-effective measures to prevent environmental degradation; and this principle, explicitly or implicitly, is endorsed in treaties on climate change, air pollution, marine pollution, transboundary movements in hazardous wastes and the conservation of biological diversity. Birnie and Boyle (2002: pp115–21) suggest that the main effect of the principle is to lower the standard of proof before preventive action is required. As the environmental consequences of some activities are often difficult to establish, particularly over the long term, the legal duty on responsible states is to acknowledge potentially dangerous effects for which there are reasonable scientific grounds for concern. Again, an absolute prohibition of the current or proposed activity is not necessarily implied; but the expectations of diligent regulation are raised for the relevant obligations of conduct – environmental standard-setting, transboundary impact assessment, international cooperation, the adoption of clean production methods, systems of prior notification or authorization, and so on.

Of course, such obligations often pertain to the behaviour of non-state actors, which raises the question whether private individuals or companies have a direct duty to cosmopolitan citizens to prevent environmental harm. In so far as the conduct of private actors causes ecological damage outside their home state, that state has 'secondary' obligations to prevent that injury by means of the diligent regulation of its activities. The global reach of this requirement is most fully established in responsibility rules for the marine environment, where states have clear duties to prevent national vessels from polluting other national maritime areas and also the high seas environment (Smith, 1988: pp72–94). Yet these are still obligations where the home state of the harm producer is ultimately answerable for any damage caused. It is only where physical damage has actually taken place, where costs have been borne, that states have been willing to step back in order to pass the compensation burden onto private operators, accepting only residual responsibility (i.e. when, for whatever reason, the private operator is able to escape the full burden of compensation for environmental damage).

A less state-centred development of *private* environmental obligations is most evident, therefore, in the growing influence of cross-border *liability and compensation rules*; for example, in liability treaties on marine pollution, nuclear damage and the transboundary movement of hazardous wastes. The private responsibility rules in operation here rely on the harmonization of national civil liability systems through international agreements. Following innovations in the oil pollution liability regime, compensation obligations on private operators have been extended beyond personal injury and property damage to environmental damage (see Chapter 5). This rule development is part of a wider shift in global governance towards hybrid public–private forms of regulation where, because of political and technical challenges to state authority, countries have proved willing to accept standard-setting (e.g. radiation protection, food quality) and licensing procedures (e.g. vessel seaworthiness) shaped to a large degree by transnational networks of experts (Sand, 1999; Falkner, 2003). However, as these techniques move towards self-regulation, the clear lines of accountability found in state responsibility rules become blurred; and the cosmopolitan principle of equal respect for all interests is eroded by authority structures and legal mechanisms inaccessible to resource-poor individuals or groups.

In contrast to these private environmental governance initiatives, recent developments in international criminal law hold more cosmopolitan promise, at least for the prevention of severe harm. The 1998 (Rome) Statute of the International Criminal Court has established an institution with universal jurisdiction over what are agreed to be the most serious crimes of concern to the international community – genocide, crimes against humanity, war crimes and the crime of aggression. By departing from the previously exclusive right of states to determine the criminal law for their national citizens, the International Criminal Court feeds into what has been labelled the 'individualization of responsibility' for human rights violations; that is, the emergence of legal obligations of direct (individual) accountability alongside existing state responsibility rules (Nollkaemper, 2003: p631). Breaches of 'peremptory norms' are deemed to be of such grave concern to the international community and all peoples that culpable individuals (as well as states) are confronted directly with the consequences of their acts. Significantly, the

Rome Statute empowers the Court with jurisdiction for intentional 'widespread, long-term and severe damage to the natural environment' as a result of planned or large-scale acts of war excessive in relation to their military objectives (Articles 8(1) and 8(2)(a)(iv)). While currently restricted to a category of war crimes, this seminal recognition of universal criminal responsibility for individuals carrying out massive (trans)national ecological destruction may well become a necessary sanction in a world facing the spread of weapons of mass destruction.

Procedural environmental entitlements

In Chapter 1 the entitlement of individuals and groups to democratic governance was argued to be a core component of accountability for transnational environmental harm. Understood in cosmopolitan terms, the democratic entitlement can be expressed as a right for all those significantly affected by a political decision to have an equal opportunity to influence the making of that decision – *wherever that decision is made*. For Thomas Pogge (2002: pp183–9), this human right to equal opportunity for political participation extends to international ecological regulation because of the significant harms and risks now placed on outsiders by the activities of national citizens. A common source of identity, as cosmopolitan citizens, for otherwise unrelated individuals is their shared experience of the cross-border ecological effects of material activities over which they typically have had little or no involvement. To recognize themselves together as transnational or even global publics, the reflexive move is that they perceive these consequences as adversely affecting their interests and therefore in need of regulation. Procedural rights and duties in support of such joint problem-solving would be expected to enable open assessments of ecological risks, inclusive deliberation among all relevant parties and consideration of the interests of those unable to contribute discursively – notably non-humans and future generations. Their lasting contribution to a 'greening' of citizenship would be to facilitate mutual learning about ecologically adaptive ways of living (Barry, 1999).

Principle 10 of the Rio Declaration, as endorsed by 176 states and the UN General Assembly, is the most widely supported international statement on procedural environmental obligations:

> *Environmental issues are best handled with the participation of all concerned citizens, at the relevant level. At the national level, each individual shall have appropriate access to information concerning the environment that is held by public authorities, including information on hazardous materials and activities in their communities, and the opportunity to participate in decision-making processes. States shall*

facilitate and encourage public awareness and participation by making information widely available. Effective access to judicial and administrative proceedings, including redress and remedy, shall be provided.

The focus on individual entitlements at the national level is in deference to established state sovereign powers and citizenship rights, yet there is also the acknowledgment that public participation may be needed at other scales of decision-making.

In its draft constitution on the prevention of transboundary harm from hazardous activities, the ILC, recalling in its preamble the Rio Declaration, codifies the relevant procedural obligations judged to have currency in international environmental law – prior authorization of risk-bearing activities, risk assessment, notification and information exchange, consultation of preventive measures and dispute-settlement measures. Significantly, there is an explicit acceptance that states originating significant risk-bearing activities are required to inform and register the concerns of all affected publics, regardless of nationality. Article 13 stipulates that states shall 'provide the public likely to be affected by an activity within the scope of the present articles with relevant information relating to that activity, the risk involved and the harm which might result and ascertain their views' (International Law Commission, 2001: p375). As with the other procedural articles, this provision essentially sets out a standard of diligent conduct expected of states to conform to agreed objectives for transboundary harm prevention.

Of course, these are all (inter)state obligations, but aside from any claim to equitable treatment between national publics, in Article 15 the ILC also expressly recognizes equal participation opportunities for individuals exposed to the risk of significant transboundary harm. Under the obligation of *non-discrimination*, these persons are to be granted access to judicial or administrative procedures of redress regardless of their nationality, residence or the place where the injury might occur. The non-discrimination principle embodies, at least for specified areas of application, the cosmopolitan ambition of individuals receiving equal access across borders to procedures with which they can protect their interests. As first formulated in the 1970s by the Organization for Economic Cooperation and Development (OECD), it calls on states to accept the transboundary effects of ecologically harmful activities located in their territories as potentially having the same legal significance as domestic effects. Explicit treaty obligations to that effect are not common – examples include Article 3 of the 1974 Nordic Convention on the Protection of the Environment and Article 9(3) of the 1992 Convention on the Transboundary Effects of Industrial Accidents – and the principle is generally regarded as not being well developed in international environmental law (Birnie and Boyle, 2002: pp147–8, 269–70).

Nevertheless, procedural rights realizing non-discrimination goals are clearly in evidence in conventions addressing transboundary environmental impact assessment. The most comprehensive treaty in this area is the 1991 (Espoo) Convention on Environmental Impact Assessment in a Transboundary Context, negotiated under the auspices of the UN Economic Commission for Europe (ECE). Its central substantive requirement on parties is to take all appropriate and effective measures to prevent, reduce and control significant adverse transboundary impacts from proposed national activities. As noted by Knox (2002: pp302–4), the procedural obligations in support of this goal directly apply norms of non-discrimination: parties are required to consider transboundary effects in their domestic environmental assessment procedures, and to open these procedures to affected non-national publics and their representatives. Like the draft ILC convention on prevention of transboundary harm, publics in affected states are entitled to notice of, and consultation on, the proposed activity, with the final decision required to take due account of their comments (albeit with no duty to refrain if the affected parties are still unhappy with the project). The positive obligation on states to conduct impact assessments for transboundary environmental effects is also found, outside the Espoo Convention, in issue-specific and regional MEAs; for example, the Nordic Environmental Protection Convention, the Law of the Sea Convention (Articles 204 to 206), the 1994 Convention on Nuclear Safety (Article 17), and the Convention on Biological Diversity (Article 14) (Sands, 1995: pp579–91; Okowa, 2000: pp132–6).

It would be misleading to presume that these state obligations to inform and consult non-national publics necessarily create cosmopolitan citizenship rights for all individuals under the protection of contracting states. Information provision, consultation and notification requirements within international environmental law are found in numerous treaties, but have traditionally centred on inter-state obligations or, in terms of reporting and compliance monitoring, the legal relations between states and international organizations. Treaty obligations are highly significant, as in spite of declarative statements like Principle 10 of the Rio Declaration, there is evidence that, in the absence of specific treaty commitments, states do not generally notify or consult other states before embarking on activities that generate transboundary environmental risks (Okowa, 2000: p169). Instruments like the Espoo Convention therefore set down detailed rules to ensure that the concerns of affected third parties are taken into account. The shift that the Espoo Convention makes in treating the public of the affected party as having separate entitlements from state representatives is pushed further by MEAs vesting explicit procedural rights in legal or natural persons. Seminal treaty obligations here include the individual access to information rights in the 1992 (Paris) Convention for the Protection of the Marine Environment of the North-East Atlantic (Article 9) and the 1993 (Lugano) Convention on Civil Liability for Damage Resulting From Activities Dangerous to the Environment (Chapter III).

The 1998 (Aarhus) Convention on Access to Information, Public Participation in Decision-making and Access to Justice in Environmental Matters, developed like the Espoo Convention by the ECE, is the most important elaboration of Principle 10 to be found in treaty law. Here procedural entitlements in environmental decision-making move beyond information rights to an expansive notion of public participation (covering specific activities, plans, programmes, policies and other legally binding instruments) and accessible review procedures. Much has been made of the ambition of the Aarhus Convention to increase citizen participation, which has clear cosmopolitan potential: a non-territorial notion of the 'public concerned' refers to those natural or legal persons affected or likely to be affected by, or having an interest in, the relevant decision-making (Article 2(4)). Under this definition, crucially, environmental NGOs are accorded a legal interest in participation and access to justice. Moreover, the non-discrimination principle is invoked in Article 3(9), stating that the provisions of the Convention apply to concerned publics whatever their nationality or domicile. To be sure, concern has been expressed that the Convention is too permissive in its treatment of public participation, deferring frequently in its provisions to 'national law requirements' (Lee and Abbot, 2003). In force since October 2001, it is still too soon to judge whether this will turn out in practice to be a major weakness, although the embrace of the Convention by the European Union and member states has already induced strong regional rule development designed to implement it effectively.

Northern European states have, within the ECE, championed the Aarhus recognition of environmental NGOs as legitimate bearers of procedural rights on behalf of affected publics. The European Eco-Forum network of environmental NGOs, which has received funding from most of these countries (e.g. Denmark, Finland, Germany, Norway, the Netherlands), participated in the ECE conferences charged with drafting the Convention and is actively involved in assisting its monitoring and implementation. This input builds on the now established practice for NGOs, as observers, to attend meetings of the parties of environmental treaties, typically permitted unless at least one-third of member states object – a (non-voting) participation right first set out in Article 11(7) of the 1973 Convention on International Trade in Endangered Species, and one since included in a sizeable number of MEAs, including those on stratospheric ozone protection, transboundary management of hazardous wastes, climate change and the conservation of biological diversity (Birnie and Boyle, 2002: pp216–17). It also reflects the wider consultative status accorded to NGOs by the UN in its international conferences and other decision-making mechanisms (e.g. the UN Human Rights Committee). And environmental NGOs have themselves of course campaigned vigorously for international recognition of environmental protection norms across numerous issue areas. If research has shown that their political influence on environmental treaty-building is often reliant on international negotiating contexts where NGOs still lack international legal personality (Arts, 1998; Corell and Betsill, 2001), the Aarhus Convention nevertheless endows them with novel entitlements in its implementation.

The transnational scope of such procedural rights has been reinforced by the ECE in its recent sponsoring of a Protocol on Strategic Environmental Assessment to the Espoo Convention. Acknowledging in its preamble the Aarhus Convention, the 2003 Kiev Protocol conjoins the public participatory intent of the former – including its requirements for contracting parties to recognize and support environmental protection groups – with the prescribed consideration of the significant environmental effects of plans, programme and policies. The Protocol reaffirms the Espoo Convention provision that its public entitlements should be exercised without discrimination to national citizenship status (Article 3(7)). As with all ECE treaty instruments, the geographical reach of this non-discrimination cannot extend beyond member states in Europe, North America and Central Asia; but geopolitical changes now mean that an unprecedented number of states could become signatories. The innovative development of environmental norms within the ECE is rooted in a historical context of western European security cooperation. With the post-Cold War emergence of democratic governance for countries in transition, the potential currency of these environmental protection rules has expanded considerably. Indeed, the Newly Independent States have been the most enthusiastic supporters of the Aarhus Convention, bringing its provisions into domestic effect ahead of implementing measures in western European states (Wates, 2003). Furthermore, the Executive Director of the UN Environment Programme has argued that these norms have a universal moral appeal warranting consideration of their legal codification outside the ECE region (Economic Commission for Europe, 2002: p4).

Compliance and enforcement entitlements

As noted above, the expectation that non-state actors can effectively contribute to the implementation of international environmental obligations is embodied in the principle of non-discrimination – expressed in Principle 10 of the Rio Declaration, the ILC draft convention on the prevention of transboundary harm and, explicitly or implicitly, in a number of MEAs. Opening up judicial and non-judicial remedies to affected persons creates at least the potential for more cosmopolitan interest representation. It also reveals an unwillingness to rely solely on state-centred mechanisms of compliance and dispute settlement in international environmental law. In part this reflects the inherent limitations of traditional compliance and enforcement procedures at this scale. Non-compliance of a state with its treaty obligations triggers a need to determine responsibility and possible remedies, yet typically this assessment requires the consent of the state in breach – a condition that holds for international adjudication more generally. Aside from grave criminal acts, only a state that has accepted the jurisdiction of an international enforcement mechanism is subject to its judgments. Assigning responsibility for transboundary environmental harm may be difficult enough within these constraints, when the causal connection between particular activities and injuries suffered may be contested between two states. When multiple source states are involved, encompassing disparate polluting activities and numerous affected parties, these problems are obviously compounded; and traditional state responsibility rules for settling disputes are found even more wanting (Okowa, 2000: pp195–7).

It is not surprising, therefore, that intergovernmental environmental litigation is rare. In cases of cross-border damage caused by high-risk activities (e.g. ship-source oil pollution, nuclear contamination, hazardous waste transport and disposal), states have tended to opt for national civil remedies and other private law arrangements, such as insurance settlements and out-of-court payments to individual claimants. As already mentioned, the role here of international treaties has been to promote consistency in environmental compensation rules. And we need not impute altruistic motives to such state behaviour: even-handed, predictable treatment respects established norms that victims of significant transboundary harm should have their interests taken into account, but is also crucial for foreign trade and investment decision-making. Indeed, while private-liability remedies are usually articulated in terms of non-discrimination, their origin in personal injury and property law reinforces the legal identification of victims as economic claimants defending individual welfare rather than citizens protecting shared ecological well-being. An innovative effort to recognize the latter role – that is, to graft public participation rights onto an international civil liability framework – is the 1993 Lugano Convention. In addition to its seminal information-access provisions mentioned above, Article 18 of the treaty enables environmental protection organizations to request national courts to issue prohibition, prevention or reinstatement orders against operators of ecologically dangerous activities (Sands, 1995: pp673–7). Yet states have not rushed to ratify this treaty and, more than ten years since it was opened for signature, the Lugano Convention has still to enter into force.

Furthermore, the existence of a non-discrimination principle within an MEA is not, by itself, sufficient to secure effective access for victims to compensation (or other remedies) for environmental damage received. Requiring the assessment of environmental compensation to be carried out in terms as favourable to non-national injured parties as domestic victims rests on national rules of protection already being adequate. It is significant that the first treaty to feature non-discrimination for environmental damage claims – the Nordic Environmental Protection Convention – does not include substantive rules on liability: it establishes for affected persons only a *right of action* against those parties in another contracting state claimed to be causing them significant environmental harm. This presumes compatible environmental damage valuations and liability coverage among the member states

(Denmark, Finland, Norway, Sweden), so that the transnational legal entitlement to seek compensation is basically a geographical extension of existing citizenship rights. For transboundary environmental risks unlikely to be confined to regions with shared liability norms, specific compensation standards acceptable to many states become necessary. As is evident in the environmental damage provisions of international liability regimes, such standards consequently tend to be modest in their coverage.

Where the causal links between risk sources and affected publics become more remote in space–time (e.g. stratospheric ozone depletion and anthropogenic climate change), civil liability systems may no longer be feasible, but problems also with invoking traditional state responsibility rules in these cases has prompted a recent emphasis in international environmental regimes on so-called 'soft compliance'. Rather than favouring judicial remedies against states in breach of their MEA obligations, the preference of many treaty bodies has been for fact-finding and practical assistance, especially where lack of technical capacity rather than intentional wrongdoing is regarded as the source of non-compliance (as is often the case with countries in transition and developing countries). Soft compliance entails recourse to non-binding commitments alongside binding targets differentiated according to state capabilities and past or present culpabilities for damage. It has also opened up spaces for NGOs and expert networks to undertake limited oversight and implementation functions. There are precedents for such input; for example, environmental NGOs have been allowed access to annual review meetings under the 1979 ECE Convention on Long-Range Transboundary Air Pollution, while transnational wildlife NGOs are directly involved in the trade-monitoring mechanisms of the Convention on International Trade in Endangered Species. The shift to non-confrontational implementation instruments is offering environmental NGOs opportunities for more sustained input, although they do not always have the resources or inclination to take these (Raustiala and Victor, 1998: pp663–9; Andersen and Sarma, 2000: pp343–4).

The soft compliance mechanism of the Aarhus Convention creates even more scope for the participation of relevant non-state actors when non-judicial and consultative methods are employed. Article 15 of the Convention, on the review of compliance, expressly allows for 'appropriate public involvement', which may include 'the option of consideration of communications from members of the public on matters related to this Convention'. The public entitlement to participate in compliance was elaborated on at the first meeting of the parties to the Aarhus Convention in October 2002 in Lucca: it includes the right of members of the public to nominate (but not vote on) candidates to the Compliance Committee, as well as the right to submit to this body allegations of non-compliance by any party and thereafter be entitled to participate in the discussions of the Committee. These are obligations clearly flowing directly towards citizens of contracting states which, given the Convention's definition of affected publics, include environmental NGOs as addressees. The novelty of these procedural entitlements was highlighted at the Lucca meeting by the US: attending as an ECE member state, but not a signatory to the Aarhus Convention, the American delegation issued a strong statement of concern about the proposed public compliance measures. They charged the participation and communication rights accorded to individuals and NGOs as an unwise 'inversion of traditional treaty practice', placing on record that the US would not recognize the compliance regime as precedent. The explicit public compliance entitlements were nevertheless adopted by acclamation at the meeting, strongly supported by European Union states (Economic Commission for Europe, 2002: pp8–9, 19–20).

Reinforcing these compliance rights, the Aarhus Convention also includes access to justice provisions for members of affected publics in the national enforcement of environmental regulations. Article 9 enables public access to legal review procedures to challenge, firstly, alleged violations of the treaty's access to information and public participation obligations and, secondly, private persons and public authorities claimed to be in contravention of national environmental laws. Again, environmental NGOs recognized by member states are, alongside members of the public, deemed to have a 'sufficient interest' in 'rights capable of being impaired', thus empowering them to initiate judicial proceedings (Article 9(3)). Lee and Abbot (2003: p195) caution that this provision may not comprise a 'citizen suit' entitlement as such, as deference to national review procedures means that a contracting state could accept, as sufficient to meeting its obligations, merely allowing citizens the opportunity to make complaints to a relevant prosecutor or regulatory authority. The transnational reach of the provision also remains untested: would the Aarhus Convention commitment to non-discrimination and a wide access to justice enable an environmental NGO representing foreign victims of damage to gain standing in the source states even if its national environmental laws had not been contravened? This seems unlikely.

Endowing public actors with direct enforcement rights is a necessary step in realizing ecological citizenship: it represents a political commitment to secure effective citizen involvement in policy compliance. The Aarhus Convention illustrates that, even with the progressive development of international environmental enforcement, the goal is no more than forging common national standards open to equal consideration of the interests of non-nationals. As there are great variations between countries in the enforcement rights afforded to environmental NGOs, any international acknowledgement that they have a legitimate public-interest role is note-worthy. The Council of Europe – responsible for developing the Lugano Convention – has, like the ECE, proved receptive in its treaty-drafting to importing civic participation norms from its liberal democratic member states into international rule-making on the environment. Building on the public enforcement provisions of the Lugano treaty, the Council of Europe has identified rights for environmental NGOs to participate in criminal proceedings under Article 11 of its 1998 (Strasbourg) Convention on the Protection of the Environment through Criminal Law. This attempted harmonization of criminal measures between states recognizes that serious environmental harm violates basic interests shared by peoples. Enabling NGO access is particularly ambitious given that criminal sanctions are an unquestioned prerogative of state sovereign authority; yet the Council of Europe cites the proven capability of environmental NGOs to represent collective ecological concerns as justifying their involvement in criminal proceedings on behalf of affected persons (Council of Europe, 1998: p17). As the criminal jurisdiction of contracting parties includes extra-territorial offences committed by their nationals, NGOs have at least a legal basis for seeking domestic criminal remedies against responsible individuals or corporations for serious environmental damage caused beyond their home country.

Article 11 of the Strasbourg Convention empowers public enforcement action, but this entitlement is at the discretion of individual member states within *national* criminal jurisdictions. There is no question of individuals or NGOs having access to criminal proceedings against the wishes of their home states. The direct access of affected parties to international environmental enforcement bodies is thus truncated – an underdevelopment of cosmopolitan rights unsurprising in the light of the potential in this area for sanctions against states. Under international law, only states have the right to bring a claim for redress before an international tribunal with compulsory jurisdiction. Even for states, there must be sufficient legal grounds to support such an action, which largely depend on the nature of the alleged breach of an international obligation and the particular remedy sought. Typically, it would have to be demonstrated that a right had been violated, which could refer, for example, to significant physical damage (e.g. from transboundary air or marine pollution) or a failure to uphold a procedural environmental duty (e.g. an obligation to consult over the use of shared natural resources) (Smith, 1988: pp5–8; Okowa, 2000: pp209–10). These are general rules of state responsibility: their application to environmental harm encompasses numerous duties within and outside treaties. What is clear is that states are entrusted with the sovereign right exclusively to represent the interests of their national publics in contentious judicial proceedings between countries.

Again, it is the propensity for soft implementation in international environmental regulation that is providing opportunities for the engagement of non-state actors. While they have no authority to become parties to contentious international proceedings, such as those at the International Court of Justice, the preference of states for less confrontational forums has created openings for NGOs across a range of institutional settings. These include international arbitration (e.g. the environmental arbitration provided by the Permanent Court of Arbitration in the Hague) and consensual proceedings (such as those available under the International Tribunal of the Law of the Sea). This relaxation of legal standing rules brings environmental enforcement closer to the structure of legal proceedings in the field of human rights (Birnie and Boyle, 2002: pp223–4). They reflect, therefore, the growing currency of the cosmopolitan notion that, where vital interests are at stake, the concerns of affected publics may be legitimately represented by NGOs.

Indeed, the precedent to grant standing for individuals or NGOs to initiate environmental enforcement measures by an international treaty body pre-dates the Aarhus Convention compliance rights by a decade. Under the citizen submission provisions of the 1993 North American Agreement on Environmental Cooperation, any member of the public (an individual or NGO) in Canada, the US or Mexico has the right to claim that a member state is failing to enforce its environmental laws effectively. Subject to at least a two-thirds majority vote of the treaty's governing council, its secretariat can request the development of a factual record on the alleged deficiencies in enforcement. The factual record is non-binding, which has provoked strong criticism from environmentalists. Nevertheless, the opening of an international treaty body to direct public access may be judged as a positive step in the growth of transnational environmental accountability (Fitzmaurice, 2003). And this provision has influenced the formulation of soft enforcement measures elsewhere; for example, the access afforded to non-state actors, at the Organization for Economic Cooperation and Development (2000), to raise alleged breaches by its member states of its 2000 Guidelines for Multinational Enterprises.

Conclusion

From this brief survey of international environmental regulation, several summary observations are possible on public mechanisms of access and redress. Firstly, international cooperation on transboundary ecological problems, while constrained by the principle that sovereign states alone legally represent their national publics, is not closed to the notion that all persons have equal standing when their vital ecological interests are threatened. Core state environmental obligations articulated in terms of harm prevention commonly register duties to humanity that have general scope beyond territorial borders and into the future. The legal obligations of MEAs constitute collective group interests safeguarding the well-being of all citizens in contracting states from selected sources of ecological harm. Where environmental damage is deliberate and massive, affected publics have a right to protection that is, at least in some circumstances, universal – legally empowering *any* state to defend this entitlement on behalf of the international community. Secondly, the evolution of procedural rights in international environmental decision-making has created some openings for non-national affected publics. Linked to the global diffusion of democratic norms of civic participation, these opportunities are most evident in the application of the non-discrimination principle in international environmental regulation, particularly in treaties developed by the ECE. However, these procedural entitlements are not common nor, thirdly, are public compliance and enforcement rights. The latter have slowly emerged in MEA soft implementation mechanisms and the legal access for non-nationals permitted in internationally harmonized domestic civil liability rules. Individuals and NGOs still cannot pursue environmental legal claims involving the compulsory jurisdiction of international courts.

Overall, then, we can observe that the prevention of significant environmental harm to non-national parties is well established as a regulative norm in international governance, but that the direct participation of affected parties in realizing the relevant rules is at best embryonic. To explain this state of affairs would of course require an in-depth examination of norm development across different issue areas, with a focus on the interplay of environmental protection values with territorial norms and institutions. The 'social fitness' thesis put forward by 'constructivist' international relations scholars to account for norm selection offers a promising starting point for research, highlighting some of the political path dependencies already alluded to in this book. Here, the truncated cosmopolitan character of international environmental obligations can be understood in the context of a dominant 'norm-complex' of liberal environmentalism favouring market-based polices and justifications, yet institutionalized within an international governance system still centred on sovereign state authority (Bernstein, 2001; also Finnemore and Sikkink, 1998). *Citizen* environmental entitlements expressed *across territorial boundaries* might seem doubly disadvantaged by this norm-complex, yet their modest progress attests to some countervailing tendencies. These include, I suggest, the resonance of cosmopolitan environmental rights with the harm prevention and equality of opportunity norms of democratic liberalism, and also the presence of international legitimating institutions receptive to more cosmopolitan public participation (e.g. ECE, Council of Europe).

The preoccupation in this chapter has been, less ambitiously, with clarifying the nature of new public entitlements in international environmental law. Obviously, this leaves open the question of which counterpart cosmopolitan obligations fall on individuals and groups. In a world of strong ecological, economic and political interdependencies, cosmopolitan environmental duties on individuals are more than a responsibility not to engage in private activities likely to degrade ecological conditions vital to their co-nationals and foreigners. These are important direct duties, and the processes of inter-cultural communication by which we may agree on their transnational content and application warrant sustained attention. Even more challenging, perhaps, is the determination of cosmopolitan responsibilities based on the indirect role of individuals in supporting political and market-based institutions that produce transboundary environmental degradation. As set out by Pogge in his discussion of responsibilities for world poverty, under a human-rights outlook individuals have a negative duty not to cooperate in upholding institutions causing significant harm to others. That all humans are now participants bound up in institutional orders with global effects renders this duty cosmopolitan. However, Pogge argues, the institutional responsibility of citizens in the more powerful, affluent countries is accentuated by their governments' role in designing and maintaining economic and political ground rules that generate systemic harm. Their collective responsibility is all too apparent in the many ways in which citizens in these countries have benefited, and continue to benefit, from activities imposing environmental (and social) costs on non-nationals (Pogge, 2002: pp169–77; Paterson, 2000: pp35–65).

Andrew Dobson (2003) argues cogently that the inequalities featured here – structurally imposing environmental costs on poorer countries – call into question the very usefulness of the cosmopolitan understanding of obligations to non-nationals, because its picture of reciprocal, rights-based entitlements veers so far from the unequal relationships of physical harm actually experienced by vulnerable individuals and communities. In short, there is a glaring gap between the moral conception of empowered cosmopolitan publics and the real world of social and ecological damage, which may not be recognized as such by the affected communities in question, let alone by those responsible for the damage. For Dobson, the latter in particular must be confronted with their complicity in harm production in terms of the duty to reduce their inflated 'ecological footprint' – their environmental resource consumption and assimilation demands (2003: pp97–117). This is a crucial reminder directly to take into account the actual material impacts generated by resource- and energy-intensive development paths as the source of environmental obligations to non-nationals (and also co-nationals). However, this framework rests itself on a cosmopolitan entitlement – the right to a fair (equal) share of 'ecological space' – which suggests that Dobson's notion of 'ecological citizenship' may be nearer than he claims to the sort of cosmopolitan outlook informing this book (see also Wall, 2003). To be sure, this is in part due to the stress I share with Dobson on harm prevention, which, he correctly observes, has not been a preoccupation of cosmopolitan authors – with the notable exception of Andrew Linklater. Obligations not to harm the vital ecological interests of distant strangers (through space or over time) in principle are owed to everyone by everyone, but in practice the duties naturally fall heavily on harm producers.

Of course, whether or not we accept these cosmopolitan duties rests on the political, rather than academic, influence of this moral interpretation of environmental problems. Transnational or global citizenship action in broad agreement with it is concerned, firstly, with openly communicating this understanding across diverse networks of human association; and secondly, by realizing as far as possible the rights to public participation already located in human rights and environmental law in order to hold to account governments and international institutions for the harmful effects of activities carried out with our implicit endorsement. This second move is but one area where cosmopolitan public entitlements meet their corresponding duties on individuals and groups. Of course, legal instruments, compromised by hierarchical power relations, may only marginally enable citizen action in pursuit of common environmental needs. Global citizenship as political participation has its own autonomy, expressed in numerous campaigning and activist practices (Gaventa, 2001; see Chapter 2). Affirmation of the cosmopolitan notion of equal respect for all persons informs these social and ecological activist networks (e.g. People's Global Action, International Forum on Globalization), but it can also serve as a moral standard by which their own constituencies, decision-making and protests can be judged. Other organizational forms – states, international organizations, multinational corporations – all make claims to act in the global public interest. The extent to which any of these actors addresses the basic environmental needs of transnational publics is ultimately judged by how far they create and/or promote conditions for egalitarian decision-making and effective, socially just problem-solving (Brunkhorst, 2002).

Chapter 4

The World Trade Regime and Environmental Accountability

The Doha Declaration, agreed in November 2001 at the fourth Ministerial Conference of the World Trade Organization (WTO), launched the current round of global trade negotiations. Such a renewal of the trade liberalization project – one with ambitious market access goals across key trade and services sectors – would have seemed inconceivable to anyone observing the street battles in Seattle two years earlier at the third WTO ministerial meeting. Yet the Doha Declaration was at least partly cognizant of the political realities represented by a decade of growing protests from anti-globalization activists and nongovernmental organization (NGO) coalitions (Williams and Ford, 1999; Weber, 2001). In the face of very public challenges to its democratic legitimacy as an intergovernmental organization, the WTO flagged up a Doha Development Agenda geared, it was claimed, to facilitating the substantial welfare gains to developing countries that would flow from dismantling trade-distorting subsidies and other protectionist barriers in industrialized countries. Not only did the Doha Declaration also reaffirm the commitment to sustainable development embedded in the 1994 (Marrakesh) Agreement Establishing the World Trade Organization, stressing the compatibility between environmental protection goals and open, non-discriminatory trade rules, it also contained a pledge to make the WTO's operations more transparent, entailing increased access to information and improved public dialogue. For the WTO the 'Seattle syndrome' had been exorcized and the organization was back in business (World Trade Organization, 2001, 2002: p3).

However, political tensions remain over the incorporation of environmental (and social) concerns into the negotiations and rulings of the WTO. Developing countries now comprise two-thirds of the WTO membership of 146 states and are generally unsympathetic to the efforts of leading industrialized countries, supported by environmental NGOs, to address at the WTO the ecological implications of international trade rules. At the same time, the significant political influence of NGO environmental constituencies within these states – notably the European Union (EU) countries – is evident in the Doha commitment of WTO member governments to launch formal negotiations on the relationships between trade rules and international environmental law. To be sure, these negotiations include the trade consequences of environmental measures, where the geopolitical alignment of member state positions has been less predictable, varying according to the measure in question and the national export interests at stake. There is also no simple correspondence between member state grievances and environmental concerns at the level of the WTO enforcement regime – its compulsory dispute settlement mechanism – where several high-profile cases have exposed competing claims over whether the unilateral use of import restrictions for environmental protection ends is legitimate under international trade law. What is clear, though, is that as the ecological impacts of economic integration receive increasing regulatory attention from states, there is an ever more pressing need for agreement over which environmental constraints, if any, can justifiably impinge on trade rule-making.

This chapter examines the opportunities within the WTO for the representation of transnational environmental interests by NGOs. Even prior to Seattle, environmental social movement pressure had prompted the WTO to increase its engagement with civil society groups (O'Brien et al, 1999: pp134–53; Scholte et al, 1999), and this communication now includes the de-restriction of documents, access to ministerial meetings, occasional meetings with the Director-General, and the facilitation of NGO-oriented symposia and briefings. Following a brief description of the key environmental provisions within the world trade system, I examine the new opportunities for environmental NGOs to interact with the WTO. Particular attention is directed at the NGO briefings on trade and environment, held at the organization's centre in Geneva: their external relations rationale for the WTO Secretariat is clarified, while a survey of the NGO participants at these briefings reveals the motivations of those taking part and their assessments of (suggested) mechanisms for enhancing WTO relations with NGOs.

Recent scholarship on WTO–civil society links has posited that there are institutional limitations to the incorporation of environmental values in the world trade regime These constraints include the dominance of producer interests in trade negotiations, the legal supremacy of free trade over environmental protection goals and the exclusion of NGOs from WTO policy deliberations (Esty, 1999; Conca, 2000; Weber, 2001). Their collective impact is to restrict the scope for assigning responsibility for trade-related environmental harms, whether this damage arises from the attributes of an imported product (e.g. genetically modified organisms) or the means of its production (e.g. pollution discharges). There is a marked accountability deficit when trade-related environmental effects are systemic and diffuse (e.g. biodiversity depletion, greenhouse gas emissions), with at best fractured chains of responsibility. Given that the WTO is accountable solely to its member states, trade restrictions in support of environmental protection can be justified only in terms of national (territorial) interests, requiring WTO legal adjudication between the export rights of the source state and the regulatory entitlements of the affected state. As we shall see, restrictions targeting ecological effects beyond the borders of the importing state test the legal limits of the trade regime.

Of course, environmental NGOs campaigning on trade issues claim to articulate and represent the concerns of transnational publics experiencing trade-generated injury. Their moral case is that WTO bodies – and their constituent member states – should be obliged to answer for the extra-territorial environmental effects of their trade policies; and that individuals or groups facing significant harm should have access to means of redress. This chapter identifies shared goals among environment and development NGOs for institutionalizing modes of environmental answerability at the WTO, which centre on new points of access for civil society actors. These reformist recommendations contrast with the calls from 'global justice' groups and networks (e.g. Our World is Not For Sale) for the WTO to be abolished: while this latter type of civil society activism has received more publicity (and is addressed in Chapter 2), the leading transnational environmental NGOs perceive WTO restructuring to be more within the realm of the possible. I shall address this issue of political feasibility as well as the depth of the new accountability gains promised – how might they promote a fairer consideration of cross-border ecological interests?

Environmental provisions within the world trade regime

The WTO presides over a multilateral trading system of which the core international treaty is the General Agreement on Tariffs and Trade (GATT), as legally consolidated in 1994. Prior to this promulgation, the GATT had served for half a century as the focus for international tariff-reduction efforts. Its durability and renewal under the WTO attests to the now global influence of neoclassical trade theory – in particular, the claim that the domestic economic benefits for states of trade liberalization outweigh any negative adjustment costs from increased competition. Net economic gains are anticipated as domestic specialization of production in areas of comparative advantage achieves, through increased efficiencies, globally competitive commodities. GATT 1994 obligations are informed, above all, by this theoretical understanding of free trade: at the heart of the trade system are the so-called non-discrimination principles of most-favoured-nation status (Article I) and national treatment provision (Article III). Their combined effect is legally to prescribe equality of treatment for globally traded products, such that contracting states agree to fair, open rules of economic interaction.

The generation of transboundary environmental degradation between and beyond countries subscribing to trade liberalization constitutes a key challenge for WTO rule-making and adjudication. In so far as economic activities within member states cause ecological damage beyond their national borders, and the affected publics are not compensated, the efficiency and welfare gains of trade liberalization are compromised. As economic globalization proceeds, increasing the scope and intensity of international trade, these external environmental costs can be expected to grow in the absence of coordinated policy responses; although their impacts vary according to the industrial sector, technologies and product characteristics involved (Jones, 1998). There remains a lively discussion in the trade–environment literature about the impacts on competitiveness of measures to externalize (or internalize) environmental costs within and between countries. Evidence is inconclusive concerning, for example, whether trade liberalization promotes a 'race to the bottom' in environmental standard-setting as polluting industries seek out jurisdictions with low compliance costs, or whether concerns about competitiveness can stall or defeat proposed national environmental regulations (e.g. Nordstöm and Vaughan, 1999; Neumayer, 2001; Ulph, 2001). This theoretical indeterminacy about the shifts in comparative advantage caused by transboundary environmental spillovers has heightened the political role of the WTO in interpreting 'environmental exceptions' to GATT trade rules.

Article XX of GATT, allowing conditional exceptions to GATT/WTO obligations, includes scope for member states to appeal to human, animal or plant health and natural resource conservation reasons. This 'general exceptions' provision reflects an attempt to balance the sovereign rights of states to prescribe national standards affecting trade with the need to safeguard the free trade principle. A strict burden of proof imposed on any party asserting an Article XX exception is reinforced by a 'chapeau' (qualifying clause), whereby the proposed trade-restrictive measures are illegal if they are applied in a manner constituting 'arbitrary' or 'unjustifiable' discrimination between countries where the same conditions apply, or act as a 'disguised restriction on international trade'. These qualifications have proved onerous for states defending environmental exceptions before the compulsory, binding Dispute Settlement Body (DSB) of the WTO, comprising independent adjudication panels and an Appellate Body. Not until a 2000 panel ruling on a French ban of asbestos imports from Canada, as necessary to protecting human life or health, has an environment-related trade restriction under Article XX been accepted (WTO Appellate Body, 2001a). Additional rules on environmental standard-setting within the GATT/WTO regime, sharing the non-discriminatory intent of Article XX, are provided under the Agreement on the Application of Sanitary and Phytosanitary Measures (SPS) and the Agreement on Technical Barriers to Trade (TBT). Both pertain to product standards and have generated several high-profile disagreements between WTO member states; for example, the SPS dispute over EU import bans on United States

(US) beef products treated with growth hormones and the combined US/Canadian opposition to EU proposals to label genetically modified foods, alleging a violation of the equal treatment provisions of the TBT agreement.

From WTO dispute settlement adjudication on Article XX exceptions, the key pronouncement on trade sanctions oriented to non-domestic environmental impacts is set out by two Appellate Body decisions in 1998 and 2001 on the legality of a US import prohibition of shrimp products from countries without certifiable means for reducing the incidental mortality of endangered sea turtles in their commercial shrimp trawling (WTO Appellate Body, 1998b, 2001b). Until these rulings, it was accepted that trade measures under GATT Article XX with environmental protection objectives could be justifiable only within the jurisdictional boundaries of the implementing state. Lives or resources affected by environmental harm outside the country imposing the trade barrier could not legitimately be the basis for exceptions to Article XX: to do so would seemingly breach the *territoriality principle* – that the sovereign right of states to protect their populations against the threat or incidence of trade-related harm is respected, but that this right has no extra-territorial reach (Mattoo and Mavroidis, 1997: pp329–32; Byron, 2001: pp31–4). The ruling out of (unilateral) state trade sanctions invoking Article XX to achieve environmental protection beyond national jurisdiction was taken to be an enduring lesson from the well-known, but unadopted, GATT panel rulings in the 1990s against US embargoes on tuna imports from countries allowing fishing practices killing large numbers of dolphins. However, as Schoenbaum (2002: pp707–13) argues, the *Shrimp–Turtle* rulings of the Appellate Body upheld the right of WTO member states to employ trade restrictions to protect environmental resources *beyond national jurisdiction*, provided that they had already undertaken good-faith efforts to reach a negotiated environmental agreement with the relevant trading states.

It is instructive that the most significant clarification of WTO environmental obligations has arisen from the decisions of the DSB panels and Appellate Body. Even though the WTO Agreement restricts exclusive authority in interpreting GATT 1994 to the majority decisions of the Ministerial Conference and General Council, and DSB rulings are treated as imposing no binding precedents on future disputes, legal commentators have argued that it is inevitable that, as the body of decisions builds, previous decisions will hold influence on the judgments of future panels (Cameron and Gray, 2001: pp272–6). In contrast to the evolving interpretation of trade–environment obligations within the dispute settlement system, the WTO body charged with exploring these linkages – the Committee on Trade and Environment (CTE) has made slow progress. Created in 1994, the CTE serves as the forum for member states to address the relationship between trade and environmental measures, with a view to determining whether rule changes are required in the multilateral trading system to enhance their positive interaction. The lack of substantive agreement in the CTE on trade–environment measures is largely attributable to divergent state priorities and positions, most notably between industrialized countries sympathetic to environmental regulations impinging on trade and developing countries fearful of a discriminatory 'green protectionism' excluding their exports from lucrative overseas markets (Olsen et al, 2001; Shaffer, 2001).

A renewed mandate for the CTE was provided by the Doha Ministerial Declaration, introducing the first formal negotiations between WTO member states on environmental issues. Discussions, launched in March 2002, centred on paragraph 31 of the declaration:

> (i)   *the relationship between existing WTO rules and specific trade obligations set out in multilateral environmental agreements (MEAs). The negotiations shall be limited in scope to the applicability of such existing WTO rules as among parties to the MEA in question. The negotiations shall not prejudice the WTO rights of any Member that is not a party to the MEA in question;*
>
> (ii)   *procedures for regular information exchange between MEA Secretariats and the relevant WTO committees, and the criteria for the granting of observer status;*
>
> (iii)   *the reduction or, as appropriate, elimination of tariff and non-tariff barriers to environmental goods and services.*

In two accompanying paragraphs on trade and environment, the CTE is instructed to retain its previous focus on the effect of environmental measures on market access, but to pay attention to the priorities of developing countries, in particular the least-developed among them, including their needs for technical assistance and capacity building in the field of trade and environment.

During 2002–3 CTE talks were dominated by paragraph 31(i) and soon exposed significant differences between states. Inclusion of this topic had been a core European Community (EC) demand at Doha and, supported by Switzerland, Norway and Japan, the EC sought support for establishing general 'principles and parameters' on the relationship between WTO and MEA obligations. This overarching approach was opposed by states – notably Australia, New Zealand and the US, along with most developing-country delegates – sceptical of rule-making or interpretation likely to impose constraints on the WTO regime. The latter group proposed instead a 'bottom-up' approach, looking case-by-case at the specific trade obligations of relevant MEAs, thus protecting WTO rules from a more wide-ranging scrutiny according to international environmental law. When discussions in 2003 moved in this direction, it was agreed that the most relevant MEAs to scrutinize were the three in force at that time containing mandatory trade measures – the 1973 Convention on International Trade in Endangered Species of Wild Flora and Fauna (CITES), the 1989 Convention on the Control of Transboundary Movement of Hazardous Wastes and Their

Disposal (Basel Convention), and the 1987 Protocol on Substances that Deplete the Ozone Layer (Montreal Protocol).

World Trade Organization engagement with environmental NGOs

The absence of consensus among member states about the nature of appropriate relations between the WTO and NGOs has coloured the organization's stance in this area since 1994. Article V.2 of the Marrakesh Agreement is noncommittal: 'The General Council may make appropriate arrangements for consultation and cooperation with non-governmental organizations concerned with matters related to those of the WTO.'

Guidelines for conducting these relations with NGOs were not issued by the General Council until July 1996 (World Trade Organization, 1996). While these included improved public access to WTO documents and an instruction to the WTO Secretariat more actively to seek direct contacts with NGOs – through such mechanisms as symposia, meetings and briefings – the guidelines conveyed also the view of most member states that the distinctive trade treaty basis of the WTO precluded any direct involvement of NGOs. According to this view, the 'special character' of the WTO means that the *national* political procedures of member states are a more legitimate focus of NGO trade-oriented concerns and lobbying than the organization itself – a stance Steve Charnovitz has labelled 'WTO exceptionalism' (2002: pp320–5) to distinguish it from the norms of greater NGO participation found, for example, in United Nations organizations. Reinforcing this position, the commitment to increased WTO transparency and public dialogue in the Doha Declaration includes no specific invitation to NGOs.

However, according to WTO Secretariat officials, the exceptionalist charge short-changes the real advances made in recent years in opening up the organization to public scrutiny. Direct relations with civil society groups are portrayed as necessary to increasing public understanding of the organization and, more generally, the benefits of rule-based trade liberalization (Werner, 2002). Political support for greater transparency initially came from the US, the EC and other advanced industrialized WTO member states (notably Norway and Switzerland), responding largely to domestic environmentalist constituencies. Developing-country member states, weary of the agenda-setting power of Northern NGOs, have tended to oppose these efforts in so far as they entail more formal WTO–NGO relations. Nevertheless, four modes of civil society access have become significant for transnational environmental NGOs – de-restriction of documents, NGO symposia on trade and environment, NGO briefings on WTO council and committee work (notably the work of the CTE), and attendance at ministerial conferences.

De-restriction of documents

In parallel with its decision in 1996 on relations with NGOs, the WTO General Council adopted procedures for the circulation and de-restriction of WTO documents, establishing the basic principle that most documents would be circulated as unrestricted. Most exceptions to this – including working documents, minutes of meetings of WTO committees and Ministerial Conference summary records – were considered for de-restriction after six months, although members retained the right to block public access for selected documents. It rapidly became apparent to NGOs that de-restriction was neither straightforward nor timely and calls were made to accelerate the process (Bellman and Gerster, 1996). The General Council discussed such proposals in 1998, with Canada and the US subsequently championing a presumption of immediate de-restriction for most WTO documents. However, developing countries proved reluctant to support this, believing that it would disproportionately benefit Northern lobbying groups – notably environmentalists and labour rights activists – at odds with their trade interests (Loy, 2001; Shaffer, 2001: p67). After four years of discussions, the General Council reached a decision in May 2002 to accelerate de-restriction of official WTO documents, cutting the time period in which most documents are publicly made available to 6–12 weeks, and also reducing significantly the list of exceptions.

As part of its express intention to increase transparency in the functioning of the WTO, the General Council also decided to make available online, in all three official WTO languages (English, French and Spanish), all de-restricted WTO documents. Since 1998 there has also been a special section of the WTO website dedicated to NGO issues (www.wto.org/english/forums_e/ngo_e/ngo_e.htm): the website itself is heavily used, receiving about 600,000 user sessions a month in 2002, and has earned praise from media and NGO representatives. For example, the UK charity, One World Trust, has commended the WTO on its range of available online documents, highlighting the access to non-technical summaries of legal texts, the provision of detailed decision-making information, and a clear information disclosure policy (Kovach et al, 2003: p15). While the Secretariat, due to staff constraints, proved unable to maintain the monthly online bulletin for NGOs launched in 2002, the gains in organizational transparency have been significant.

NGO symposia on trade and environment

Under the 1996 General Council decision on relations with NGOs, the Secretariat was allowed significant discretion to experiment with different modes of interaction, both informal and formal (Werner, 2002). Perhaps the most high profile in the trade and environment area has been the organization of Geneva-based symposia oriented to environmental NGOs and other interested non-state actors. A GATT symposium on trade, environment and sustainable development had been held in 1994, in response to an environmentalist backlash against a dispute settlement panel ruling on the tuna–dolphin US import controls: unsurprisingly, this symposium facilitated only vocal disquiet from the attending NGOs. In September 1996, the first WTO symposium with NGOs on trade and environment, attended by 35 NGOs, featured more constructive exchanges with the Secretariat (O'Brien et al, 1999: p139). Nine months later, the number of NGOs attending a second symposium on trade and environment had doubled, with, significantly, the participation of developing-country NGOs funded by the Australian, Canadian and Dutch governments. Since then, prompted by US and EU proposals, NGO input has been encouraged in more formal WTO symposia (including environment and development themes), featuring the participation also of member states and high-ranking representatives from other international organizations. Environmental NGOs have welcomed the opportunity to participate in these high-level symposia and, in line with its public awareness remit, the Secretariat has carried on organizing informal symposia and seminars dedicated to NGOs, including regional meetings.

WTO Secretariat briefings for NGOs

The success of the trade–environment symposia, combined with European and US calls for increased WTO transparency, persuaded Director-General Renato Ruggiero to convene an internal taskforce in May 1998 to suggest ways of enhancing cooperation with civil society actors. As endorsed by the General Council, the key innovation to emerge from this taskforce was the creation of regular briefings for NGOs on the work of WTO committees and working groups. As the Secretariat already organized press briefings in Geneva, it was deemed to be both feasible and legitimate to extend this opportunity to relevant NGOs (Marceau and Pedersen, 1999: pp19–20). The first NGO briefing, in September 1998, was delivered to over 20 environment and development NGOs on the deliberations of the CTE, and briefings were soon rolled out to cover the activities of other WTO committees. The Secretariat has, in addition, responded to strong interest in the special sessions mandated by the Doha Ministerial Declaration, briefing NGOs on the negotiations taking place in the Committee on Agriculture, the Committee on Trade and Development, the CTE and the Council for Trade in Services.

NGO briefings are organized by the External Relations Division – a relatively small division of the WTO Secretariat comprising one director and eight regular staff in 2002–3. In recent years, External Relations has become the focal point for NGO interactions with the WTO, and is charged with developing relationships with civil society groups (alongside liaison with international intergovernmental organizations and national legislative representatives). Initial NGO contacts with the CTE were facilitated by the WTO

Trade and Environment Division, which organises the NGO symposia in this thematic area. However, in 1996 Director-General Ruggiero entrusted External Relations with coordinating transparency and NGO input activities across the WTO: subsequent Directors-General (Mike Moore, 1999–2002; Supachai Panitchpakdi since 2002) have maintained this division of labour within the Secretariat. As the briefings have become regularized, External Relations has experimented with other points of contact, from invited NGO seminars and position papers to occasional meetings with the Director-General.

NGO attendance at WTO ministerial conferences

The first WTO Ministerial Conference, in December 1996 in Singapore, followed the publication of WTO guidelines for arrangements on relations with NGOs; but these guidelines contained no instructions on participation at ministerial meetings. Again, it was pressure coming from European and North American member states that prodded the General Council to mandate the Secretariat to coordinate civil society representation. Lacking the legal template available to United Nations bodies for accrediting NGOs to participate in relevant conferences (see Chapter 2), the Secretariat invited NGO registration on the basis of Article V.2 of the Marrakesh Agreement – that they were non-profit organizations 'concerned with matters related to those of the WTO'. In practice, the Secretariat sent registration forms to all 159 NGOs expressing an interest in attending the Singapore Ministerial Conference. Almost all were accepted and 108 NGOs turned up (including 10 environment/development NGOs, in contrast to 48 business lobbying groups). The provision of an NGO centre at the meeting, with office and media facilities, was praised by the NGO attendees, and has become a regular feature of ministerial conferences. NGOs were less happy to be restricted to observing plenary sessions but excluded from negotiations (Marceau and Pedersen, 1999: pp12–15; O'Brien et al, 1999: pp92–7).

With no support among WTO members for NGO access to negotiations, the organization has maintained its strategy of truncated NGO involvement. Subsequent ministerial conferences in Geneva (1998), Seattle (1999), Doha (2001) and Cancún (2003) have nevertheless seen NGO registration become the norm with, Doha excepted, an increasing number of NGOs represented. These include a growing number of environmental NGOs: interestingly, the high-profile transnational groups and activist coalitions (e.g. Friends of the Earth International, Greenpeace International, International Forum on Globalization, Third World Network) have all received recognition status at WTO ministerial meetings despite their challenges to the existing system of trade rule-making.

Attendance at ministerial meetings enables NGOs to lobby member state representatives, which the more reformist transnational environmental groups

(e.g. WWF International, World Conservation Union) favour over demonstrations. Moreover, some WTO member states have drawn consistently on
transnational NGOs for trade-related research and media assistance. Since the
Seattle meeting, developing-country delegations in particular have forged
lobbying alliances with Northern development NGOs (e.g. Médicins sans
Frontières, Oxfam International, CAFOD) over issues such as access to generic
medicines and opposition to agricultural subsidies in the US and EU. These
NGOs have also benefited from the willingness of some developing countries
(e.g. Uganda, Kenya) to accept domestic development (and other) NGOs on
their national trade delegations (Ddamilura and Abdi, 2003). Where, occa-
sionally, domestic environmental NGOs have been invited onto Southern
trade delegations, this has been above all in order to make use of their expertise
(e.g. the Bangladeshi Environmental Lawyers Association). Northern-based
environmental NGOs, often working closely with sympathetic European
states, have tended to find it more difficult to harmonize campaigning
objectives with developing countries, in spite of the growing presence of
transnational environmental NGOs from the global South (e.g. ECONEWS
Africa, Third World Network). As I note in the conclusion to this chapter,
though, a North–South trade–environment agenda conversant with human
development needs is emerging.

NGO involvement in CTE briefings: reasons for attendance and assessments of WTO–civil society relations

As the only routine locus of physical interaction between NGOs and the
Secretariat in Geneva, the regular briefings on WTO work provide an
opportunity to gauge the usefulness of this information access tool from the
perspective of NGO participants, as well as their broader views on the
openness of the organization. The Doha negotiating agenda on trade and
environment has heightened the significance of the CTE meetings and, in
response to outside interest, the WTO Secretariat has maintained regular
NGO briefings to report on the progress of member state discussions (as well
as developments in other WTO committees). In 2002 there were three
briefings for interested NGOs on CTE meetings, centred on member state
discussions of paragraph 31 of the Doha Declaration. I attended, as an
observer, the CTE briefings for NGOs in October and November. In
addition, the WTO External Relations Division consented to me contacting
relevant NGOs on their briefings mailing list, in order to undertake a short
questionnaire survey. The questionnaire was designed to elicit from NGOs
their reasons for attending the CTE briefings, their assessment of these
meetings as an outreach tool, and their position on WTO–civil society

relations, including attitudes on various recommendations for extending or formalizing NGO participation in the WTO.

The questionnaire was administered in October–November 2002 and directed at all 30 NGOs that participated in the 2001–2002 CTE briefings; 14 replies and 12 completed questionnaires were received. Two replies were from organizations that had almost entirely attended NGO briefings on other WTO committees, so their responses were taken into account only for the issue of general WTO–civil society relations. Ten replies were CTE-relevant, representing most of the dozen regular attendees at the CTE briefing sessions in 2001–2002. They comprise five environment and development NGOs, two international business associations, an international trade union federation, a global faith alliance and a university law professor. With the exception of the trade union federation (based in France) and one environmental NGO (located elsewhere in Switzerland), all the respondents were from organizations with headquarters or offices in Geneva.

From the survey it is clear that NGOs are turning up at the WTO with the expectations that the briefings will provide important, up-to-date information on the state of play of negotiations within the CTE. All respondents gave this as a reason for attending. However, the one-way information dissemination of the briefings – receiving feedback from WTO Secretariat External Relations and Trade and Environment staff – does not preclude NGOs from making full use of opportunities for questions to ascertain the positions of particular member states, which are often not specified in the official reports of meetings. Questions are also used to convey views to Secretariat staff, pushing briefings in a more interactive direction, even if, in line with Secretariat norms of impartiality and confidentiality, WTO staff are able only to express personal assessments. Furthermore, three respondents also acknowledged the opportunity to network with other participants as a reason for attending the briefings: from personal observation, this side-benefit of participation is evident in the briefing room before and after the official business; and points to a circle of professional familiarity among the Geneva-based NGOs.

Table 4.1 summarizes from questionnaire replies the satisfaction of NGO participants with various aspects of the 2001–2002 briefings. The organization of the briefings, in terms of advance notice to interested parties and meeting times (during office hours), finds favour with all respondents. Of course, the modest information-disclosure function of the briefings means that the regular attendees are those transnational NGOs located in Geneva. There is widespread satisfaction with the usefulness of the verbal reports from WTO Secretariat staff on the work of the CTE. Both direct observations of the author and survey results attest that time was made available for Secretariat staff to receive all questions and also to answer as thoroughly as possible. The only significant (albeit minority) source of NGO disquiet is that there is insufficient opportunity during or after briefings to consult WTO Secretariat staff servicing the CTE. Two respondents (both environmental NGO

Table 4.1 *NGO satisfaction with 2001–2002 WTO briefings on CTE negotiations*

Aspect of NGO briefings on CTE	Satisfied	Not satisfied	Don't know
Advance notice of meetings	10		
Convenience of meeting times	10		
Usefulness of verbal reports on CTE negotiations	9	1	
Opportunities for questions to WTO representatives	8	1	1
Response of WTO representatives to questions	9	1	
Opportunity to talk to WTO CTE representatives	6	4	

Total: 10 responses.

representatives) registered a separate concern that the member state representative chairing the CTE had not attended briefings, even though provision is made in the 1996 General Council guidelines for chairpersons to participate in briefings in a personal capacity.

Not surprisingly, when prompted to make any recommendations for change in the organization or delivery of the NGO briefings, these two respondents suggested formal opportunities to interact with the CTE chair and/or other member state representatives active in the work of that committee. Another environmental NGO recommended that time and space should be made available after the briefings for participants to consult WTO Secretariat staff on a bilateral basis – a proposal that stretches beyond the terms of reference for the meetings, signifying a desire for more formal WTO–NGO consultative relations. A fourth environmental NGO representative, who had expressed the sole note of dissatisfaction with the response of the Secretariat staff to participant questions in the briefings, wanted a more detailed account of member state positions during CTE discussions, including some analysis both of their development and their purchase on other states. However, most participants were satisfied with the organization and content of the meetings: both international business federations and the global faith alliance expressed a preference for no change. The only remaining respondent with reform proposals was the university law professor, who stated that there should also be briefings on environmental discussions in other WTO committees and councils, noting that these forums (e.g. the SPS, TBT, Trade-Related Aspects of Intellectual Property Rights (TRIPS) and the Trade Negotiating Committee) were more important in world trade rule-making than the CTE.

During recent years, commentators (e.g. Scholte et al, 1999; Olsen et al, 1999; Charnovitz, 2002), alongside environment and development NGOs (e.g. Greenpeace International, 2002; Oxfam, 2002), have put forward various suggestions for opening up the WTO to public scrutiny and increased NGO participation. Ten of the most prominent reform recommendations were distilled from this literature and included in the questionnaire to NGO briefing attendees: Table 4.2 summarizes their responses.

Table 4.2 *NGOs' positions on WTO–civil society relations*

Statement on WTO–civil society relations	Strongly support	Support	Don't support	Don't know
The current level of public access to WTO documents is satisfactory	1	2	9	
There needs to be further de-restriction of WTO documents for public access	7	4	1	
There should be regular WTO meetings with NGOs on trade and environment issues	9	3		
There should be a permanent WTO–civil society liaison group	5	4	2	1
NGOs formally liaising with the WTO should be internationally accredited	5	5	1	1
There should be observer status for recognized NGOs on WTO committees	9	1	2	
NGOs should have a right to submit briefs to WTO dispute settlement hearings	8	3	1	
There should be regular WTO regional symposia with relevant civil society actors	6	5	1	
Southern NGOs should be supported by WTO members to attend Geneva briefings/symposia	9	2	1	
The WTO should become a member of the UN Non-Governmental Liaison Service	4	2	1	5

Total: 12 responses.

While it is not unexpected to find NGOs supporting measures that would increase their access to WTO documentation and meetings, the table records some notable differences in emphasis. The majority of respondents, especially environmental NGOs, favour further de-restriction of WTO documents. There is strongest support for proposals related to greater NGO participation in existing WTO decision-making – regular meetings with NGOs on trade and environment issues, the conferral of observer status for recognized NGOs at WTO committee meetings, and the right of NGOs to submit briefs to WTO dispute settlement hearings. Perhaps in realization of the current practical bias at briefings in favour of European-based NGOs, strong aggregate approval is expressed (with the exception of a business federation) for enabling Southern NGOs to attend WTO briefings and symposia in Geneva. This concern to ensure more equitable geographical inclusion of relevant non-state interests is reinforced by significant (though less strong) support for making routine the WTO regional symposia with civil society actors. Increasing NGO interest in engaging with the WTO centrally has prompted the organization's Secretariat to consider ways of formalizing their input, while retaining the valued flexibility of existing arrangements. Both the idea of a permanent

WTO–global civil society liaison group and accreditation of transnational NGOs are being actively considered (Werner, 2002). Responses to the questionnaire indicate majority endorsement for both.

There is concern that the WTO lacks the technical capacity to facilitate more systematic relations with transnational NGOs, hence the limited support – arising mainly from the environment and development NGO respondents – for the proposal that the WTO becomes a subscribing member of the United Nations Non-Governmental Liaison Service (NGLS), in order to draw on acknowledged expertise in this area of capacity-building. In fact the WTO External Relations Division has periodically consulted with the NGLS on, for example, identifying relevant NGOs and the preparation of briefing papers on NGO accreditation for member states (H Jenkins, 2002). But the key challenge is more political than technical: WTO Secretariat commitments to develop NGO dialogue have persistently been checked by influential Southern member states (notably the Arab League), frustrating efforts to find a consensus on transnational civil society relations. Some support has been given to NGO capacity-building where this does not encroach on existing WTO decision-making in Geneva; for example, WTO efforts – under the Joint Integrated Technical Assistance Programme – to improve the capacity of African countries to accommodate civil society interests in *national* trade policy design (Ddamilura and Abdi, 2003).

Finally, the questionnaire invited respondents to offer any further suggestions for strengthening WTO–civil society relations. Three environmental NGOs made overlapping observations – registering satisfaction with the progress achieved in the past few years by the WTO in fostering improved central access for civil society groupings, but noting that there now needs to be an 'institutionalization' or 'mainstreaming' of these links. There is also the charge that the WTO propensity for discretionary relations with NGOs has allowed the Secretariat to select non-state participants for technical trade meetings on a private and partial basis:

> For example, the WTO is holding a two day seminar on investment – a topic of crucial importance for NGOs; nevertheless, an NGO representative asking to participate was refused access. This has happened on several occasions. On other occasions, some NGO representatives were allowed in on an informal, ad hoc and individual/personal basis.

Interestingly, there is a convergence between environmental NGOs and transnational business associations on the need to build up trade policy dialogue within civil society at the national level. However, whereas for the former this is one of various scales admitting interest representation, for the latter it is the only appropriate forum. As articulated by one of the business associations:

> *Such [WTO–civil society] relations should not be formalized but nurtured at a national level between the public/private sectors and NGOs. Otherwise, a parallel structure seeking input into the WTO is created that has neither a legitimate, coherent knowledge base nor a meaningful mandate. At the level of the WTO such input could be provided sensibly only by its members.*

This last point raises the critical issue of the legitimacy of NGOs representing transnational environmental interests in WTO rule-making and enforcement. How can moves to formalize WTO–civil society relations be seen more openly and fairly to address cross-border environmental impacts attributable to international trade policy? In other words, we need to consider now the potential role within the WTO for new norms of accountability for transnational environmental harm – and how these would be applied. The focus will be on the immediate outlook for reform priorities suggested by the survey, while the concluding discussion will highlight the broader political context of transnational environmental NGO interaction with the WTO.

WTO rule-making and cross-border environmental harm: new norms of accountability?

The expectation of NGOs that the WTO should accelerate opportunities for the representation and communication of environmental interests raises the prospect of applying new accountability norms to the organization. Of course, NGO demands that multilateral economic institutions be made publicly accountable for the environmental (and social) effects of their policy decisions have been directed elsewhere, including at the International Monetary Fund (IMF) and the World Bank. Both organizations have faced challenges in recent years from activist networks that their lending activities have harmed vulnerable communities and ecosystems. The weighted majority voting governing the two Bretton Woods institutions has encouraged environmental NGOs to lobby the domestic legislative bodies of those states providing the most funding (in particular the US and Germany), which has provoked a modest realignment in World Bank lending but negligible changes in IMF structural adjustment programmes. Significantly, the IMF has shared the WTO philosophy of delegating civil society liaison to its Public Affairs Division, while responsibility for NGO dialogue within the World Bank has long since moved from External Relations to the Strategic Planning and Review Department (Scholte, 2001; Covey, 1998: pp95–100). In organizational terms, environmental questioning of its policies remains for the WTO, like the IMF, more an issue of reputation management than internal regulation.

All multilateral economic organizations are formally accountable to member governments and therefore to the national publics of these states, but environmental NGOs assert that this is insufficient to deliver accountability to affected parties for the cross-border effects of their policies and practices. As regards the WTO, environmentalists claim that the ecological consequences of trade rule-making impact beyond as well as between national territories (e.g. on the global atmosphere and the high seas), and that these systemic consequences are neglected by WTO members. NGOs argue that both the extra-territorial reach and routine production of environmental externalities promoted by current trade rule warrant their representation of damaged communities on the basis of their expertise and moral commitment to prevent ecological damage. If by transnational environmental accountability we mean mechanisms of public answerability and redress against responsible actors for significant environmental harms involuntarily received, then it would have to be demonstrated that these mechanisms are needed in WTO rule-making. Schematically, this can be discussed according to our accountability norms (see Chapter 1) of environmental harm prevention, the legitimate inclusion of affected parties, and the impartial consideration of environmental claims.

Prevention of environmental damage

The obligation on states to prevent damage to the environment of other states or areas beyond the limits of national jurisdiction is, as outlined in Chapter 1, now a widely accepted norm in international law. With the preamble to the Marrakesh Agreement and the restated commitment to environmental protection (and sustainable development) in the Doha Declaration, the obligation to prevent transboundary or global environmental damage is, at least in principle, one internal to the aims of the WTO. The accountability challenge to the WTO presented by environmental NGOs is that the organization is not addressing the harmful ecological consequences arising from its rule-making and enforcement. Above all, the key GATT/WTO principle of non-discrimination allegedly undermines the efforts of countries to employ trade measures against imports produced in an ecologically unsustainable manner. Furthermore, environmentalists charge that, in arbitrating trade disputes over conflicting national TBT and SPS standards, WTO dispute settlement panels make or endorse environmental risk assessments in a closed, ill-equipped manner (Byron, 2001).

The recent preoccupation of the CTE with the relationship between WTO rules and specific trade measures in MEAs attests to concerns that there are international ecological obligations existing in potential conflict with trade rules. Under a restrictive legal definition of specific trade obligations promoted within the CTE by the US, Canada and India, WTO incompatibility is a possibility for at least six MEAs in force – CITES, the Basel Convention, the Montreal Protocol, the 1998 Rotterdam Convention on Prior Informed

Consent Procedure for Certain Hazardous Chemicals and Pesticides in International Trade, the 2000 Cartagena Protocol on Biosafety, and the 2001 Stockholm Convention on Persistent Organic Pollutants. The 2003 move by the WTO to confer *ad hoc* observer status on relevant MEA Secretariats at CTE meetings acknowledges their legal and technical authority in representing particular transnational environmental interests, although the EU push to extend this involvement to other negotiating committees has not found favour among WTO member states.

It is certainly evident from the regular information exchange and meetings between MEA secretariats and the WTO Secretariat that, even with legal uncertainties remaining over rule compatibilities, cooperation is enhancing perceptions of mutual trust (World Trade Organization Committee on Trade and Environment, 2002). As environmental NGOs remain excluded from the CTE itself, the MEA secretariats are seen as the most promising channel to communicate ecological concerns over WTO rules; after all, these NGOs are typically a core constituency of political support for MEAs outside contracting states. However, the strict remit of the CTE prevents a more fundamental interrogation of WTO accountability for the ecological consequences of trade rule-making. MEA secretariats themselves have stated that while observer status in WTO negotiations is important, and real tensions remain over formalizing this, the priority is convincing national trade representatives to the WTO of the need to embed environmental protection norms in trade negotiations (Abaza, 2002; Zedan, 2002). For example, just prior to the 2003 WTO Ministerial, UNEP and the Secretariat to the Convention on Biological Diversity helped organize a Global Biodiversity Forum in Cancún in order to facilitate communication of biodiversity conservation issues between (governmental and nongovernmental) environmental representatives and national trade ministers.

A key claim of transnational environmental groups is that policies designed to prevent ecological harm from material trade flows cannot be legitimately recognized by the WTO as long as the precautionary principle is not explicitly incorporated into trade rule-making (e.g. Friends of the Earth International, 2002; Greenpeace International, 2002). The charge that precautionary norms are discounted by the WTO finds support, it is argued, in a 1998 ruling of the Appellate Body, stating that the European Communities violated the SPS Agreement by banning imports from the US of beef treated with growth-promoting hormones. Crucially, the dispute settlement body struck down the European argument that the trade barrier was justified on precautionary grounds on account of purported health risks. It noted that the precautionary principle finds reflection in Article 5.7 of the SPS Agreement: but pulled the European Communities up for failing to conduct a required scientific risk assessment (WTO Appellate Body, 1998a: pp44–7). However, for environmental NGOs this confirmed the WTO's unwillingness to acknowledge the precautionary principle as a customary rule of international environmental law (e.g. Friends of the Earth International, 2001).

Perceived WTO threats to the conservation goals of the Convention on Biological Diversity and its 2000 (Cartagena) Protocol on Biodiversity are also a high-profile area of concern for these groups. In terms of the convention, the claim is that the WTO TRIPS Agreement, by strengthening patenting of genetic resources, may well accelerate the displacement of biologically diverse traditional farming practices (in developing countries) for high-yield monoculture systems (Friends of the Earth International, 2002: p8). And as regards the Biosafety Protocol, the worry is that a US legal challenge – tabled at the WTO in 2003 – to the EU ban on imports of genetically modified crops pre-empts and thus potentially undermines the protocol. This agreement, which entered into force in September 2003, empowers states to impose precautionary import restrictions on 'living modified organisms' to avoid or minimize possible adverse biodiversity (and health) effects. The consistency of these unilateral trade measures with WTO rules is by no means assured, and awaits clarification in CTE negotiations and DSB adjudication decisions. Their fate in the face of WTO interrogation will be a key litmus test for gauging the legal standing of trade obligations embedded in international environmental agreements.

Inclusion of affected parties

The inclusion of the concerns of citizens in decisions significantly affecting them is a core principle of political legitimacy in liberal democratic states. By maintaining that member states remain the only legitimate bodies for representing relevant interests in trade rule-making and enforcement, the WTO resists the trend in global governance to admit at least the arguments of non-state actors – NGOs, activist networks, epistemic communities, etc. (see Chapter 3). Robert Howse (2002: pp114–15) claims that these types of actors present a particular challenge for the WTO at the transnational level, where the third-party effects of trade policy-making routinely extend beyond national borders and, crucially, where domestic political systems often fail to register transnational ecological and social impacts. The continuing WTO reliance on the indirect representation of public values through member governments, Howse argues, seems incapable of working effectively towards mutual understanding of trade-related externalities. For the communication of environmental interests and values, NGOs and activist networks claim to expose the full ecological impacts of trade policy – for example, the external sink costs associated with climate change not included in the pricing, use and international trade of fossil fuels (Greenpeace International, 2002: p2). The democratic legitimacy of including environmentalist voices rests on their authority as 'intellectual competitors' – that is, the veracity of their claims to represent otherwise unacknowledged trade impacts on valued ecosystem goods and services (Esty, 1999).

Recent moves to greater transparency in WTO decision-making have certainly improved the capacity of environmental NGOs to scrutinize its work and publicly communicate their concerns. Trade and environment issues have been at the centre of tentative innovations in civil society interaction – notably the NGO symposia and briefings – while it has also been shown above that NGO participants of CTE briefings have an appetite for more institutionalized involvement in WTO business. Perhaps the most realistic focus for the next step in evolving WTO–NGO relations is the creation of an NGO advisory committee, which is already under consideration by the WTO Secretariat. Director-General Panitchpakdi has endorsed the recent work of the WTO Secretariat in building up civil society links and has expressed a preference for more regular NGO exchanges. However, there remains the firm position that the appropriate target for NGO lobbying is member states rather than the WTO itself. The granting of observer status for environmental NGOs at the CTE seems unlikely and is certainly ruled out of the key trade negotiation and policy review bodies. This stance has been strengthened within the General Council since the Bush administration reversed the Clinton-led initiative to encourage more NGO involvement in the work of the organization.

While dispute resolution within the WTO remains a purely inter-state mechanism, in practice private groups alleging economic injury arising from trade restrictions frequently lobby their national trade representatives to initiate litigation. Not surprisingly, member states – particularly powerful ones – have not hesitated to defend the interests of domestic industrial and commercial constituencies, even if wider geopolitical calculations impinge on the timing and nature of legal proceedings (Keohane et al, 2000: pp486–7). State-controlled access to WTO dispute resolution acts as a significant constraint on the inclusion of issues not easily translatable into national economic interests. Yet transnational NGOs have found encouragement in the occasional recourse of dispute settlement panels to *amicus curiae* (friend of the court) briefs as a legitimate input into their deliberations. Provision for panels to seek information from any relevant source, and to consult appropriate experts, is enabled by the dispute settlement understanding annexed to the Marrakesh agreement (Article 13.2). However, it was the 1998 *Shrimp–Turtle* ruling of the Appellate Body that interpreted this provision to include the right of dispute settlement bodies to request briefs from NGOs, and also to accept unsolicited submissions from them. As this case involved the submission of three environmental NGOs, and entailed extra-territorial trade and environment effects, it holds particular relevance for the ability of NGOs to represent collective ecological values. Since this and other supportive rulings on NGO briefs, numerous developing country members at the WTO have expressed criticism of the practice, fearing an additional source of legal leverage against them by well-resourced environment and development NGOs (Charnovitz, 2002: pp344–52). This disquiet was made vocal during the Doha dispute settlement review and, until these fears can be allayed, there will not be enough political support among WTO member states to realize NGOs' aspirations to formal rights to submit such briefs.

Impartial consideration of transnational environmental claims

To recall from Chapter 1, impartiality as an accountability norm denotes that decisions in the 'public interest' are those that can be accepted by all affected parties as reasonable according to even-handed procedures and the avoidance of unjust distributive outcomes. In international law it is linked to the widening embrace by state actors of fairness standards in global governance. Despite the pervasive presence of power-based motives in international negotiations, there is evidence that such fairness dialogue has some purchase in both multilateral trade and environment rule-making. The core principles of the GATT/WTO regime – sovereign equality, consensus decision-making, non-discrimination, special and differential treatment for developing countries – inform WTO claims to even-handed trade governance (Albin, 2001: pp100–40). And international environmental agreements covering ozone depletion, climate change, transboundary air pollution, the high seas and Antarctica share these governing principles (Franck, 1995: pp380–412; Albin, 2001: pp54–99). This *fairness overlap* between the trade and environmental governance domains questions the stance of WTO exceptionalism in addressing trade-related ecological matters. In order to further the impartial consideration of transnational environmental interests in WTO policy and judicial forums, it suggests the need to formalize opportunities for environmental NGOs to make regular representations to the relevant bodies – a reform strongly supported by the respondents to our survey.

It is widely acknowledged that, in spite of recent moves to increase transparency in the WTO, trade rule-making is still secretive – particularly in relation to comprehensive 'single undertaking' negotiations, such as the Doha Round, where proposals are presented in an 'all-or-nothing' framework package for member states. The single undertaking approach, first employed by the US and European Communities in the early 1990s to pressure developing countries to accept new trade obligations under the Uruguay Round, has been argued to favour the exercise of power-based bargaining by leading industrialized countries under the cloak of consensus decision-making (Steinberg, 2002: pp359–65; Jawara and Kwa, 2003). It has been argued that allowing transnational NGOs access as observers to trade negotiating rooms could advance impartiality by enabling them to monitor the behaviour of national representatives (Howse, 2002: p107). However, given that business NGOs and lobbyists already enjoy internal access to national trade delegations, some mechanism would need to be in place to ensure representative participation of environmental NGOs without overloading the negotiating sessions with numerous observers. Given the opposition of developing countries to greater involvement by environmental NGOs in WTO decision-making, this is not politically feasible at present, and exposes the need within the WTO to examine more broadly the extent to which its organization of trade negotiations enables the non-national identification of trade-related effects (economic, social and environmental).

A fairer consideration of environmental concerns in trade rule-making is more likely to be advanced by systemic revisions in rule-making and interpretation, notably the explicit recognition of the authority of key international environmental agreements in WTO law. One promising suggestion is the introduction of an MEA exception clause in a renegotiated GATT, stating explicitly which obligations with potential WTO inconsistency are exempted from GATT/WTO rules, and providing a decision-making rule for adding others (Neumayer, 2001: pp177–80). Interestingly, the evolution of dispute settlement case law may also support reinforcement of the influence of international environmental obligations on the basis of authoritative interpretations of Article XX exceptions. Here the *Shrimp–Turtle* Appellate Body decisions are important, given their acceptance that unilateral trade controls to achieve conservation goals beyond national jurisdiction could sometimes be permitted in so far as they are directed against states wilfully undermining those goals through their process and production methods (Howse, 2002: pp11–14). An acknowledgment of extra-territorial environmental impacts is even more reason to render the WTO dispute settlement process more transparent, and accept our survey finding in Table 4.2 above that transnational NGOs should have a right to submit briefs to dispute settlement hearings. The impartiality gains to be made here rest on the fact that WTO panel and Appellate Body decisions have significant legal independence, enabling them in principle to reach fair judgments in support of regime integrity. Embedding ecological provisions or exceptions in WTO law is thus essential to promoting structural redress for environmentally injurious trade rule-making that would otherwise be deemed acceptable.

Conclusion: Cancún and beyond

There are grounds for predicting the emergence of less asymmetric bargaining within the WTO, which would favour openness to trade-related concerns from a wider range of member states. For example, Steinberg (2002: pp368–9) forecasts an erosion of the established dominance of EU and US interests in WTO rule-making, facilitated by the expanding membership of the organization and more sustained cooperation among developing countries. This claim finds support in the failure of the September 2003 Ministerial Conference in Cancún, where the so-called Group of 23 (led by Brazil, China, India and South Africa) blocked agreement on further trade liberalization in the absence of significant European and US moves to address the debilitating impacts on developing countries of their agricultural subsidies, textile import quotas and tariff levels. With the increasing negotiating competence and combined clout of developing states, the 'double standards' of the industrialized countries are becoming less defensible in practice. Ironically, the shift to fairer trade bargaining threatens the Doha trade and environment negotiations at the WTO, as their very existence rests on EU agenda-setting power and a Northern perception of trade-related ecological issues. Without meaningful input by developing countries into the CTE, which would undoubtedly fuse ecological protection with development-oriented priorities, the notion of environmental accountability for WTO decision-making is politically vulnerable.

Environmental NGOs routinely claim to represent those transnational (and future) publics negatively affected by international trade rules. The support of our survey respondents for the new informational openings at the WTO is self-evident, as is their commitment to more interactive, institutionalized NGO access. These groups themselves nevertheless face open interrogation of their global civil society legitimacy – their constituencies, decision-making and financing, as well as the universality of their arguments. For some observers, the claims of transnational environmental NGOs often embody unquestioned assumptions, constructing 'global' environmental problems – suffused with unexamined European or North American values – which may run against the economic development interests of poorer countries (see Chapter 2). Furthermore, none of the five transnational environment and development NGOs participating in the survey on WTO briefings currently holds NGO accreditation with the United Nations Economic and Social Council (although one is officially recognized by the United Nations Conference on Trade and Development). To be sure, all support independent accreditation as the price for more formal interactions with the WTO in Geneva, and the WTO Secretariat is also willing to entrust this accreditation to an impartial international body (Werner, 2002). This may go some way to reassuring Southern member states that there will be objective scrutiny of transnational NGOs engaging with the organization, especially if it is accompanied by capacity-building for Southern NGO involvement in Geneva meetings.

However, the criteria for assessing on what basis, and to whom, Northern-based NGOs speak is only now receiving sustained attention. As discussed in Chapter 2, it is increasingly recognized that, in so far as these NGOs claim to represent the needs of ecologically threatened or damaged communities outside their membership constituencies, their advocacy invites external scrutiny according to norms of accountability applied to state and private actors – for example, stakeholder consultation, external social and environmental impacts, relations with partners and access to information. Interestingly, models of external NGO accountability so far have been developed most fully in Southern states: these mechanisms include self-regulation (South Africa), certification (the Philippines) and registration (India) (Clark, 2003: pp169–85; SustainAbility, 2003). This trend suggests that the receptiveness of Southern member states to arguments for environmental NGO involvement in (Geneva-based) WTO deliberations may be encouraged by a statement of governance principles in which parity of representation for Southern trade-related civil society organizations is accompanied by independent NGO accreditation criteria (as indeed envisaged by the WTO Secretariat).

Such a shift in political support of Southern member states for NGO access at the WTO would also be assisted by Northern-based environmental NGOs demonstrating that they can help deliver tangible benefits to these states. The obvious precedent here has been set by Northern development NGOs, in active partnership with Southern state and civil society actors, who have addressed the incidence or potential for specific injuries to local populations arising from WTO decisions – for example, the campaign of Médicins sans Frontières and Oxfam International (against the lobbying of US drug companies) to ensure that poor countries are able to import affordable generic medicines. In this case, the NGOs aligned themselves with Southern (mostly African) members of the WTO in a largely successful effort to waive state licensing obligations under the Trade Related Aspects of Intellectual Property Rights Agreement when the protection of public health might otherwise be jeopardized. Presented by Supachai Panitchpakdi as an example of the flexibility of WTO intellectual property rules, it represented more accurately the application of concerted global pressure to prevent the organization backsliding on a commitment made to developing countries at Doha.

There are also signs that Northern environmental NGOs concerned with international trade are finding common ground with Southern civil society groups and states. In part this is due to growing cooperation between environment and development NGOs within advanced industrialized states. For example, drawing on Dutch and Danish experience with environment/ development NGO participation on national trade delegations, the UK NGO Trade Network has, since 1999, coordinated trade-related lobbying and been allowed to send nominated representatives to WTO ministerial conferences as part of the UK official trade delegation. Such participation is governed by formal protocols of confidentiality and does not include access to trade-negotiating sessions. While its political significance is minor compared with the considerable lobbying activity publicly undertaken by NGOs at ministerial conferences, it has enabled an integrated representation of the environment and development concerns of UK-based NGOs, facilitating more meaningful dialogue with Southern state representatives. It complements wider Northern NGO initiatives to identify the ecological needs of the latter, as with the ambitious round of consultations with developing countries being undertaken by the Geneva-based International Centre for Trade and Sustainable Development, in order to promote united communication of a 'Southern agenda on trade and environment' (Cameron, 2003).

It is notable that according to environmental NGOs in attendance at Cancún, from both the global North and South, ecological issues as such were not a major issue at the conference. EU attempts to revive the CTE Doha mandate were frustrated. But the lobbying efforts of Northern environment and development groups, in alliance with Southern NGO partners, assisted the Group of 23 in blocking the negotiations. Prior to the conference, in February 2003, environment and development NGOs from over 30 countries held an 'international civil society hearing' in Geneva to voice opposition to the proposed WTO Agreement on Agriculture, charging the US and EU with supporting inequitable farming systems that endanger food security and rural livelihoods in developing countries (Friends of the Earth Europe, 2003). In a trade rule-making regime where state preferences are paramount, the mobilization of sovereignty-based claims is an effective, if paradoxical, strategy for NGOs claiming to represent interests transcending national borders. It is also a strategy in evidence in the efforts of Greenpeace and Friends of the Earth, in alliance with Oxfam and other development NGOs, to help developing countries (notably the African Group) prevent WTO-sanctioned private intellectual property rights encroaching on their perceived genetic resource entitlements (e.g. Oxfam, 2002: pp219–24).

These points of political convergence between Southern states and transnational environmental groups are at least expedient for both sets of parties in the 'all-or-nothing' Doha trade negotiations, yet they fall short of a comprehensive trade agenda compatible both with ecological and development-oriented needs. And they are isolated further by the lack of progress of the formal trade and environment negotiations taking place within the CTE – including the crucial issue of the relationship between WTO rules and trade obligations set out in international environmental agreements. Excluded from CTE deliberations, transnational environmental NGOs still face significant resistance from Southern member states to their requests for greater access to WTO decision-making in Geneva. This means that even the incremental reform proposals supported by these NGOs (notably, the creation of a WTO–civil society liaison group, observer status for NGOs in WTO deliberations, granting a formal right for NGOs to submit briefs to dispute settlement hearings, a WTO–civil society liaison group and connecting the WTO to UN NGO liaison norms) are by no means probable. In so far as the WTO is becoming more receptive to Southern state concerns, a more effective representation of Northern NGO-articulated environmental claims in Geneva will therefore rest on the force of their appeal beyond European publics and their congruence with human development goals.

Chapter 5

Transnational Liability for Environmental Damage

The ability of affected publics to hold to account those responsible for cross-border environmental harm rests not only, as set out in previous chapters, on having their interests incorporated into international rule-making such that ecological risks are prevented or minimized; it also turns on effective rules of liability and compensation – that is to say, the legal capacity of injured parties to seek redress in cases where environmental damage has actually occurred. Responsibility for damage, in other words, refers to the fact that actors are both answerable and *liable* for their actions. Yet while the last thirty years has seen the negotiation and implementation of numerous international environmental agreements, most of these treaties lack detailed provisions stipulating the responsibility of state and non-state actors for environmental damage. In terms of existing international law, the central deficiency relates to the means of financial accountability for environmental harm across national boundaries and to the global commons. Principle 13 of the 1992 Rio Declaration on Environment and Development registered this deficiency, calling on states to cooperate in developing liability and compensation rules for environmental damage caused by activities both within and beyond their areas of territorial jurisdiction or control (United Nations, 1993: p10).

Even the nature of environmental liability remains unsettled in international governance: it is possible, broadly, to distinguish between state-centred and civil liability frameworks. *State-centred* liability denotes state responsibility for breaching some international obligation (whether based on customary or treaty law) or for the adverse environmental consequences of otherwise legal activities. *Civil* liability may include states as responsible parties but extends this accountability also to relevant non-state actors: liability rules are private law obligations imposed by national laws implementing the procedural and substantive obligations of an international treaty. As Sands (1995: p629) notes, the boundary between the two systems is becoming blurred as states often pick up a residual responsibility for providing funds under civil liability schemes when full compensation of environmental losses is not available from private operators. Nevertheless, the general trend in international rule development for environmental liability has been to de-emphasize state responsibility by channelling liability directly onto those culpable for the damage (Birnie and Boyle, 2002: pp186–7).

The development of state liability provisions in public international law has thus progressed haltingly for transnational ecological harm. Most multilateral environmental treaties stipulate that signatory parties should act in accordance with the principle of state responsibility for environmental damage, but specific liability and compensation provisions are rarely prescribed. The 1972 Convention on International Liability for Damage Caused by Space Objects remains one of the few treaties with explicit state liability obligations – rules which supported a successful claim by Canada against the USSR for the clean-up of radioactive debris following the break-up of a Soviet satellite over Canadian territory in 1979 (Sands, 1995: pp646–8). Outside treaty law, the most significant recent precedent featuring state liability for environmental damage was United Nations Security Council Resolution 687 (1991) stating Iraq's liability for environmental damage resulting from its invasion and occupation of Kuwait. There are also occasional instances of international awards of environmental compensation for transboundary pollution damage, which typically cite the 1938 precedent of an international tribunal's finding for the United States against Canada for material damage from pollution – the *Trail Smelter* decision. Overall, though, state practice reveals a widespread reluctance routinely to pursue environmental liability through inter-state claims: indeed, the International Law Commission – the United Nations body charged since 1978 with the codification of general legal principles of international liability – has reflected state preferences for increasing the importance of private liability attached to operators of risk-bearing activities as the main mechanism for progressing environmental liability (International Law Commission, 2002: pp225–6).

This international understanding is evident above all in the development of civil liability treaties, which have emerged to facilitate risk management for economic activities considered hazardous, notably (potential) damage arising from the peaceful use of nuclear energy, oil pollution, the transportation of dangerous goods and the transboundary movement of hazardous wastes (Sands, 1995: pp652–78). The civil liability regime for ship-source oil pollution was the first of these regimes to broaden compensation obligations beyond personal injury and property damage provisions to *environmental impairment*, and has served as an influential model for liability rule development for the carriage of dangerous goods, the maritime carriage of hazardous and noxious substances, and revisions to civil liability provisions for nuclear damage (Sandvik and Suikkari, 1997: pp64–5). Moreover, the method of compensation entitlement under this regime – strict liability (without the need to prove negligence) – has become the norm for pollution damage liability rules applicable to hazardous activities. And it has also been rationalized as an effective and equitable means of incorporating the 'polluter pays' principle into the field of environmental liability (Gauci, 1997: pp18–20; 1999: p30). For these reasons, in this chapter the marine oil pollution civil liability regime is examined in detail as a formative vehicle for transnational environmental accountability: to what extent has it promoted legal norms serving to protect third parties suffering transboundary injury?

To recall a central normative claim of this book, democratic accountability requires the effective and equitable treatment of the claims of affected publics. For oil pollution liability, this relates above all to claims for financial compensation arising from physical damage. My focus here is on the international harmonization of legal rules of entitlement for environmental compensation under multilateral treaties on civil liability and compensation for oil pollution damage. These treaties legally empower victims of oil-spill damage to make financial claims against culpable tanker owners and, in certain circumstances, against the global oil cargo industry. Transnational environmental accountability under this regime means the facilitation of third-party redress for ecological damage received in national waters (wherever the spillage). Even if the spillage itself has not been physically transmitted across maritime borders, there may still be a transnational relationship of responsibility in terms of a foreign operator answerable and financially liable to domestic victims for local damage. As we shall see, there is no secure international consensus on the nature and geographical scope of this environmental responsibility.

Nevertheless, the international oil pollution liability regime introduced a significant innovation in transnational environmental compensation – the harmonization of private law remedies for environmental damage; and this type of accountability mechanism is achieving a growing governance role in managing hazardous transboundary risks. The experience with the oil pollution liability treaties points to important issues concerning the adequacy of civil law suits as an instrument of environmental accountability; for example, whether their restriction to particular types of ecological compensation and to proximate affected publics is a necessary feature of the architecture of these regimes, or whether this is contingent on an alterable balance of geopolitical interests. Uptake by states of standardized civil liability rules in the regulation of hazardous transboundary practices and processes indicates strong international support for adapting existing legal principles to cover serious environmental harm. At the same time, however, the reliance on private international law to achieve regulatory goals prompts concerns about the contribution of private authority (operators, certification societies, insurance companies) to delivering this new form of environmental accountability. Is it possible in such a regulatory system to ensure the full representation and protection of affected environmental interests? A first step in broaching this question, prior to looking at the oil pollution liability case study, is to note the general principles of transboundary liability identified by the International Law Commission.

Principles of international liability

It is by no means straightforward to locate general principles of cross-border liability for environmental harm production. In 2002, after a five-year hiatus, the International Law Commission (ILC) resumed its protracted consideration of 'international liability in case of loss from transboundary harm arising out of hazardous activities' (International Law Commission, 2002: pp220–7). Given competing state perspectives, the Commission has struggled to facilitate international consensus on a unified framework for liability rule-making applied to transboundary hazards. Indeed, some commentators have charged the ILC with a confused understanding of international liability, notably in its treatment of the topic as distinct from questions of state responsibility (Taylor, 1998: pp144–53; Boyle, 1999). The Commission maintains that international liability pertains to the occurrence of significant harm or damage arising from acts which international law does not prohibit, while state responsibility is concerned with internationally wrongful acts. In other words, liability rule-making is directed at the regulation, without recourse to prohibition, of activities perceived to entail substantial danger of a transboundary nature (Rao, 1998a: pp16–17). Since 1982 the ILC has limited the scope of its liability work to *physical effects giving rise to harm*, heightening its relevance to addressing environmental damage.

Of course, what constitutes 'significant' (potential or actual) harm is crucial to constituting environmental liability for transnational practices. Here the ILC has looked to the formulations of professional legal associations and existing treaty practice. To take the first source, the work of the International Law Association has directly influenced the ILC recommendations on levels of transboundary harm deemed necessary to trigger liability: in order to allow for the inevitability of certain levels of harm in the conduct of many industrial activities, the ILC has followed the lead of the International Law Association in identifying thresholds of significant harm as those triggering 'real detrimental effects on such aspects as human health, industry, property, environment or agriculture in other States' (Rao, 1998a: p30). The risk of causing significant transboundary harm is seen to extend from low probabilities of causing disastrous harm (e.g. nuclear power generation) to high probabilities of causing significant harm (e.g. waste incineration emissions). Relevant thresholds of harm are deemed measurable by scientific criteria, but subject to context-bound judgments on, for example, prevailing technical standards in source and recipient areas, estimated pollutant trajectories and national legal definitions of loss or injury. Faced with this variability in determining harm thresholds, in 1995 the ILC convened a working group to clarify matters by identifying inherently dangerous substances and processes. The working group deferred to the indicative lists of risk-bearing activities annexed to existing treaties on transboundary harm, such as the 1991 (Espoo) Convention on Environmental

Impact Assessment in a Transboundary Context and the 1993 (Lugano) Convention on Civil Liability for Damage Resulting from Activities Dangerous to the Environment (Rao, 2003: pp13–14). Endorsing this approach, the ILC has opted not to specify thresholds of harm, suggesting that this is best left to international agreements on particular hazards and risks.

For the ILC, the liability arising from significant transboundary harm caused by lawful activities is essentially *no-fault liability*. The key principle here is that liability is triggered by unavoidable harm, whether this harm was unforeseeable for the source state or, if foreseeable, was not amenable to reasonable measures of risk prevention or minimization by that state (Boyle, 1999: pp76–9; Birnie and Boyle, 2002: pp188–90). Acceptance by states of obligations for no-fault liability is represented by the Commission as part of their general obligation to prevent transboundary damage. As discussed in Chapter 3, this obligation is one of due diligence – due care and regulatory attention in environmental harm prevention – connected to prevailing technical standards of environmental management. It is demonstrated by such requirements as prior authorization by states of risk-bearing activities entering their territory, international environmental impact assessment, dispute settlement and principles of cooperation, information exchange, notification and consultation. And the more hazardous an activity is perceived to be, the higher the standards of care and regulatory vigour reasonably expected of states. The principle of no-fault liability deems that even if a source state of transboundary harm has demonstrated due diligence, that liability still stands, although due diligence may be offered by states or private parties under their jurisdiction as a reason for limiting their liability.

In a situation where liability arises under no-fault cover, the Commission argues that international law supports the fundamental principle that individuals who have suffered harm or injury due to the activities of others should be granted relief. But that compensation or relief may not always be full; rather 'the victim of harm should not be left to bear the entire loss' (International Law Commission, 1996: pp243, 320–2). The judgment is that an *equitable balance of interests* must guide the communication between states to determine the nature and extent of compensation for significant transboundary harm. The balance is designed to respect the sovereign right of the state of origin to permit lawful activities which may nevertheless cause unavoidable harm to others beyond its borders, yet not to cause uncompensated losses on these parties. In negotiations between states, relevant factors to achieving an equitable balance of interests include the risk of significant transboundary harm, the importance of the activity and its economic viability in relation to costs of prevention, the degree to which states likely to be affected are prepared to contribute to preventive costs, and prevailing standards of protection (International Law Commission, 1996: pp242, 313–16). While support is still lacking for the international legal codification of the principle of equitable compensation for significant transboundary harm, it is acknowledged by commentators that it would be a valuable advance in cross-border environmental accountability (Boyle, 1999: p78; Birnie and Boyle, 2002: p190).

In addition to bilateral or multilateral negotiations between states, the ILC has endorsed transnational procedures for determining the nature and extent of compensation. The principle of *non-discrimination* stipulates that states originating the threat or incidence of significant transboundary harm are obliged to provide treatment for non-national affected parties on a par with nationals in respect to judicial and administrative remedies (International Law Commission, 1996: pp243, 269–75). Precedents for this principle are identified in various international agreements (e.g. Article 3 of the 1974 Nordic Convention on the Protection of the Environment) as well as recommendations of the Organization for Economic Cooperation and Development and the Economic Commission for Europe. As discussed in Chapter 3, the principle has gained international currency in recent years, enabling growing legal representation of the interests of affected publics. Its transnational character is the opening up of local remedies to foreign actors, whether these are non-state parties or even affected states: in the latter case, the state takes up a private law position by bringing a civil suit, often on the grounds of its sovereign authority to represent collective ecological interests (e.g. the environmental trustee role, noted below, asserted under the oil pollution liability regime). To be sure, equal access by no means guarantees satisfactory substantive and procedural entitlements (Birnie and Boyle, 2002: pp274–5), but it has certainly secured widespread recognition as a necessary component of global rule-making for environmental liability.

Non-discrimination intensifies the (environmental) liability of the operators of activities bearing transboundary risks by exposing them to the potential claims of actors beyond the national borders of the source state. It has also been noted that such equal treatment for all claimants is a particular priority for ecological effects given the tendency of environmental damage towards mass group harm: the *common spatial position of the affected parties* is in these circumstances more relevant than their nationality or place of residence (Von Bar, 1997: p364). There is a neat alignment here between ILC recommendations and the international harmonization on national liability laws for environmental harm. Yet the Commission has confined the application of the non-discrimination principle to affected parties within national jurisdictions. There has been no effort to codify the nascent international liability rules being developed for those areas – the global commons – falling outside the exclusive spaces of state sovereignty (Arsanjani and Reisman, 1998). This reticence reflects clear differences in opinion between states over the legitimacy of the topic, although the ILC has left open the possibility of addressing damage to the global commons once it has finalized its current work on international liability (International Law Commission, 2003: pp117, 128). Restricting liability for transboundary environmental damage to national territorial spaces defers to existing treaty and customary law but raises critical questions regarding the adequacy of this new tool of responsibility for addressing extra-territorial ecological harm. An examination of the international oil pollution liability regime – the seminal source of rule development for cross-border environmental compensation – allows a substantive examination of these issues.

The marine oil pollution liability regime

Prevention of ship-source oil pollution has been an international regulatory goal since 1954, giving rise to various conventions, resolutions and codes developed under the auspices of the United Nations International Maritime Organization (IMO). The 1973/78 International Convention for the Prevention of Pollution from Ships (the MARPOL Convention) stands as the core treaty regulating harmful emissions from ships: Annex I, concerned with oil pollution, contains detailed technical provisions designed to eliminate intentional discharges. MARPOL is credited as instrumental in significantly reducing discharges from marine transportation, achieved by focusing international regulatory control on mandatory equipment standards for oil tankers – notably segregated ballast tanks and crude-oil washing. Such regulatory progress has taken decades, though, punctuated by intensive IMO rule development in reaction to occasional catastrophic oil spills (Mitchell et al, 1999).

It was the political fallout following the 1967 *Torrey Canyon* oil tanker disaster off the southwest coast of Britain that provoked the IMO to review state systems of civil liability for oil pollution damage. National claims processes were overwhelmingly structured by the traditional law of tort, leaving potential claimants with the onerous task of proving shipowner negligence. And the restriction of damage claims to personal injury and property damage typically excluded environmental mitigation and reinstatement costs. For oil spills caused by non-national vessels, even personal and property damage claims could be frustrated by the unwillingness of domestic courts to assume enforceable jurisdiction or the shipowner registering only limited assets (Churchill and Lowe, 1999: pp358–9). In a time prior to the codification of coastal state environmental jurisdiction in the 1982 United Nations Law of the Sea (LOS) Convention, the international negotiations to draft an oil pollution liability convention had to defer strongly to the long-established navigation rights of flag state vessels. Even western European states such as the United Kingdom (UK) and France, pushed by public pressure to support new international obligations on liability for oil pollution damage, had to balance this against their domestic shipping interests and their economic reliance on maritime trade.

Not surprisingly, then, the civil liability convention adopted at a diplomatic conference in Brussels in 1969 (entry into force June 1975) proved to be a political compromise. The International Convention on Civil Liability for Oil Pollution Damage (CLC) 1969 places liability for oil pollution damage squarely on the registered owner of the ship from which the oil escapes or is discharged: this liability is strict in the sense that the claimant only has to demonstrate that (s)he has suffered damage as a result of the spill, removing the need to prove that the shipowner was at fault. The intent here was to facilitate prompt, equitable compensation payments to victims for damage suffered in the territory, including the territorial sea, of any contracting state. To aid this, ships carrying more than 2000 tons of persistent oil as cargo are required to carry appropriate liability insurance. For owners of oil-carrying vessels the new burden of strict liability was mitigated by the limitation of their liability under CLC 1969 (up to 133 Special Drawing Rights for each ton of a ship's gross tonnage, capped by a maximum of 14 million Special Drawing Rights for each incident): claimants are only able to breach that limit – and sue for more – if the incident is a result of the 'actual fault or privity' of the owner. Furthermore, the shipowner avoids any liability if the damage is: (i) attributable to acts of war or exceptional natural phenomena, or is wholly caused either (ii) by an act of omission of a third party done with the intent to cause damage or (iii) the negligence or other wrongful act of an authority in its function of maintaining navigational aids.

Despite the move to strict liability at the Brussels Conference, states animated by marine protection interests had expressed reservations that CLC 1969 might not be adequate to meeting the damage claims arising from large-scale oil pollution incidents: there was also an assertion that oil cargo interests should bear some of the economic consequences of oil pollution damage. As part of the Brussels compromise, the IMO was entrusted therefore with the creation of a new international fund to supplement the liability coverage of CLC 1969. The 1971 International Convention on the Establishment of an International Fund for Compensation for Oil Pollution Damage (Fund Convention) (entry into force October 1978), sharing a strict liability and compensation ceiling framework (limited to 60 million Special Drawing Rights, depending on shipowner liability payments), established a statutory system compelling oil cargo interests in contracting states to pay a levy, calculated on the basis of their national share of international oil receipts, towards the International Oil Pollution Compensation (IOPC) Fund 1971. In operation until May 2002, the IOPC Fund 1971 provided compensation for oil pollution damage not fully available under CLC 1969 because of the responsible shipowner being exempt from liability or being financially incapable of meeting compensation obligations or, alternatively, that the damage exceeded the limits of shipowner liability. Up to 31 December 2001, the 1971 Fund had approved the settlement of pollution damage claims arising out of 96 incidents, amounting to over £280 million in total compensation payments (International Oil Pollution Compensation Funds, 2002: pp37–9).

That tanker owners and oil companies were in favour of uniform, limited liability rules for oil pollution damage is evident in their global cooperation in establishing two private schemes – the Tanker Owners Voluntary Agreement Concerning Liability for Oil Pollution (1969–97) and the Contract Regarding a Supplement to Tanker Liability for Oil Pollution (1971–97) – which complemented the oil pollution liability treaties (Sands, 1995: pp665–7; Gauci, 1997: pp25–7). Tensions emerged in the 1980s, though, with the perception of oil cargo interests that shipowners' limited liability was lagging behind rising damage mitigation costs and inflation, pushing the compensation burden for major spillages onto the oil importers. In contrast, CLC 1969 contracting states with sizeable tanker interests (e.g. Greece, Korea, Liberia) were expressing alarm at incidences of national courts breaking shipowner rights to limit liability under the convention, undermining in their view both the economic viability of their shipping industries and the much-vaunted equity of application of CLC 1969. An IMO diplomatic conference in London in 1984 reviewed the liability and compensation provisions of both CLC 1969 and the Fund Convention 1971, adopting significant increases in both shipowner liability and the IOPC Fund 1971 compensation ceiling, although the former was linked to a narrowing of the conditions under which the shipowner could lose the right to limit liability – a significant concession to shipping interests. Concerns had also been raised by contracting states at the London Conference about a growing number of substantial claims for environmental damage compensation allowed by national courts under the international liability regime (International Maritime Organization, 1993b: pp475–83). Here delegates identified a convergence of flag state (shipping) and coastal state (environmental protection) interests in redefining the parameters of liability for oil pollution damage to standardize cover of transnational environmental harm. The agreed amendments featured the explicit inclusion of environmental impairment as constitutive of pollution damage under CLC and the extension of the geographical scope of both liability conventions beyond the territorial seas of contracting states to cover their exclusive economic zones (EEZs) (or equivalent) and the costs of measures wherever taken to prevent damage to their national maritime areas.

These and other amendments were formulated within legal protocols but their entry into force (based on minimum thresholds of national tanker tonnage and oil receipts) failed to take place. As the leading oil importer in the world, United States ratification was desirable for global acceptance of the 1984 CLC and Oil Pollution Fund Protocols, but the extensive damage caused by the grounding of the *Exxon Valdez* in Prince William Sound, Alaska, in 1989 prompted the unilateral introduction of an American oil pollution liability regime. The strength of environmentalist sentiment in the aftermath of the *Exxon Valdez* incident is evident in the comprehensive liability provisions of the Oil Pollution Act (OPA) 1990, which imposes stronger duties of care on shipowners than CLC 1969 – and includes a right of action against operators. In contrast to moves to strengthen limited liability defences under the 1984 CLC Protocol, OPA 1990 shifts the burden of accountability towards the harm producer – for example, incident-related failures in reporting, cooperation and compliance can all leave a responsible party facing unlimited liability for damage. Furthermore, individual US states had opposed national ratification of the 1984 protocols because this would have pre-empted their rights to establish their own oil pollution liability rules; and many have indeed imposed additional liability for oil pollution damage beyond that established by OPA 1990 (Little and Hamilton, 1997: pp394–7). As discussed below, the critics of the international oil pollution regime have claimed that its ecological remediation provisions are weaker than OPA 1990, rendering it less effective in compensating affected environmental interests. The 1984 amendments were finally incorporated into the international liability system when another IMO diplomatic conference in 1992 reduced their conditions of entry into force to facilitate early regime adoption without American ratification. As framed by these revised protocols, CLC 1992 and the Fund Convention 1992 (both in force May 1996) set the current terms of application of claims for compensation within contracting states: the focus will now fall on their provisions on environmental damage and geographical scope.

Environmental liability for oil pollution I: defining environmental losses

Article I(6) of CLC 1969 defines pollution damage as:

> *loss or damage caused outside the ship carrying oil by contamination resulting from the escape or discharge of oil from the ship, wherever such escape or discharge may occur, and includes the cost of preventive measures and further loss of damage caused by preventive measures.*

While it was clear from the beginning that this wording covered economic losses connected with personal injury or property damage, the absence of any reference to environmental damage left this aspect to the interpretation of national courts according to the domestic implementation of the convention (Wetterstein, 1994: p234). Concerns expressed by states at the 1984 IMO Conference on Marine Liability and Compensation that some liberal court rulings on damage were destabilizing the regime's uniformity of application, led to the formulation of a new clause on environmental damage. As incorporated into Article I(6) of CLC 1992, pollution damage is defined as:

(a)   *loss or damage caused outside the ship by contamination resulting from the escape or discharge of oil from the ship, wherever such escape or discharge may occur,* provided that compensation for impairment of the environment other than losses of profit from such impairment shall be limited to costs of reasonable measures of reinstatement actually undertaken or to be undertaken *(emphasis added)*.

(b)   *the costs of preventive measures and further loss or damage caused by preventive measures.*

The statement on environmental impairment was shaped by experience with the IOPC Fund 1971 and was therefore designed to limit environmental claims against both shipowners under CLC 1992 and oil receivers under the Oil Fund Convention 1992. National courts in states that had ratified the 1992 protocols would not be able to find coherently for environmental damage claims beyond loss of profit and reasonable measures of reinstatement; this would rule out, it was planned, claims for environmental damage *per se* (Gauci, 1997: pp55–6).

According to the chair of the committee charged at the 1984 IMO conference with formulating the substantive changes to CLC 1969, it proved too difficult to reconcile divergent state positions on Article I(6), so the environmental impairment amendment was more a clarification than an innovation. Conference records demonstrate this lack of agreement, from states with prominent shipping interests (e.g. Greece, Liberia) preoccupied with ruling out the possibility of excessive environmental damage claims, to those states (e.g. Australia, Netherlands, Poland) pushing for a broader definition of pollution damage to encompass liability claims for ecological impairment and restoration (International Maritime Organization, 1993b: pp347–57, 479–83). Shipping and oil industry observers to the work of the committee aligned themselves with the former position, while the two observing environmental groups – Friends of the Earth International (FOEI) and the International Union for the Conservation of Nature and Natural Resources (IUCN) – supported the latter stance. Significantly, a transnational network of maritime law associations, the International Maritime Committee – which had played an active part in formulating the original text of CLC 1969 – actively participated in refining the text of the amended definition of pollution damage. It is clear, though, that this gave a legal sheen to what was a political compromise mediating between divergent state interests.

Not surprisingly, states that domestically had to balance shipping, oil industry and environmental interests shaped the negotiated compromise on pollution damage incorporated into the 1984 CLC Protocol (International Maritime Organization, 1993c: p205). Heightened public concern about oil pollution informed UK moves to strengthen transnational environmental liability for pollution damage, but strong maritime trade interests moderated its ecological protection agenda. Supported by the Federal Republic of Germany, the UK delegation argued successfully for a broad understanding of economic loss and an explicit acknowledgment of reasonable cost recovery for environmental reinstatement measures (International Maritime Organization, 1993b: pp347–9, 479–80). Thus, 'losses of profit' under Article I(6) was agreed to encompass not only *consequential loss* claims (loss of earnings by owners/users of property contaminated by oil) but also claims for *pure economic loss* (loss of earnings suffered by parties whose property has not been damaged, e.g. coastal hoteliers, fishery concerns): this formalized for the CLC and Fund Convention an extension of liability norms beyond their traditional restriction to property damage (White, 2002). However, while representing a legal recognition of environmental compensation, the clause 'reasonable measure of [environmental] reinstatement' failed to prevent subsequent inter-state disputes as to the application of the oil pollution liability regime to ecological damage. Disagreements in practice can be identified over: (i) quantification of damage, (ii) the state as environmental trustee, and (iii) ecological restoration.

Quantification of damage

As a system of economic compensation for oil-spill damage, the recovery of environmental reinstatement costs under the CLC/Oil Fund Convention regime has turned on whether they are deemed acceptable according to the international rules. Resolution No. 3 of the IOPC Fund Assembly, adopted in 1980, as clarified by the 1984/1992 environmental amendment, has informed the efforts of the IOPC Fund Executive Committee to ensure consistent implementation of the environmental damage provisions of the oil pollution liability treaties. This resolution had been prompted by Soviet claims for ecological compensation arising from the grounding of a tanker, the *Antonio Gramsci*, off Ventspils (Baltic Sea) in 1979, whereby the USSR government attempted to recover estimated costs for environmental damage beyond demonstrated economic loss. Although the USSR was at that time not party to the 1971 Oil Fund Convention, its claims against the shipowner under CLC 1969 had consequences for the Fund by consuming a major part of the shipowner's limitation amount. In the light of this claim, the 1971 Fund Assembly adopted Resolution No. 3 stating that 'the assessment of compensation to be paid by the International Oil Pollution Compensation Fund is not to be made on the basis of an abstract quantification of damage in accordance with theoretical models' (International Oil Pollution Compensation Fund, 1980).

Claims for environmental compensation not related to quantifiable economic loss have consistently been opposed by the IOPC Funds on the basis of Resolution No. 3. Such claims are rare although by no means insignificant in amount; for example, environmental damage claims of 5,000 million lire (*Patmos* spillage – 1985) and 100,000 million lire (*Haven* spillage – 1991) from the Italian government, and $3.2 million from Indonesia (*Evoikos* spillage – 1997). The 1971 IOPC Fund declared all these inadmissible because of the abstract manner of their calculations; however, the Italian government still pursued its environmental claims through its national courts. Although the Italian Court of Appeal accepted a claim, which included *inter alia* non-use environmental values assessed by expert testimony, the Fund appealed against the judgment and the claim was settled out of court. In the Settlement Agreement, the Fund made it clear that it neither accepted nor made payments for such environmental claims (International Oil Pollution Compensation Fund, 1994; Bianchi, 1997: pp113–28). It is worth noting that Italy's adoption of CLC 1992 and the Fund Convention 1992 (in force in Italy by September 2000) had to await resolution of the *Patmos* and *Haven* claims: at the 1992 IMO conference Italy had expressed its reservation that only accepting environmental damage claims quantifiable in terms of concrete economic loss prevented the legitimate recognition of damage 'in terms of fair remuneration according to prior understandings between the parties' (International Maritime Organization, 1993d: p176). The position on environmental damage quantification within the CLC/Fund Convention regime is in contrast with OPA 1990, where abstract quantification of non-market environmental damage is allowed in accordance with prescribed assessment standards. Whatever the merits of the American model, the lack of clear damage assessment and compensation standards within the international regime has presented a significant obstacle to the uniform application of environmental compensation rules (Little and Hamilton, 1997; Sandvik and Suikkari, 1997: p68).

The state as environmental trustee

The *Patmos* case highlighted the possibility of a state's right to environmental compensation as *parens patriae* (guardian) of collective interests; that is, as representative of its affected public as a national community. In that case the Italian courts stated that CLC 1969 made no distinction between private property damages and public property damages: they found, moreover, that direct public ownership was not necessary to justify environmental compensation claims because the state as a trustee for national or local publics has a right of action beyond economic loss (Bianchi, 1997: p126; Gauci, 1997: p254). While the IOPC Fund has recognized that public bodies can be legitimate claimants under the oil pollution liability regime, it has not accepted trusteeship claims divorced from quantifiable elements of economic damage. In the *Haven* case the Fund Executive Committee observed a punitive element in the environmental damage claims neither admissible under the civil liability rules nor of any consequence to the shipowner (protected by limitation of liability) (International Oil Pollution Compensation Fund, 1994: pp5–7).

More recently, the right of a state as public trustee to claim environmental compensation has been championed by the French government – within an

IOPC Fund 1992 Working Group established in 2000 to review the international oil pollution liability conventions. Despite being one of the first states to ratify the 1992 protocols and incorporate their rules into domestic law, French ministers – facing a public outcry following the break-up in December 1999 of a Maltese-registered tanker, the *Erika*, which badly contaminated with heavy fuel oil an extensive section of the Brittany coast – severely criticized the 1992 Fund over its claims handling and fixed compensation ceilings (International Oil Pollution Compensation Fund, 2001: pp113–14). In its submission to the Working Group, the French delegation recommended incorporating into the IOPC Fund 1992 Claims Manual a concept of compensation for environmental damage as a violation of state rights over collective marine assets. The submission cited in support a provision of OPA 1990 – Section 1006(b)(2)(A) – stipulating that the federal or foreign governments, individual states and Indian tribes can pursue environmental liability claims for oil pollution damage as trustees (as well as owners and managers) on behalf of their respective affected publics. However, the French public trustee proposal failed to receive significant support within the Working Group, as it was judged to fall outside the scope of pollution damage defined in CLC 1992 (Third Intersessional Working Group, 2001c, 2001d: pp32–3). The Fund continues to maintain that such theoretical formulations of public or collective environmental damage would open up liability determination to arbitrary decisions in national courts, perhaps even hindering private victims in their own claims for compensation.

Ecological restoration

French moves to liberalize the environmental reinstatement rules of the international oil pollution regime conjoined the state trusteeship principle with a broader notion of compensation. They argued that international and national developments in the field of environmental liability demonstrated increasing acceptance of ecological rehabilitation norms. If this was only implicit in Article 235(3) of the LOS Convention requiring states to assure 'prompt and adequate compensation in respect of all damage caused by pollution of the marine environment' then, the French government main-tained, it was certainly clear in constitutional and legal obligations embraced by many countries (e.g. Brazil, France, Italy, Spain, United States). Once again, OPA 1990 served as the key comparator; in particular, the eligibility accorded to restoration costs for the loss of natural resources and services which, by allowing the acquisition of equivalent habitats away from the damage site, go beyond CLC 1992 provisions on environmental reinstatement. Supported above all by the Italian delegation, the French called for the oil pollution liability conventions to be amended to allow member states to permit claims for introducing 'identical' or 'equivalent' ecological attributes in an adjacent marine area should reinstatement at the damage site be physically or economically infeasible (Third Intersessional Working Group, 2001c: pp12–14; 2001d: pp31–4). This is also a position endorsed by the IUCN observer (de la Fayette, 2002). Encouraged by the French presidency of the European Union in the second half of 2000, the European Commission added to the political pressure on the international oil pollution liability system. In the wake of the *Erika* incident, the Commission published its own proposals for European maritime safety: one of its key recommendations, echoing French and Italian concerns, called for CLC 1992 to be amended to enable restorative compensation for damage to the environment in a manner consistent with wider Commission proposals on civil liability for environmental damage (Ringbom, 2001).

These proposals ran up against the fact that the oil pollution liability conventions were not designed to provide full compensation for environmental damage (Gauci, 1999). While the review of the environmental impairment provisions by the 1992 Fund Working Group identified scope for more innovative recovery measures, the French proposals prompted serious concerns about their compatibility with the established rules on economic loss and environmental reinstatement. Furthermore, telling practical criticisms against compensatory restoration came from the observer delegation with the greatest experience of coordinating damage assessments and environmental recovery following oil spills – the International Tanker Owners Pollution Federation Limited (ITOPF). An ITOPF submission to the Working Group had noted the ecological risks of introducing new species into an area or engineering new habitat areas – both of which could upset those natural recovery processes relied on after most oil spills to degrade post-cleanup residual oil (Third Intersessional Working Group, 2001a; White, 2002). In the absence of references to marine ecological research in the arguments of those pushing for compensatory restoration, the technical authority of the ITOPF proved influential in setting a scientific case against it.

Although the 1992 Fund Working Group did not accept the French and Italian proposals to allow environmental compensation beyond economic loss, the delegations of Australia, Canada, Sweden and the UK sponsored a more modest recommendation to liberalize the criteria for admissibility of reinstatement costs to include recovery efforts centred on the damaged area (short of substitute habitat enhancement or creation). It was anticipated that this broadening of environmental impairment norms would prove more receptive to new ecological rehabilitation techniques, while staying within the parameters of environmental damage set by the oil pollution liability conventions. After initial opposition from Japan and Korea (both major contributors to the 1992 Fund), the proposal was approved by the 1992 Fund governing Assembly in October 2002. Fearing speculative environmental claims, the Japanese and Koreans were won over with the stipulation that only reasonable measures of ecological reinstatement directly linked to the damaged area would be admissible for compensation. This decision represented a cautious but significant advance for the application of environmental liability norms to transnational oil pollution damage, although it failed to meet French and Italian demands for more generous ecological rehabilitation provisions.

Environmental liability for oil pollution II: broadening geographical scope

The spatial delimitation of oil pollution liability under the international conventions has always deferred to the sovereign rights of contracting states: both CLC 1969 (Article II) and the Fund Convention 1971 (Article 3) apply only to pollution damage caused or impacting on the territory, including the territorial sea, of member states. At the time of the original conventions, there was no international consensus on the breadth of the territorial sea, which militated against the uniformity of geographical application of the liability regime. Article 3 of the LOS Convention 1982 set the limit of the territorial sea of a state at twelve nautical miles, which is now widely accepted as the international norm (Churchill and Lowe, 1999: pp79–80), although both CLC 1992 and the Fund Convention 1992 do not refer to the twelve-mile limit in deference to the autonomy of state maritime claims (e.g. Liberia, which is a member of the oil pollution liability conventions but not the LOS Convention, claims a 200-mile territorial sea). Nevertheless, at the 1984 IMO London Conference on Maritime Liability and Compensation, various states successfully lobbied for an amendment to the oil pollution liability conventions to recognize the exclusive economic zone (EEZ) rights accorded to coastal states by the LOS Convention (Part V): these entitlements extend up to 200 nautical miles from the baseline from which the breadth of the territorial sea is measured (Article 57). The broadening of the geographical scope of the liability conventions was reinforced at the 1984 conference by international agreement clarifying that the liability conventions cover measures, wherever taken, to prevent oil pollution damage within a territorial sea or EEZ.

As eventually incorporated into CLC 1992 as Article II, and the Fund Convention 1992 as Article 3, the oil pollution liability conventions are geographically defined as applying exclusively:

> (a) *to pollution damage caused:*
> > (i) *in the territory, including the territorial sea, of a Contracting State, and*
> > (ii) *in the exclusive economic zone of a Contracting State, established in accordance with international law, or, if a Contracting State has not established such a zone, in an area beyond and adjacent to the territorial sea of that State determined by that State in accordance with international law*

> and extending not more than 200 nautical miles from the
> baselines from which the breadth of the territorial sea is
> measured;
>
> (b) to preventive measures, wherever taken, to prevent or minimize
> such damage.

In respect of geographical coverage, OPA 1990 is broadly in conformity with the international regime, applying to internal navigable rivers, bays and lakes, coastal waters and the 200-mile EEZ of the United States. This consolidates at least a global recognition that (environmental) liability rules for oil pollution extend coastal state jurisdiction beyond territorial waters.

The political pressure on the oil pollution liability regime to acknowledge the distinctive legal import of the EEZ must be placed in the context of its wider geopolitical significance as:

> a reflection of the aspiration of the developing countries for economic
> development and their desire to gain greater control over the economic
> resources off their coasts, particularly fish stocks, which in many areas were
> largely exploited by the distant-water fleets of developed States (Church-
> ill and Lowe, 1999: pp160–1).

With several Latin American and African countries pushing for 200-mile territorial seas in the 1970s, the EEZ represented the political compromise extracted from states in the global North who viewed the extension of coastal state sovereign powers as a threat to their maritime freedoms. EEZ entitlements, as codified in the LOS Convention, stop short of territorial rights, granting coastal states:

> sovereign rights for the purpose of exploring and exploiting, conserving
> and managing the natural resources, whether living or non-living, of the
> waters superjacent to the sea-bed and of the sea-bed and its subsoil, and
> with regard to other activities for the economic exploitation and
> exploration of the zone (Article 56(1)(a)).

Moreover, Article 56(1)(b)(iii) of the LOS Convention recognized for the first time coastal state jurisdiction in the EEZ over protection and preservation of the marine environment, raising the prospect of the environmental liability provisions within CLC 1969 and the Fund Convention 1971 falling behind the evolution of international maritime law on extra-territorial rights.

Although the LOS Convention had at that time not entered into force, several delegations at the 1984 London conference cited its EEZ provisions in support of an extension of the geographical coverage of the oil pollution liability treaties. A south–north division of interests is discernible in conference minutes: African (Gabon, Nigeria, Morocco), Asian (China, India, Indonesia,

Korea) and Latin American (Argentina, Brazil, Chile, Mexico, Peru) delegations lined up to assert their EEZ natural resource rights and environmental protection jurisdiction, as recognized in the LOS Convention. Key industrial states dependent on unimpeded maritime traffic, such as Belgium, Denmark, Federal Republic of Germany, Japan, Sweden and the UK (joined by significant Eastern bloc powers – German Democratic Republic and the USSR), opposed extension of oil pollution liability rules to EEZs, arguing on legal grounds that CLC 1969 and the Fund Convention 1971 were autonomous from the LOS Convention and, in a replay of objections to liberalizing environmental reinstatement rules, maintaining also that any such change would in practice invite speculative claims (International Maritime Organization, 1993a: pp147–8, 338–9, 365; 1993b: pp361–72). Shipping, maritime insurance and oil cargo interests, all attending as observers, lobbied in support of this position. For a time the EEZ proposal lacked the two-thirds majority of states necessary to adopt it. However, cross-cutting the south–north cleavage, and proving pivotal to acceptance of the EEZ adjustment, a North American/Australasian alignment of states with rich offshore marine resource endowments (Canada, United States, Australia, New Zealand) successfully pressed home the majority state support for the amendments to CLC and the Fund Convention, ensuring also that their final drafting was informed by the LOS Convention (International Maritime Organization, 1993b: pp520–2, 599–602).

Unlike the environmental damage provision clause of the oil pollution liability conventions, the EEZ amendment has not provoked disputes in practice over its application to transnational harm: the growing international consensus over both its legitimacy and delimitation has prevented unilateral national variance from the norm. And maritime oil trading companies have, in spite of their initial opposition, adapted themselves to the extended geographical scope of the 1992 oil pollution civil liability regime. The only issues to arise over implementation of the designation relate to areas where coastal states have not chosen to exercise their right under the LOS Convention to claim an EEZ, falling instead under the coverage of an area equivalent to such a designation under Article II(a)(ii) of CLC 1992 and Article 3(a)(ii) of the Fund Convention 1992. Most recently, this has applied to the Mediterranean area where, in a region of interlocking maritime interests, coastal states have yet to agree on mutually exclusive EEZs. In September 2000, France, Italy and Spain issued a tripartite declaration signalling the applicability of the oil pollution liability treaties to an area beyond and adjacent to their respective territorial seas in the Mediterranean, up to the 200-mile limit. This has provoked concerns from member states that the designation is not 'in accordance with international law' as stipulated by the conventions; firstly, because it might jeopardize the legitimate EEZ claims of other Mediterranean states and, secondly, because it establishes overlapping areas of jurisdiction incompatible with the conventional delimitation of maritime boundaries. However, France, Italy and Spain have stressed that the zone is only germane to the oil pollution liability conventions, without prejudice to EEZ claims (International Oil Pollution Compensation Fund, 2001: pp17–19).

While the extension of the geographical coverage of the oil pollution liability regime is generally acknowledged by member states to enhance the rights of victims by admitting extra-territorial claims (impacting on the EEZ), its spatial resonance to transnational harm may still be questioned in relation to marine protected areas and marine common spaces.

Marine protected areas

In recent years the notion of marine protected areas has gained growing currency in international law. Article 211(6) of the LOS Convention allows coastal states to designate special areas, whereby they can prescribe particular standards and navigational practices to prevent ship-source pollution. Within the United Nations Environment Programme, the Regional Seas Programme has advanced specially protected marine areas through protocols to its East African, Mediterranean, South-East Pacific and Caribbean Conventions. In addition, Annex I of the MARPOL Convention has facilitated the designation of extensive Special Areas where oil discharges are strictly controlled or prohibited – for example, the North West European Waters Special Area created in 1999. Lastly, there has been the parallel, albeit more halting, development by the IMO of the designation of Particularly Sensitive Sea Areas (PSSAs) – marine protected areas established to protect recognized ecological, socio-economic or scientific values. An important catalyst for the current flurry of activity on marine protected areas came from the 1992 United Nations Conference on Environment and Development (UNCED), notably the Convention on Biological Diversity and Chapter 17 ('Protection of the Oceans') of the sustainable development programme, Agenda 21. The overarching UNCED Rio Declaration provided an endorsement of precautionary norms and the concept of common but differentiated responsibility, which explicitly informed subsequent IMO work, including that on marine protected areas (Wonham, 1998).

The range of marine protected areas – all with different geographical scope, criteria for designation and protective measures – has undoubtedly caused confusion, but consolidation work within the IMO has now clarified at least the respective roles of MARPOL Special Areas and PSSAs (de la Fayette, 2001: pp185–94). While the global network of marine protected areas expands further, their impact on oil pollution liability claims has yet to be systematically examined, both for the CLC/Fund Convention executive bodies and member states. The IOPC Funds in practice have long acknowledged the need to meet more demanding clean-up standards in areas identified with high tourism and/or wildlife values. While oil-spill damage in ecologically sensitive PSSAs has so far not been an issue for the 1992 Fund Executive Committee (the six PSSAs currently designated are the Australian Great Barrier Reef; the Cuban Sabana–Camagüey Archipelago; Malpelo Island, Colombia; the Florida Keys, US; the Wadden Sea, Germany/Netherlands/Denmark; and the Paracas National Reserve, Peru), the committee is likely to take a more generous view of 'reasonableness' in order to meet stringent environmental reinstatement costs. Were that to be the case, the preventive environmental rationale of marine protected areas would at least prompt a sympathetic realignment in the economic compensation system for oil pollution damage, although the high biodiversity value of such areas is likely to expose more acutely the absence of recompense for ecosystem damage *per se*.

Marine common spaces

Outside territorial seas and exclusive economic zones, use of the high seas is above all governed by open access and the near-exclusivity of flag state jurisdiction over maritime vessels. This *laissez-faire* regime has not only generated widespread over-fishing and marine pollution, but also prompted concerns over piracy, drug trafficking and the movement of asylum seekers (Churchill and Lowe, 1999: pp203–22). For the oil pollution liability system, the collective action problem resides in the absence of incentives for actors to mitigate damage not affecting any state rights or interests. According to the IOPC Fund 1992 Claims Manual, responses on the high seas to an oil spill in principle would qualify for compensation only if they succeed in preventing or reducing pollution damage within the territorial sea or exclusive economic zone of a contracting state (International Oil Pollution Compensation Fund, 2000: p7). The Fund position is that, given world shipping lanes, such spills are rare. Furthermore, the difficulty of mounting a practical response to an oil discharge on the high seas means that natural dispersal is normally relied on for such incidents: any adverse consequences would manifest themselves in national claims systems – for example, the pure economic loss of a reduced fish catch in the EEZ of a member state. Nevertheless, there is a preventive need for oil pollution liability mechanisms to cover significant harm in marine common spaces (Boyle, 1997: p93).

Regardless of the practical rationale for restricting liability for high seas oil pollution damage to its impact on national interests, the LOS Convention affords states the right of intervention on the high seas in the case of maritime casualties threatening harmful pollution (Article 221(1)) and, more radically, the right of port states to take legal proceedings against visiting vessels alleged to have illegally discharged oil outside the state's own maritime zones, including the high seas (Article 218(1)). An increasing reliance on port state enforcement in maritime governance is evident in the evolving network of regional Memoranda of Understanding which coordinate port state regulation of safety and environmental rules – including MARPOL provisions on oil pollution discharges (Keselj, 1999). Port state control has established a significant precedent for the development of transnational accountability for marine pollution, acknowledging situations where states can take action against polluters for non-national harm. While these actions are likely to favour criminal liability sanctions, they render the oil pollution civil liability regime open to interrogation for its confinement of environmental compensation to damage in coastal state maritime zones.

A new accountability? Oil pollution compensation and affected publics

Is it possible to identify, in the evolution of the oil pollution liability regime, movement towards a more effective and equitable institutionalization of accountability for transboundary harm? The changing environmental and spatial parameters of the international liability conventions suggest increased resonance with the consequences of oil pollution damage; and although the relevant legal norms remain firmly within a system of economic compensation, they operate according to rules of uniform coverage and the equal treatment of claimants. In other words, the financial accountability promoted by CLC 1992 and the Fund Convention 1992 is structured to protect the interests of all third parties materially affected by significant oil discharges as they impact on the maritime zones of contracting states. This impartial orientation to *affected publics* suggests a promising platform for securing transnational environmental liability and compensation. To consider its consistency with the model of accountability advanced in this volume, we need to consider the extent to which the interests of affected publics are represented and incorporated in the governance regime. As argued in Chapter 1, this can be assessed in general terms according to standards of harm prevention, inclusiveness and impartiality. Reference to these criteria enables a summary review of the oil pollution liability regime as a tool for progressing responsibility for transnational environmental harm.

Harm prevention

The obligation of conduct on actors to prevent damage to the marine environment is evident in the growing repertoire of international maritime regulation. While in practice a reactive regulatory tool, environmental liability treaties can contribute to preventive goals by providing additional economic incentives for actors to take into account the potential social and ecological consequences of their activities. The conjunction of strict liability and compulsory insurance in the oil pollution liability regime is widely acknowledged by most contracting states to have proved effective in meeting quantifiable claims for environmental (and other) damage from oil spills. However, there are continuing concerns, as noted above, that the environmental reinstatement provisions of CLC are too restrictive. Nevertheless, as at 31 December 2003, 93 states had ratified CLC 1992 and 84 states had ratified the Fund Convention 1992 – figures indicating the global reach of the liability regime. In effect, all international tankers now require certification and insurance consistent with the coverage of the conventions, though under MARPOL rules single-hull tankers are permitted to operate outside US waters until 2015. A recent study of the main vehicle by which shipowners mutually insure their third-party liabilities – the Protection and Indemnity Clubs – demonstrates the significant incentives afforded by compulsory oil pollution liability insurance to penalizing shipowners with poor environmental performance (Bennett, 2001: p20). If the precise influence here on shipowners' commercial viability has yet to be ascertained, the higher duty of care it imposes has at least partially incorporated marine protection incentives. And it is a plausible thesis that this has contributed to the sharp decline in major tanker spills since the 1970s (National Research Council, 2002).

For critics of the international compensation framework advanced in the oil pollution field, its economic incentives to avoid discharges are weakened by the channelling of (limited) liability to the registered shipowner – a charge levelled by the European Commission in its post-*Erika* review of CLC/Fund Convention and one re-ignited following the *Prestige* spillage off the northwest Spanish coast in November 2002. Marine insurance and oil company representatives have rejected European Commission proposals to make charterers and operators directly liable, arguing that the resultant fragmentation of accountability would dilute shipowners' responsibilities, serving also as a disincentive for insurers to take a proactive interest in the condition and operation of the insured. A more fundamental criticism, perhaps, is that in spite of strict liability standards, the preventive force of the oil pollution liability regime is reduced by the heavy burden of proof imposed on victims to demonstrate a causal link between specific oil contamination and the alleged damage. Monitoring of ship movements, combined with long-distance sourcing of oil types, could collectively facilitate more compensation claims against shipowners and the 1992 Fund. An additional argument deserving consideration is that, in order to set a burden of proof in line with precautionary environmental norms, a statutory presumption of causality in favour of the claimant could be invoked where, in addition to strong (but inconclusive) evidence of a vessel in the proximity of a spill being responsible for the alleged damage, there is a proof of breach of anti-pollution regulations by that vessel (Gauci, 1997: p85). One benefit of such a move would be to integrate more closely the oil pollution liability conventions with the MARPOL rules on oil tanker equipment standards, combining their incentive effects on shipowners.

Inclusiveness

The issue of establishing proof of damage exposes the individualistic structure of accountability informing the international oil pollution liability framework, for its inclusion of affected environmental interests is registered through particular economic claims. It is important here to credit the system for its non-discriminatory application, such that national court judgments on compensation claims must, if fairly reached, be recognized in any contracting state (CLC 1992, Article X(1); Fund Convention 1992, Articles 7(6) and (8)). This equality of treatment promotes inclusive representation of liability claims across national maritime zones. As already stated, though, the *jurisdictional selectivity* of the liability conventions points to problems in invoking financial responsibility for oil pollution in marine common spaces. The International Law Commission, in its work formalizing new state responsibility rules, has recommended that states be given legal standing to seek remedies for breach of obligations *erga omnes* (collective obligations owed to the international community as a whole). However, short of international crimes (which could conceivably include intentional massive marine pollution), the Commission has cautioned against 'third party' states being able to seek compensation as a form of reparation for such breaches (Peel, 2001: pp93–4). In the area of marine law, where Article 192 of the LOS Convention – 'States have the obligation to protect and preserve the marine environment' – has already been identified by some commentators as an obligation *erga omnes* (see Ragazzi, 1997: p159), this might seem to exclude environmental liability for major oil pollution damage to marine common spaces. A counter-proposal is that such reparations, sought by proactive states on behalf of the world community, could be awarded to an international organization to utilize in accordance with the collective environmental interests harmed (Peel 2001). In other words, criminal fines imposed under principles of state responsibility could facilitate direct redress for *extra-territorial* environmental damage, supplementing the existing territorial scope of the oil pollution civil liability conventions. This would secure globally inclusive coverage for oil pollution damage.

Non-state advocacy for collective ecological interests is evident from the involvement of environmental organizations in the oil pollution liability regime. Revision and amendment of CLC is undertaken through committee work and diplomatic conferences convened by the IMO, which has approved observer status for environmental interest-group involvement in both policy arenas. FOEI and IUCN were active at the key 1984 IMO international conference on CLC 1969 and the Oil Fund Convention 1971, lobbying for the inclusion of ecosystem values in the environmental liability amendments, while these and other environmental interest groups have some influence on the development within the IMO of marine environment protection instruments. The legal autonomy of the IOPC Funds has resulted in narrower scope for environmental nongovernmental organizations to be accredited as observers (International Oil Pollution Compensation Fund, 1996). To be sure, their administrative focus admits less scope for political lobbying: FOEI has become less active in recent years, leaving IUCN as the only active environmental interest group among a significant number of industry-related observers.

Consultative status for environmental groups allows at best an indirect representation of their own ecological agendas, relying for influence at the international rule-making level on the support of sympathetic member states. The IOPC Funds in practice have admitted environmental clean-up claims from voluntary organizations, suggesting to some commentators that the effective inclusion of collective ecological interests in the liability process is best sought through granting a direct right to individuals or groups to seek public damages for environmental harm, separate from compensation for individual economic loss or reinstatement payments (Wetterstein, 1994: p240; Gauci, 1997: pp256–60). Legal initiatives in line with this include the standing afforded to environmental organizations by the 1993 Convention on Civil Liability for Damage Resulting from Activities Dangerous to the Environment (Article 18) and also recommended by the European Commission in its proposed directive on environmental liability (Commission of the European Communities, 2002: pp44–5). Not surprisingly, shipping interests have rejected any move to detach environmental compensation entitlements from site-specific reinstatement costs, forecasting a tide of speculative claims (Howlett, 2002). This position holds sway within the oil pollution liability regime: at the present time, there is no significant constituency of support among member states to enact such a public interest right.

Impartiality

As a component of transnational environmental accountability, *impartiality* denotes the extent to which affected publics could reasonably accept that their interests have been taken into account in the relevant area of governance. The oil pollution liability framework, constituted through majoritarian norms of international rule-making and, in the practice of the IOPC Funds, striving for consensual rule application, deepens its democratic legitimacy with its deliberative transparency and openness to the representations of non-state actors. IMO conferences and committees, along with IOPC Fund decision-making, reveal lively argumentation on the incorporation of environmental costs into maritime liability regimes. Of course, there is nevertheless an asymmetry of power between the lobbying force of shipping/oil cargo interests and the dispersed, ever-changing constituency of transnational publics affected by environmental harm, who must rely on the sponsorship of affected states and environmental organizations. Ecological concerns are routinely registered in rule-making and implementation only through the advocacy of 'coastal' states, representing their own national maritime priorities.

Furthermore, even within its own parameters of liability, the core capacity of the international regime fairly to make provision for entitled environmental claimants has been questioned. In recent years there has been a considerable increase in oil damage compensation claimed from the IOPC Funds, including cases exceeding the maximum compensation limits of the 1971 Fund (60 million Special Drawing Rights) and the 1992 Fund (135 million Special Drawing Rights) – notably, claims arising from the *Braer* (UK, 1993), *Nakhodka* (Japan, 1997), *Erika* and *Prestige* spills. In these cases the Executive Committees of the IOPC Funds have made interim pro rata payments to ensure that no admissible claims – including environmental ones – are excluded, but this laudable impartiality in claims processing means that losses may not always be fully compensated. Amendments to CLC 1992 and the Fund Convention 1992 agreed in 2000 by the Legal Committee of IMO saw compensation limits raised by 50 per cent in November 2003; while IMO also approved in 2003 a new supplementary or third-tier fund for compensation (also funded by oil receivers), in order more fully to meet admissible claims for damage. Both initiatives are seen by member states as vital to maintaining the viability and credibility of the international oil pollution liability system. By increasing the pool of compensation funds (up to 750 million Special Drawing Rights), they may well allow scope for IOPC Fund discretion in favour of more innovative environmental reinstatement claims, should the balance of member state interests facilitate that.

These increases in compensation limits were prompted by moves within the European Commission to establish a separate European Community compensation fund (up to one billion euros), in response to the perceived shortfall of the international oil pollution liability funds. The Commission has criticized the central role played by private organizations in the area of maritime safety, developing rules more directly to regulate classification societies (responsible for verifying the seaworthiness of vessels) and recommending amendments to CLC 1992 to weaken the right of liability limitation of the shipowner. Behind the latter proposal lies the view that the tight interdependence between the Protection and Indemnity Clubs and shipowners, characterized by a tradition of self-regulation in maritime insurance coverage, may compromise the impartial consideration of public (environmental) interests in liability rule development and implementation (Bennett, 2001; Ringbom, 2001). Indeed, in an attempt to stave off the prospect of additional liability burdens on tanker owners, the International Group of Protection and Indemnity Clubs has proposed voluntary increases in the limits of liability for smaller vessels under CLC 1992, to be applicable to damage in states opting for the new third-tier compensation fund. Following the *Erika* and *Prestige* spills, the close cooperation of private shipping actors in the oil pollution liability regime is being scrutinized over its public answerability.

The growing governance role of transnational civil liability rules

The marine oil pollution civil liability regime stands at the forefront of rule development for transnational environmental compensation, advancing private law remedies to enable national victims of oil spillage damage to make financial claims against domestic/non-domestic tanker owners and companies receiving oil after sea transport. Its widely acknowledged effectiveness can be attributed to a vehicle of liability that facilitates prompt and equitable compensation recovery for affected third parties, although this rests on a financial capacity that has struggled fully to meet the costs of occasional catastrophic spills. In the arena of marine oil pollution, this strict liability model has been extended to the International Convention on Liability and Compensation for Damage in Connection with the Carriage of Hazardous and Noxious Substances by Sea, 1996, and the International Convention on Liability for Bunker Oil Pollution Damage, 2001. Both conventions (still to enter force) broadly share the environmental reinstatement provisions and jurisdictional scope of CLC 1992. Significantly, though, the bunker oil liability convention – covering fuel oil spills from vessels other than tankers – breaks with the liability channelling provisions of CLC 1992, exposing to compensation claims operators and charterers, as well as registered owners (all with rights of limitation). This notable shift to multiple liabilities has been judged by some authorities to indicate pressure from the United States and the European Commission on IMO to accord more with American liability norms in this area of oil pollution, although it also reflects the need to make up for the absence of a second tier of supplementary compensation – as under the Fund Convention (Wu, 2001; Kim, 2002).

A comprehensive account of the evolution of the international oil pollution liability conventions would need to map out the changing balance of geopolitical power between coastal and flag-state interests. The threat of unilateral action by key coastal states (notably the UK and the United States) created the incentive for flag states to sign up to CLC 1969 and then the Fund Convention 1971, reinforced by the preference of tanker owners and oil importers for uniform, predictable oil pollution liability rules across the world. While American disengagement from the international process delayed the adoption of the 1984 liability amendments, their eventual incorporation into CLC 1992 and the Fund Convention 1992 allowed a seminal acknowledgment of transnational environmental compensation and a significant expansion of the geographical scope of the oil pollution liability norms. For developing countries, the revised international regime recognized their enlarged maritime zones of interest (EEZs), offering them also the economic incentive of low-cost or no-cost insurance coverage for oil pollution damage – the costs of major spills being covered above all by oil companies in industrialized countries. Ironically, European Commission efforts to set up a regional oil pollution compensation fund would, if successful, ultimately reduce the transfer of liability funds from European oil importers to injured and affected parties in member states from the global South. This would increase the burden on oil receivers in these countries, prompting their state authorities to disengage from the Fund Convention (building on the precedent set by those Southern states joining CLC but not the Fund Convention; e.g. Brazil, Chile, Senegal, South Africa). The international oil pollution liability regime constitutes a finely balanced geopolitical equilibrium of mutual state interests: further fragmentation could quickly unravel its intricate network of responsibilities and entitlements.

Reference only to the interplay of geopolitical interests would fail to explain the currency and character of the oil pollution liability regime: its environmental compensation provisions, as obligations, draw legitimacy from private law concepts of responsibility and fair treatment. Overlapping civil liability traditions between states have facilitated the extension of these familiar legal norms to transnational damage claims and environmental harm from oil spills. The relatively rapid acceptance of international oil pollution liability norms by the majority of tanker owners and oil-importing states attests to their 'fit' with existing normative frameworks. Of course, this also sets constraints on the further growth of environmental compensation for oil pollution damage, because private liability norms tend to register only certain types of claim (economic loss) from individualized victims. Both the ecological and jurisdictional selectivity of the current oil pollution liability regime have been highlighted, which limit its competence to address collective environmental interests. For marine common spaces in particular, there is currently no direct civil liability coverage for oil pollution damage. The creation of marine protected spaces and port state control instruments indicates that environmental protection for such areas is emerging; yet there remains room for innovation in civil and criminal liability norms to encompass environmental compensation for damage to common marine spaces.

Development of environmental liability norms for other areas of transboundary risk, albeit slow, illustrates the formative influence of the oil pollution treaty provisions on civil liability and compensation. The absence of liability coverage for environmental damage following accidents at nuclear installations was starkly exposed in 1986 by the Chernobyl disaster. Hampered by the sensitivities of nuclear-power states, it took the International Atomic Energy Authority almost ten years to broker international agreement on amendments to the 1963 (Vienna) Convention on Civil Liability for Nuclear Damage covering new liability rules. Under a 1997 Protocol the Convention has broadened its definition of compensatable nuclear damage to include the costs of reinstatement of an impaired environment, the loss of income deriving from an economic interest in any use or enjoyment of the environment and the costs of preventive measures (Article I(1)k): these provisions are explicitly informed by the environmental liability sections of the 1992 oil pollution liability protocols. Similarly, the 1999 (Basel) Protocol on Liability and Compensation for Damage resulting from Transboundary Movements of Hazardous Wastes and their Disposal also imports the environmental damage coverage of the oil pollution treaties: Article II(2)c of the Protocol recognizes environmental reinstatement costs, loss of income and preventive costs. Negotiations over this protocol took seven years, largely reflecting the resistance of advanced industrialized states to general liability for exported wastes. It is significant that, for environmental liability within both these two issue areas, the oil pollution model offered a governance option acceptable to powerful states on account of its private law structure – notably operator-based liability, limitations on liability (except for negligent behaviour) and the compulsory requirement on operators to take out insurance or some other financial guarantee covering their liability.

As with the oil pollution regime, though, this recourse to private international law (through the harmonization of national liability rules) builds responsibility for environmental harm on the basis of individual victims being able to prove legally that the damage caused is attributable to a discrete incident – a burden of proof that favours border-impact or point-source transboundary risks, where lines of causality are relatively clear. Not surprisingly, where environmental harm is linked to multiple sources and diffuse, often extra-territorial ecological effects, adapting private liability norms presents an imposing challenge. This is apparent from current intergovernmental efforts to elaborate liability rules determining compensation for damages resulting from the transboundary movement of living (genetically) modified organisms under the 2000 Cartagena Protocol on Biosafety. The protracted, as yet unsuccessful, negotiations to agree environmental liability rules under the 1991 Protocol on Environmental Protection to the Antarctica Treaty illustrate also how common international spaces – here the Antarctic Treaty area – prevent the simple allocation of financial losses to affected parties. Indeed, in those instances where the cause of environmental damage cannot be disaggregated in terms of individual responsibility (e.g. culpability for ozone depletion or global warming), it has become widely accepted by governments that responsibility is best apportioned nationally by means of inter-state commitments (see Chapter 3). As argued by Prue Taylor (1998: pp178–9), given that environmental risk generation in these circumstances is typically the consequence of routine economic activity, positive incentives for cooperation and mutual assistance are more important for redressing breaches of relevant international agreements than automatic financial penalties (civil or criminal). This point taken, I want to conclude by stressing the necessary function still served by environmental liability for transnational harm.

Conclusion

Environmental liability is a relatively new instrument as applied to addressing physical damage arising from transnational decisions and activities. As a regulatory tool, it has been associated above all with establishing and securing financial accountability for transboundary harm to private economic interests. This reflects the deference of international rule-making to existing national systems of *civil liability*, which are typically rooted in the good-neighbour principles of property law. In other words, environmental liability obligations are understood as imperatives of answerability and compensation owed to neighbouring parties by those directly responsible for activities causing them significant damage. The international elaboration of environmental liability has favoured the harmonization of domestic civil remedies, as should be clear from the substantive discussion in this chapter. Under this framework, responsibility falls squarely on the private operator of risk-bearing activities:

> *those civil liability treaties that have been adapted do suggest a preference in international policy and state practice for the direct accountability of the polluter in national law as the best means of facilitating recovery of compensation for environmental damage, without having resort to interstate claims or the complexities of the law of state responsibility* (Birnie and Boyle, 2002: p281).

State responsibility enters as a last recourse where private remedies are inappropriate or insufficient.

The property law basis of civil liability thus conditions its responsiveness to environmental damage. Firstly, as demonstrated by the oil pollution liability regime, civil liability remedies can, through compulsory insurance, create internal incentives for set standards of environmental responsibility. These incentives are conveyed and reinforced by market signals (e.g. reduced insurance costs for careful operators), which enhances their flexibility, although the employment of private insurance depends on predictable probabilities of risk and agreed calculations of damage. International liability treaties have attempted to accommodate in a predictable way the risks attached to the transmission of selected hazardous products. This has been accomplished by defining environmental harm in terms of financial losses to individual parties. While this is in line with traditional private law principles, and has therefore benefited from the authority of established jurisprudence, it has systematically excluded non-commodity environmental values – in particular, ecological damage not affecting property rights and other sources of economic income. The extension of civil liability rules to environmental impairment has therefore not altered the theoretical parameters of compensation law, and could be considered as out of step with environmental policy objectives concerned with protecting ecosystem integrity for non-economic reasons.

Secondly, given that no-fault liability still requires a clear causal link to be demonstrated between the activities of a risk-generating operator and quantifiable economic losses, civil remedies seem to be most appropriate for addressing near-term, point-source transboundary damage. This favours accountability to *proximate affected individuals* (Wilde, 2002) clustered around the immediate hazard, as opposed to third parties harmed by longer-term, more diffuse impacts. Under international liability law, the source of the physical damage – or, more precisely, the tort – is where legal responsibility is traditionally established, which prioritizes adjacent effects. It can also work against the claimants when the alleged wrongdoer is based in another country. Rules of non-discrimination, as endorsed by the International Law Commission, have been incorporated into liability treaties to enable transnational environmental claims against offending operators in either their home state or the affected state. Of course there may still be practical and legal hurdles to such action, but it is still a necessary procedural rule conducive to building responsibility for transboundary environmental damage. More seriously, the accountability gains made here by treaties addressing hazardous processes and substances have not been matched in the general area of foreign direct investment. Outside the civil liability treaties, where significant environmental damage in a state arises from decisions made in other countries, transnational claims for compensation are rare. Holding parent companies accountable in home countries for harm to foreign affected parties is an onerous task, typically pitching poorly resourced victims against powerful corporations. This suggests the need to extend transnational environmental liability beyond specific risk-bearing activities to routine corporate decision-making (see Chapter 6).

A third structural characteristic of civil liability as a tool of accountability for transnational environmental damage is its *territoriality*, such that affected parties receive legal entitlements through their membership of states that have ratified the relevant treaties. Affected parties here are invariably (sub)national individuals and groups, although their interests are, under civil liability agreements, recognized in other contracting states. The case study on marine oil pollution highlighted the spatial extension of liability rules to EEZs, including damage received in these areas from pollution incidents on the high seas. These are significant gains in accountability for environmental damage, yet they still fall short of comprehensive geographical coverage (a selectivity arguably now inconsistent with the marine environment protection responsibilities set by the LOS Convention). Extra-territorial environmental impacts are beyond the current scope of civil liability norms and, given the absence of clear property rights for the marine and atmospheric commons, there is a strong argument that this is a systemic limitation. Indeed, several commentators have claimed that, where treaty prescriptions are absent, the most promising legal avenue to pursue liability for extra-territorial ecological damage caused by private parties is through the use of criminal penalties, even though their transnational potential is very much untested (Boyle, 1999; Cane, 2001). The environmental interests of wide-ranging, planetary publics are, according to this approach, most effectively represented by proactive states acting on behalf of the international community under the 'common heritage' of 'common concern' doctrines already mentioned in conventions pertaining to the deep seabed, global climate change and biodiversity protection. Here criminal fines and other possible sanctions are de-linked from property entitlements and can be applied more directly to significant environmental damage *per se*.

As mentioned in the marine oil pollution case study, the rights accorded to states under the LOS Convention to intervene on the high seas to prevent serious pollution and to take legal proceedings against visiting vessels for illegal oil discharges outside territorial waters both represent significant precedents in extra-territorial jurisdiction for environmental crimes. However, criminal liability for environmental damage has barely progressed beyond these powers. Article 8 of the 1998 Statute of the International Criminal Court (in force July 2002) only recognizes widespread, long-term and severe environmental damage during armed conflict as an offence entitling any state, in the interests of global order, to seek legal redress. Also noteworthy, transnational criminal liability for less grave environmental harm has been promoted by the Council of Europe through the 1998 (Strasbourg) Convention on the Protection of the Environment through Criminal Law. Significantly, under Article 11 environmental NGOs are given the right to participate in proceedings concerning environmental offences, challenging the notion that only states can legally represent the concerns of affected publics. In its rationale for this provision, the Council of Europe cites the proven capability of environmental groups as representatives of collective ecological concerns as legitimating their involvement in criminal proceedings on behalf of affected interests (Council of Europe, 1998: p17). However, while innovative in an international treaty, this provision is non-binding on contracting states, while the Convention itself is still some way from entering into force.

If, in conclusion, there is now a widespread agreement among states on the need for modalities of liability where transnational practices incur environmental damage that would otherwise go uncompensated or unchallenged, there is no consensus on the precise scope and mix of civil and criminal remedies. Transnational liability for environmental harm is a necessary pillar of the new environmental accountability, one only gradually evolving beyond its private law origins in property entitlements. There remains real potential for the extension of civil liability rules to additional point-source transboundary hazards: the most significant transnational regulatory challenge now is the incorporation of liability constraints (civil and criminal) on routine economic activities falling outside the reach of existing treaties, particularly where the damaging environmental effects are extra-territorial.

Chapter 6

The Environmental Accountability of Transnational Corporations

It is beyond dispute that transnational corporations (TNCs) are now the leading vehicles of economic globalization. Their cross-border financial flows of foreign direct investment (FDI) – comprising equity acquisitions, intra-company loans and reinvested earnings – are more important than global trade in realizing economic value. According to the United Nations Conference on Trade and Development (UNCTAD), in 2002 global sales of TNCs reached $18 trillion, compared with $8 trillion for world exports. While the start of the twenty-first century has seen the fourth major downturn in FDI since 1970 (down almost a third during 2001–02), in line with weak global economic growth, the stock of FDI is at unprecedented historical levels: the 2002 value of $7.1 trillion represented more than a tenfold increase since 1980. This stock – two-thirds of which is controlled by developed-world corporations (dominated by European, US and Japanese firms) – structures transnational production networks and investment chains affecting the livelihoods and living conditions of millions of people. In an immediate way, over 53 million people in 2002 were employed overseas by 64,000 TNCs through 870,000 foreign affiliates: the world's top 100 TNCs alone, with total assets approaching $6 trillion, employed 6.9 million foreign employees (UNCTAD, 2003: ppxvi, 5). More widely, the social and ecological effects of TNC activity impact beyond the working lives of their employees, encompassing contractors, communities and ecosystems.

The environmental consequences of TNC behaviour are multiple and substantial, if also contested. Clearly TNC investment decisions, production processes and resource transfers all impinge directly on social and ecological development paths. On one side is the familiar charge levelled by many environmentalists, and reinforced by 'anti-globalization' activists, that TNCs are ecologically irresponsible. The vivid image often employed here is of a 'race to the bottom', with global economic competition driving footloose corporations to seek locational advantages from investing in jurisdictions with minimal environmental regulation (e.g. Korten, 1995: pp229–37; Retallack,

2001). As three-quarters of FDI flows into developing countries, a major concern is that ecologically damaging practices are concentrated in states least willing or able to mitigate their impacts on vulnerable populations, while the economic benefits generated by the domestic sectors receiving that FDI are, it is claimed, typically skewed towards local elites. Against this highly critical perspective is the view that TNCs have been voluntarily harmonizing ambitious environmental production and process standards across their different territories of operation. From the cost savings of more efficient material and energy usage, or the global market benefits of building a green reputation, 'corporate environmentalism' is seen to give at least some TNCs a competitive advantage (Porter and van der Linde, 1995; Mol, 2001: pp97–100).

Underlying the standoff between these two approaches are contrasting ideas on how corporations should be publicly accountable for the ecological and social effects of their activities. It is commonly acknowledged that there are growing external pressures on TNCs to recognize that, while they may formally be outside the decision-making of large corporations, domestic or foreign publics negatively affected by these decisions have a moral stake in having their concerns taken into account. However, there are competing opinions about the nature of that incorporation. In the next section I outline the rise of voluntary initiatives for environmental self-reporting and self-regulation developed by TNCs. These are informed by a 'soft' accountability framework, where answerability to affected publics and any form of redress are solely at the discretion of the company. Their non-legally binding status belies the enduring influence of a market liberal or *contractual* model of the firm. Despite moves to register the claims of public stakeholders (e.g. local communities, environmental advocacy groups) in their corporate communications, US and UK TNCs in particular continue to operate under contractual rules and norms, which downplay negative environmental externalities and legally recognize only shareholders as the guardians of the public interest in legitimate corporate governance (Dine, 2000: pp1–36; Warren, 2000).

Critics of the market-based contractual model of the firm argue that it is structurally incapable of addressing shortfalls in ecological and social responsibility to affected publics. And as TNCs build up their global private authority, the contention is that they are out of control, usurping power from democratically constituted states (Korten, 1995; Hertz, 2001). In the absence of international regulation of TNCs, several commentators have identified new forms of control set in play by civil society actors, notably environment and development nongovernmental organizations (NGOs). Firstly, so-called *civil regulation* strengthens the external accountability demands of business behaviour by generating independent standards for corporate responsibility to affected communities (Newell, 2001; Bendell and Murphy, 2002). As discussed below, it entails various non-statutory means by which non-state actors put pressure on TNCs for public answerability and redress. Secondly, albeit less developed, individual and group claimants have recently been pressing TNCs in their home countries to accept legal responsibility for significant harm received as a result of their activities overseas. I address the emergence of this *foreign direct liability* (Ward, 2001) and its contribution to extra-territorial accountability for environmental harm.

Both civil regulation and transnational liability encompass efforts to open TNCs to new accountability demands – moral and legal claims on them effectively to register the interests of foreign publics negatively affected by their investment decisions. The emergence of these attempts to control the environmental impacts of TNC practices outside their home countries points to growing social expectations that major corporations should act responsibly. Looking at the most high-profile international initiative on corporate citizenship, the United Nations (UN) Global Compact partnership model, I consider finally how soft accountability frameworks like this one can promote the integration of ecological and social goals with transnational corporate objectives, and whether they deflect from or complement political moves to deepen and widen the public interest regulation of TNCs.

Corporate environmentalism

Corporate environmentalism comprises actions taken by firms that have a substantive and/or symbolic commitment to ecological protection. In his insightful history of this phenomenon since the 1960s, Andrew Hoffman (2001) explains how it evolved from an ancillary aspect of doing business, through a 1970s compliance-led response to new environmental regulations, then a major organizational shift in the 1980s as corporations embraced self-regulatory codes and standards until, finally, their adoption of strategic, proactive environmental management. This last transformation of corporate environmentalism, dated from about 1988 in the US, heralded the strongest internalization of ecological performance goals within many major firms. Environmental considerations now permeate, it is argued, executive level planning, influencing decisions on production technologies, product development and corporate branding. For major corporations operating across national borders, this new orthodoxy of strategic environmentalism is leading to the transnational standardization of their environmental practices, triggering also the greening of supply chains and client companies.

To be sure, Hoffman's stylized account is empirically informed by a study of the chemical and petroleum industries, particularly US-based TNCs in these sectors. Arguably his most striking claim is that, contrary to rational economic explanations, the move to corporate strategic environmentalism was driven neither by regulatory burdens nor efficiency-motivated technological innovations, but rather social pressure from external actors. In other words, broader institutional structures and events: 'how companies define their responsibility toward the environment is a direct reflection of how society views the environmental issue and thus of how the organizational field defines the role of business in responding to it' (Hoffman, 2001: p197). The organizational field is populated by other leading companies, government regulators, professional and trade associations, pressure groups and other sources of influence on corporate rules and norms. Hoffman's institutional theory explains the rise of corporate environmentalism as the product of the often contested negotiation between internal members of the firm and external actors. At the strategic level, it represents a composite of business responses to multiple constituencies, who frame their concerns according to their own interests and values. Thus, among other sources, environmental pressures may be imposed on firms from insurance companies in order to reduce liabilities; from consumers in terms of demand for greener products; from competitors in terms of reputation management; and from human resource management circles in terms of the motivation of current and prospective employees.

The precedent for globalizing environmental responsibility standards under a self-regulatory framework was set by the chemical industry, in response to the 1984 disaster at a Union Carbide India Plant in Bhopal. Here the heightened public concern registered in many countries, along with company concerns about possible new regulatory and private legal burdens, catalysed the US Chemical Manufacturers Association to create a voluntary environmental code of conduct called Responsible Care. As then taken up by the International Council of Chemical Associations, and adopted now by over 40 national chemical associations, Responsible Care requires member companies to follow particular environmental, health and safety guidelines. It also includes explicit public accountability principles, oriented to communicating openly with businesses, government, employees and communities about process and product risks. However, affected communities are taken only to be local publics in the vicinity of chemical plants rather than those further afield impacted by chemical emissions or product waste and, even at this local scale in the US, criticisms have been levelled about the lack of meaningful dialogue. Elsewhere, national chemical industry associations have also been less than transparent in revealing details of member companies deemed to be in breach of Responsible Care norms (Garcia-Johnson, 2000: pp72–8; Haufler, 2001: p33).

Responsible Care has been the main vehicle for the transnational promotion of environmentalist norms within the chemical industry. Garcia-Johnson (2000) shows in detail how US TNCs exported this voluntarist brand of corporate environmentalism to their subsidiaries in Brazil and Mexico, as well as promoting its wider diffusion through national industry associations in Latin America. Trade liberalization was instrumental in this dissemination, she claims, so that American chemical companies could exploit new markets without being at a competitive disadvantage from domestic companies with lower environmental standards. They could also anticipate a competitive 'first mover' advantage from being in the technological lead. More important than both, though, is suggested to be the need to block or weaken regulatory interventions by host countries or the international community (Garcia-Johnson, 2000: p191). For the environmental responsibility framed by Responsible Care is entirely consistent with prevailing market liberal notions of corporate governance. Their contractual take on responsibility rejects state power as a legitimate device for holding corporations to account for their external ecological and social costs. Indeed, it is not difficult to uncover gaps between what Responsible Care delivers and what governments want in terms of public interest regulation of the chemical industry. For example, the US TNC Dow Chemicals is a leading supporter of Responsible Care yet has spent the past two decades opposing US legislative moves to control dioxins.

Hoffman notes how the 1989 *Exxon Valdez* oil spill in Prince William Sound, Alaska, served, like Bhopal, as a triggering event for the formation of global guidelines on corporate environmental responsibility, though this time applying across industrial sectors (Hoffman, 2001: pp165–6). Known initially as the Valdez Principles, these became the CERES Principles after the network of actors responsible for authoring them – the Coalition for Environmentally Responsible Economies. Unlike Responsible Care, the CERES process was started by pension funds (and other institutional investors) concerned at the uncertainties and cost exposures being thrown up by new environmental liabilities. Environmental NGOs promptly joined other advocacy groups and labour unions in aligning with the coalition, in recognition of its potential economic clout in signalling new expectations of companies from capital markets. It nevertheless was designed to be compatible with existing corporate reporting duties to shareholders. Despite the support of leading environmental NGOs, including Greenpeace, this business orthodoxy underpinning CERES is evident in its latest manifestation – the Global Reporting Initiative (GRI), introduced in collaboration with UNEP in 1997 and launched as a separate reporting institution in 2002. GRI is a framework for fostering voluntary reporting on the ecological and social sustainability performance of corporations. While presented as an advance in accountability for TNCs, it essentially serves to complement annual financial statements issued by companies but, unlike the latter, without the need to be independently audited.

Behind GRI, then, is the need identified by some TNCs to respond to sensitivities in capital markets about ecological and social risks that may well hit investor returns. It is clear that certain industrial sectors and firms see the protection of corporate reputation and preventive risk management as justifying the additional scrutiny of their operations made possible by GRI guidelines. The first major companies not only to have undertaken sustainability reporting but also to have financially sponsored the transnational diffusion of the GRI process include Baxter International, Ford, Nike and Shell. Of these, Shell has arguably developed the most comprehensive environmental reporting, covering air emissions (including greenhouse gases and ozone-depleting substances), marine effluents, oil and chemical spills, energy efficiency, water use, waste generation and equipment recycling (Shell International Limited, 2002: pp26–33). As is noted below, in a sector where the leading US-based oil company, Exxon Mobil, actively opposes international calls for the control of greenhouse gas emissions, the goal of Shell unilaterally to reduce its carbon dioxide emissions demonstrates that competitors may not share predicted reputational payoffs for environmental commitments.

Over 95 per cent of Shell's major installations are externally certified to regional or global environmental management systems (EMSs) including the European Union's Eco-Management and Audit Scheme (EMAS) and the International Organization for Standardization's ISO 14001. EMSs have become the major means by which corporations demonstrate a beyond-compliance stance on environmental performance, as scrutinized and confirmed by outside auditors. ISO 14001 is by far the most popular corporate environmental management standard, with 50,000 certifications worldwide in 2004. Transnational environmental NGOs have been highly critical of ISO 14001: the development and revision of the standard has been portrayed as closed to environmental groups, while the standard itself obliges companies only to respect domestic regulatory standards within operating territories and to seek continual improvement in environmental performance (Krut and Gleckman, 1998). Uptake of the standard has been strongest in Europe and increasingly in East Asia – both regions with relatively high levels of government–business cooperation in regulatory development. It is revealing, though, that European corporations are increasingly abandoning EMAS, which diverges from ISO 14001 in requiring publication of an annual statement on environmental performance. In early 2004 there were about 3,500 EMAS certifications – down 11 per cent on the scheme's peak in December 2001 – compared with over 20,000 European certifications to ISO 14001 (ENDS, 2004).

Whatever their global currency, EMSs are vulnerable to the charge that their standard-setting lacks legitimacy in the eyes of outsiders, undermining any claim to be serving a transnational public interest. First is the argument that such environmental self-regulation could benefit Northern-based TNCs by excluding or marginalizing the concerns of developing-country industries. There is no need here to impute collusive, market-restrictive motivations to leading TNCs, for the consequences of their corporate voluntarism may anyway systematically disadvantage industries in poorer countries. To export to advanced industrialized countries, or to serve as suppliers or sub-contractors to EMS-accredited TNCs, is increasingly to be asked to accord with *de facto* global environmental standards, which is beyond the technological know-how and capital expenditure of many Southern-based corporations (Clapp, 1998; Hansen, 2002). In effect, these standards become trade restrictive. Support for ISO 14001 by East Asian countries (e.g. Malaysia, Taiwan, Thailand, South

Korea) indicates that industrializing countries with major domestic corporations are aware of the potential market benefits, and promote EMS registration for these firms.

Second, and central to the protection of public environmental interests, is the observation that the design and implementation of EMSs is not transparent. Not only is there no formal (territorial) accountability in terms of political answerability to state institutions, the exclusion also of environmental NGOs prevents effective scrutiny from civil society representatives. For example, as ISO 14001-accredited companies are not obliged to release detailed environmental performance and compliance information, they have a weakened basis for proclaiming to be ecologically responsible. The lack of publicly accessible data on the impacts of voluntary codes is not confined to EMSs and highlights an enduring accountability problem with private self-regulation (Haufler, 2001: pp118–20; Archer and Piper, 2003). It is partly in response to this accountability deficit and the wider regulatory vacuum it exposes that civil society organizations have intervened with their own ideas about what constitutes appropriate corporate behaviour. This is the realm of civil regulation.

Civil regulation

Environmental NGOs directly pressure TNCs because they attribute negative environmental impacts to the practices of powerful corporations, and they view existing state-based regulation as ineffective in controlling these activities. Civil regulation occurs when NGOs, and other civil society groupings or networks, set new standards for business behaviour. Simon Zadek (2001: p56) captures well the informal, often unsettled, nature of rule-making at play here:

> *Civil regulations in the main involve collective processes, albeit often through loose forms of social organization. They are manifestations of essentially political acts that can affect business performance through their influence on market conditions ... they can best be understood as non-statutory regulatory frameworks governing corporate affairs. They lie between the formal structures of public (statutory) regulation, and market signals generated by more conventional individual and collective preferences underpinned by the use and exchange value of goods and services.*

As an instrument of accountability for ecological performance, civil regulation moves beyond the limited ambition of voluntary environmentalism, which at best promises greater transparency and answerability for TNC behaviour. The crucial additional element is *civil redress*, whereby corporations choosing to ignore new proposed standards are subject to disruptive actions (e.g. consumer boycotts, investor pressure) organized by advocacy groups. Unpredictable, but potentially damaging to firms' profitability and societal standing, this type of coercive move from civil society actors hardens the environmental accountability demands levelled at corporations.

This is not to state that there are no positive reasons for TNCs to support at least cooperative forms of civil regulation for environmental accountability. These reasons overlap with business motivations driving the development of voluntary environmental codes, but are reinforced by informational and reputational gains perceived to be available from working in partnership with NGOs. Bendell and Murphy (2002: pp254–57) identify three sorts of expected benefits: first, to add credibility to companies' accounts of their environmental commitments and performance; second, to reap potential financial and resource savings (eco-efficiency gains) from expertise offered by NGOs; and third, to undergo organizational learning about new ecological and social challenges impinging on their spaces of operation. These benefits are not restricted to TNCs located in Northern countries. In so far as Southern companies seek lucrative overseas markets, particularly in ecologically conscious European countries, adherence to raised environmental standards may help to win new contracts. However, the additional costs incurred in aligning business practices to transnational civil regulation may still be a competitive gamble for the first companies to adopt them, which is why the potential nature and scope of sanctions to be applied to 'rogue' companies remains pivotal: 'the benefits of civil regulation will only be realized if NGOs and activist groups are able to organize, obstruct and protest when a company fails to perform' (Bendell and Murphy, 2002: p257).

At the confrontational end of civil regulation are those *direct action* protests highlighting in dramatic fashion the alleged wrongdoings of companies. In recent years, it has not been uncommon for TNCs engaged in natural resource extraction in Southern countries to face civil disobedience from locally affected communities undergoing ecological and social degradation of their living conditions. The indifference or outright hostility to these local publics from their own governments, sometimes accompanied by the violent suppression of protests, is typically the trigger for the involvement of Northern NGOs. Consumer pressure is then mobilized against the TNCs involved, with activists calling for boycotts of their products. The well-known case is of Shell pulling out of oil extraction in the Niger Delta, Nigeria, in 1993 as a result of a transnational campaign centred on the environmental plight of the Ogoni people (Boele et al, 2001). Indigenous and other minority peoples involved in struggles against TNCs and domestic political elites are a potent source of environmental victims for transnational activists: their distinctive ethnic identities and long-term attachments to the land make them easily identifiable to Northern consumers as vulnerable foreign publics. Reputational shaming over the alleged damage to these communities from the operations of TNCs can certainly erode the social credibility of the companies involved, as in campaigns against Rio Tinto (copper and gold mining in Grasberg, Indonesia), Asia Pulp and Paper, Mitsubishi and Rimbunan Hijau (logging across Southeast Asia) and Noranda (aluminium mining in Peru).

However, even sustained transnational activism may not dent corporate reputations enough to inflict the type of revenue losses that would shift long-term investment priorities: the susceptibility of companies to external pressure from NGO campaigns depends very much on their economic size and constitution, including relationship to other firms in their industrial sector. One way of civil society actors exerting also internal influence on TNCs is through *investor action* (Oliviero and Simmons, 2002: pp87–8). On specific issues, and usually combined with other tactics, corporate accountability activists have become adept at acquiring token equity in a company in order to gain access to annual general meetings. While these meetings are sometimes used to stage vocal demonstrations, more often campaigners use their shareholder status to sponsor resolutions calling for public answerability and policy changes from executive boards. High-profile TNCs like BP, Rio Tinto and Shell have experienced repeated shareholder activist charges over their environmental performance. Few activist resolutions succeed, but they have more than symbolic value. Corporations weary of repeated challenges may withdraw from controversial projects not linked to their core revenue streams.

Some NGOs, such as the Interfaith Center of Corporate Responsibility, focus on shareholder activism as a means to promote more accountable corporate governance across a wide range of areas. Nevertheless, the favoured route for long-term investor action is socially responsible investing (SRI). This entails negative screening – not buying stock in companies known to be associated with harmful practices – and, more positively, seeking out and investing in corporations associated with raised ecological and social standards of performance. SRI is facilitated by formal stock market listings, such as the Dow Sustainability Group Index in the US and FTSE4Good in the UK, as well as the commitment of investment funds (e.g. pension and mutual funds) concerned with minimizing future environmental liabilities. Zadek's (2001: p63) observation that the investment community is neither greatly troubled nor enticed by corporate ecological and social responsibility still holds: in 2003 in the US – the leading country for SRI – it amounted to no more than 11.3 per cent ($2.16 trillion) of professionally managed funds (Social Investment Forum, 2003: p1), but its growth is rapid. And it is also taking root in other major stock market locales, such as Singapore and Johannesburg.

Further market-oriented engagement with TNCs by environmental groups targets more directly particular production processes and product choices. Of a range of cooperative forms of civil regulation, *stewardship regimes* are among the more developed. They comprise environmental standards agreed to consensually by corporations, NGOs and other stakeholders, then subject in their application to independent verification and accreditation. Two of the leading regimes, the Forest Stewardship Council and the Marine Stewardship

Council, were developed by WWF – a transnational NGO with much expertise in collaborating with large companies. Established in 1993, the Forest Stewardship Council was designed to set up an authoritative global standard with which to certify wood products sourced from forests managed according to agreed principles of ecological and social sustainability (Newell, 2001: pp911–12). Following the successful diffusion of this scheme (now present in over 50 countries), in 1997 WWF teamed up with Unilever Corporation, the world's largest buyer of seafood, to establish the Marine Stewardship Council. Like the forest stewardship regime, resource management practices must be verified as sustainable, allowing a clear and credible certification of fish products for consumers.

Alongside stewardship regimes, civil regulation includes various other types of formal cooperation between environmental NGOs and TNCs, which include 'good neighbour' agreements, community development initiatives and environmental dispute resolution. Most ambitious, perhaps, are *multi-stake-holder environmental partnerships* seeking to identify enduring ways in which corporations can advance ecological and social responsibility. Prominent examples involving major TNCs include the Mining, Minerals and Sustainable Development Project and the Energy and Biodiversity Initiative. Both partnerships have generated environmental management frameworks for businesses engaged in extractive industries. However, such exercises have attracted strong criticisms from environmental activists. For example, Conservation International and the Nature Conservancy, the US-based environmental NGOs active in the Energy and Biodiversity Initiative, were charged in 2003 by the Oilwatch activist network with weakening efforts by Southern civil society groups to seek redress for harm caused by participating TNCs – notably Chevron Texaco for substantial damage alleged to have been caused by its oil extraction activities in northeastern Ecuador (Ruiz-Marrero, 2003). More generally, Poncelet (2003: pp110–11) confirms that the fear that specific claims of environmental responsibility against TNCs will be displaced or diluted by multi-stakeholder partnerships informs much NGO opposition to this form of civil regulation:

> *In resisting these partnerships, NGOs are protesting the fact that, although they are being asked to share in the responsibility for past damage done, they are not being asked to share in the power of corporate decision-making that they believe leads to these problems in the first place.*

Yet even if this power imbalance were somehow to be redressed, public accountability gains from environmental partnerships would still not be guaranteed. Several commentators have cautioned that collaborations between TNCs and NGOs often take place privately, removing them from broader civil society scrutiny and participation (e.g. Newell, 2001: p913; Bendell and Murphy, 2002: pp259–62). This democratic deficit is most apparent from the way in which Northern NGOs dominate environmental partnerships with TNCs, gaining leverage from their proven capacity to relay criticisms of corporations to key consumer markets in wealthier countries. But while Northern activists may be addressing environmental harm received in the global South, NGOs from the impacted areas are typically perceived by TNCs as too weak or ephemeral to warrant engaging with in strategic cooperation. These NGOs are thus reliant on Northern groups to communicate their interests, which at best is indirect and unreliable. On other occasions, there may be no domestic advocacy groups present to voice local grievances. As Hirschland (2003: pp92–3) argues, these gaps in civil society representation reveal the need for not just the greater involvement of Southern NGOs, but also a more direct input from local or regional publics actually affected by the civil regulation itself.

While sometimes discussed as a form of civil regulation, lawsuits launched by civil society groups against TNCs for causing serious environmental harm are properly a separate arena of social control: they invoke obligations embedded in formal systems of legal rights and responsibilities. At least in principle, they suggest a means for empowering affected publics in a more certain way than civil regulation and, given that impacted groups or communities are usually the plaintiffs, their public representiveness would seem to be more direct. It is to environmental litigation against TNCs that I now turn, with a focus on transnational legal actions.

Foreign direct liability of TNCs for environmental harm

The exposure of TNCs to civil liability claims as a result of environmental impacts arising from their FDI has generally not been extensive. There is of course great variation between national legal and regulatory systems: some Southern states – for example, Costa Rica, India and the Philippines – assert that direct TNC accountability for ecological damage is expressly enabled by environmental rights enshrined in their national constitutions (Oliviero and Simmons, 2002: p85). Furthermore, most countries now possess their own regulatory regimes oriented to environmental protection, which establish standards for corporate conduct. And while there continues to be intense debate about whether developing countries reduce or ignore ecological obligations on TNCs in order to attract FDI, the empirical evidence in support of this position remains limited, restricted to certain industries (Neumayer, 2001; Jenkins, 2002). What is more discernible is that, as most developing countries continue to liberalize FDI policies – through domestic reforms and bilateral investment treaties – there is pressure on them to defer to established legal personalities for TNCs in which environmental liability is limited.

To recall, the dominant capitalist model of corporate governance for TNCs is contractual, whereby regulatory interference for public environmental aims is viewed as an unnecessary burden on free enterprise and third parties negatively affected by externalities have little if any legal redress against offending companies. This understanding has routinely applied to corporate harms committed by TNCs outside their home country. For issues like evasion and anti-competitive practices, home states have been prepared to exercise extra-territorial control over their corporate nationals operating abroad as foreign investors, but this scrutiny has not been extended to the production of ecological harm. Protection against environmental injury caused by non-nationals is seen as a task for negotiated international agreements, with TNCs indirectly regulated through state-based controls in the territories in which they operate. As discussed in the last chapter, states have elected to rely on civil liability rules when it comes to coordinating cross-border compensation claims for environmental damage, yet these regimes have emerged only slowly and are largely restricted to the transboundary transportation of hazardous wastes. Moreover, their development has been motivated in part by the need to accommodate business demands for cross-border consistency in legal treatment where environmental liability issues are unavoidable. In an era in which neoliberal economic policy is still in the ascendancy in the G7 states – home to the most powerful TNCs – there has been no political desire to concede the more far-reaching argument that the core rules governing FDI should be tempered by global environmental liability standards.

Environmental liability for TNCs, like other areas of non-contractual (tort) liability confronting them (e.g. human rights harms), is instead being driven by activist networks and public-interest lawyers. Their goal is the creation of legal precedents for holding corporations to account for harm caused outside the territorial space of their home state (country of incorporation). Halina Ward (2002: p2) describes this as *foreign direct liability* – 'holding parent companies accountable in home country courts to people affected by their environmental, social or human rights impacts in other countries'. By apportioning responsibility to private actors across national borders, foreign direct liability advances a horizontal mechanism of corporate accountability. Scott (2001) examines justifications for applying such transnational tort liability to corporations. Although his focus is on violations of human rights, his identification of grounds for the extra-territorial application of harm prevention norms holds for ecological damage, or so I will argue. Two areas particularly relevant to increasing efforts to establish foreign direct liability for environmental harm are, firstly, the assertion of a duty of transnational care by a parent company and, secondly, a duty of home-state courts to prevent activities by TNCs violating universal norms and standards.

Parent company liability

Informing efforts to secure TNC liability for environmental harm caused in countries hosting their FDI is the fairness-based premise that their parent companies should be obliged to ensure that their behaviour as direct investors in these countries matches standards of care that would be expected in their home states (Ward, 2001). However, the complex nature of TNC organizational structures has typically militated against the firm allocation of legal responsibility for transnational torts. Intricate networks of ownership and control have basically enabled these businesses to shift liability exposure from the central parent company onto local subsidiaries. The underlying principle of contractual accountability, limited liability, has here served to insulate from liability separately incorporated entities within the same business network: this makes it difficult for the involuntary victims of corporate harm arising from FDI to hold a parent company legally responsible (Muchlinski, 2001: p16). In their attempts to seek answerability and redress, not only are the victims dealing with different countries of operation, they are frequently dealing with different companies. Litigation to obtain parent company liability must demonstrate, therefore, that duties of care still pertain even where there are devolved structures of corporate control or coordination.

Foreign direct liability actions, supported by public-interest lawyers, have become a key testing ground for transnational corporate accountability in Australia, Canada and England. Leading TNCs targeted include such major mining companies from these countries as Broken Hill Proprietary (Australia) for alleged pollution from copper extraction in Papua New Guinea; Cambior (Canada) charged with tailings pollution from gold mining in Guyana; and Anglo-American (England) for alleged silica dust poisoning arising from gold mining in South Africa. Arguably the most significant precedents have been set by English courts, notably in the Thor Chemicals and Cape cases involving South African claimants seeking compensation, respectively, for work-related poisoning from mercury reprocessing and worker/community ill-health from asbestos mining. As Ward (2001, 2002) notes, in both cases the plaintiffs overcame attempts by the parent companies to stay the action in England in favour of South African courts. The plaintiffs' lawyers managed also to demonstrate that both parent companies had effectively controlled the operations of their South African subsidiaries, and were therefore responsible for their failure to prevent foreseeable environmental health dangers. It should be stressed that, in both cases, the parent companies settled out of court (1994 and 1998 for Thor and 2001 for the Cape action) under a condition that they would not be liable for costs incurred in clearing up the contaminated land on their former industrial sites. Yet transnational environmental liability was clearly established and the cases are already serving as precedents for claims against other English-based TNCs.

Corporate liability for breaching universal norms

Another form of transnational corporate liability derives from their engagement in breaches of peremptory (*jus cogens*) norms of international law, such as violations of human rights and, arguably, vital ecological protection standards (Sornarajah, 2001: p495). In the US, the crucial precedent was set in 1997 by a federal district court in *Doe* v.*Unocal*, which held that private corporations could be held responsible for human rights violations arising out of their activities abroad. This case involved a group of farmers from Myanmar alleging that the California-based oil company, Unocal Corporation, was liable for compensation for assisting the military in forcing them to work on a natural-gas pipeline. The court accepted that liability for serious violations of international law under the US Alien Tort Claims Act could be extended to companies and, in 2002, a federal court allowed the plaintiffs to proceed to trial. While one of the human rights groups serving the initial Unocal lawsuit set out the violation of relevant international environmental norms – including a failure to let those local publics affected by the ecological impacts of pipeline development have their interests represented and taken into account (Mason, 1999: pp231–2), the legal focus centred on the most serious alleged human rights breaches (forced labour and torture).

Other lawsuits by foreign claimants invoking the Alien Tort Claims Act (e.g. against Exxon Mobil in Indonesia) have similarly focused on the most serious human rights violations alleged to have taken place, although ecological concerns have been raised. Should any of these suits ultimately be ruled in favour of the plaintiffs, the way may well be open for testing more assertively corporate liability for breaches of internationally recognized environmental standards. One option would be to stress their human rights import. For example, Scott (2001: p62) suggests that transnational civil liability claims related to environmental harms could be justified indirectly in human rights terms. The erosion of vital ecological conditions for persons or communities as a result of particular corporate practices could be judged to be detrimentally affecting core human rights (e.g. rights to health, nutrition and adequate standards of living). This position corresponds with the argument in favour of human environmental rights presented in Chapter 1.

Of course, regardless of the strength of the case for progressing foreign direct liability of TNCs, challenges are thrown up by the nature and level of culpability required to trigger opportunities for redress for injured parties. Peter Newell (2001: p915) rightly highlights as a major problem the need to identify strong causal relationships between particular pollutants and manifest health or ecological effects:

> *Common law traditions, in particular, establish high requirements for*
> *scientific evidence. The technical nature of the industrial processes and the*
> *fact that the burden of proof rests on the plaintiff to establish that an*

environmental standard has been violated, by recourse to independent and reliable technical and scientific data, excludes all but the most wealthy or technically competent.

It is significant that the foreign plaintiffs in the Thor Chemicals and Cape cases benefited from legal aid, as the courts ruled this necessary to realizing a just representation of their claims, but this assistance had to be argued for on the merits and is by no means an automatic entitlement in common law jurisdictions for foreign liability claimants. This leaves resource-poor potential plaintiffs dependent on funding support from sympathetic activist groups or on finding lawyers prepared to represent them on a *pro bono* or conditional fee basis.

Environmental NGOs have certainly picked up on transnational tort litigation as a promising, albeit still marginal, course of action for holding TNCs to account for causing ecological harm. Indeed, their more ambitious strategizing on corporate environmental liability has now broached the idea of TNC accountability for greenhouse gas emissions leading to global climate change. This has been made possible by advances in scientific understanding, including more sophisticated data analysis and modelling of environmental processes. For example, in 2004 Friends of the Earth International released a report claiming to set out the contribution of Exxon Mobil to climate change since its corporate origins as the Standard Oil Trust in 1882 (Friends of the Earth International, 2004). Collecting comprehensive data on carbon dioxide and methane emissions from the company's operations and burning of its products, the NGO ran these figures through a recognized climate model to estimate that Exxon Mobil's 20.3 billion tonnes of carbon dioxide emissions contributed in 2002 to 4.8–5.5 per cent of global carbon dioxide emissions. Almost a quarter of total emissions have come, significantly, since the Framework Convention for Climate Change was opened for signature in 1992; in other words, since the international community embraced the norm of preventing dangerous anthropogenic interference with the global climate system. Friends of the Earth recommend in the report that Exxon Mobil be held legally liable for harm posed by its activities to affected publics, suggesting financial reparations derived, for example, from damage and rising insurance costs associated with recent weather-related disasters.

There was a clear political motive for Friends of the Earth targeting a Texas-based corporate oil giant actively lobbying against international rule-making on climate change – one also closely aligned with the climate-sceptic stance of the Bush administration in the US. The feasibility of transnational tort litigation against it for greenhouse gas emissions is, at least at present, remote. To be sure, in an innovative legal move Friends of the Earth, Greenpeace and an American municipality are suing the US export credit agencies for their financial backing of fossil fuel projects overseas (see www.climatelawsuit.org), but the defendants in this case are charged with violating federal law by not conducting adequate environmental assessments. This demonstrates that accountability for carbon emissions is still understood, above all, in terms of state responsibility. While it has been argued that home states should accept responsibility for ecological harm caused in other countries by their corporate nationals (Sornarajah, 2001), this principle is not endorsed in international environmental treaties; for example, there are no explicit obligations within the climate change regime for advanced industrialized states to accept responsibility to compensate other states for harm caused by their greenhouse gas emissions (past or present). The need, then, is to see whether international standards of corporate environmental accountability emerging elsewhere might more directly protect the interests of affected publics.

International corporate accountability: the case of the UN Global Compact

International efforts to agree a common framework for the environmental regulation of TNCs go back to the 1980s, with the United Nations Centre on Transnational Corporations (UNCTC) initiating both a research project on the environmental impacts of FDI and also work on a draft code of corporate conduct. These moves need to be understood in the context of contemporaneous debates about the need to regulate TNCs, which up to that point had been dominated by developing countries arguing for the legitimacy of domestic policy constraints on inward investment (Tolentino, 1999). Being itself a product of this international political climate, UNCTC developed draft recommendations on the environmental responsibilities of TNCs, which distilled best practice corporate norms on environmental management, reporting and performance. The draft recommendations were ultimately proposed for consideration by states at the UN Conference on Environment and Development in Rio in 1992. However, the UNCTC proposals were rejected by conservative Western governments (notably the US and UK), aligned closely with the interests of major corporations. To all intents and purposes, this was the last gasp of what Hansen (2002) calls the era of regulatory activism. Since then international rule-making has focused on the protection and promotion of FDI, while the prospect of international environmental regulation of TNCs has receded.

Symptomatic of this ideological switch has been the shift to 'soft' (legally non-binding) rule-making on the rights and responsibilities of TNCs. The Organization for Economic Cooperation and Development (OECD) – representing countries that are the source of most FDI and home to the major TNCs – had first tried to seize the initiative in this area in 1976 with its Declaration on International Investment and Multinational Enterprises, which included Guidelines for Multinational Enterprises (Tolentino, 1999: pp178–9). Embracing the OECD mission of facilitating trade and investment liberalization, the Guidelines served in the 1980s and 1990s as an influential tool for deflecting continuing arguments from environment and development NGOs for stronger international legal norms governing the impacts of TNCs. The environmental recommendations within the Guidelines embodied process-based management standards. Only at the turn of the century, with the build-up of international environmental law and the unyielding opposition to neoliberalism by the global justice movement, did the OECD concede some ground on corporate environmental responsibility. Its revised Guidelines for Multinational Enterprises, issued in 2000, include an invitation to TNCs to apply high-quality standards for environmental and social reporting, as well as to seek to improve their corporate environmental performance (Organization for Economic Cooperation and Development, 2000).

If the OECD Guidelines indicate the substantial weight of opinion of political representatives from wealthy countries in favour of soft intergovernmental agreements on corporate responsibility, this position is informed, and reinforced, by transnational business networks. The most important of these is the World Business Council for Sustainable Development (WBCSD), formed in 1995 as a merger between an International Chamber of Commerce body and an environmental business network led by Swiss industrialist Stephan Schmidheiny. Since Maurice Strong, Secretary-General of the 1992 Rio Conference, invited Schmidheiny to serve as the principal business community contact for the UN meeting (Strong, 2000: p199), the mobilization by the latter of leading executives from major TNCs has proved influential in UN debates on corporate social responsibility. This is evident from the leading role of the WBCSD in the 2002 World Summit on Sustainable Development, where it lobbied forcefully to head off calls from Friends of the Earth International for a global convention on corporate accountability. Instead the WBCSD championed a voluntary notion of corporate responsibility in which businesses actively choose to go beyond regulatory compliance to improve their ecological and social performance (Holliday et al, 2002; Harmann et al, 2003).

Partnerships between businesses, governments and civil society actors have been the governance mechanism of choice for the WBCSD in its efforts to steer debates about the non-contractual responsibilities of TNCs, and over 200 such arrangements were flagged up by the UN at the Johannesburg meeting as instrumental in delivering sustainable development. UN receptiveness to voluntary business engagement as a vehicle for promoting corporate responsibility increased following the closure of the UNCTC in 1992. As an overarching framework to facilitate 'more inclusive' economic globalization, Secretary-General Kofi Annan first proposed the idea of a Global Compact at the 1999 World Economic Forum in Davos. Its chief architects, serving at the Secretary-General's office, were Roger Kell, a senior UN bureaucrat with expertise in trade and development issues, and John Ruggie, a professor from the Kennedy School of Government, Harvard University (Bendell, 2004: pp3–4). The Global Compact revived the notion of 'network solutions' to international governance problems, first articulated within the UN by Maurice Strong in the 1970s as he guided the organization's response to environmental problems. Ruggie combined this idea with his assessment that market liberalism needs to be 're-embedded' in universal principles pertaining to human rights, labour and the environment. Thus, the Global Compact represents a 'social learning network' for inducing corporate responsibility: it provides a loosely structured global forum in which the private sector works directly with the UN, in partnership with civil society stakeholders, to identify and promote good corporate practices (Ruggie, 2002; Kell, 2003).

As a voluntary initiative, the Global Compact eschews rule-making in favour of value-based commitments from companies. The universal principles endorsed in the Compact are derived from the Universal Declaration of Human Rights, the International Labour Organization's Declaration on Fundamental Principles and Rights at Work, and the Rio Declaration on Environment and Development (see www.unglobalcompact.org). The three environment principles are that businesses should:

- support a precautionary approach to environmental challenges (Principle 7);
- undertake initiatives to promote greater environmental responsibility (Principle 8); and
- encourage the development and diffusion of environmentally friendly technologies (Principle 9).

In its short commentary on Principles 7–9, the Global Compact Office notes their presence in Chapter 30 of Agenda 21 – the soft law programme of action for sustainable development agreed at the Rio Conference. Strong input from Schmidheiny's Business Council for Sustainable Development shaped the emphasis in this chapter on cleaner production and responsible entrepreneurship motivated by enlightened self-interest. In harmony with this, the Global Compact Office suggests that the environment principles direct businesses to areas such as research, innovation, cooperation, education and self-regulation.

At the heart of the Global Compact process is, Ruggie (2002: p34) argues, a 'bargain' – 'that the UN provides a degree of legitimacy and helps to solve co-ordination problems, while the companies and other social actors provide the capacity to produce the desired changes'. For any company, the price of entry to the process is a letter of commitment from its chief executive officer indicating a high-level commitment to the Global Compact principles, and then regular public communication of the progress of the enterprise in adhering to these principles. That over a thousand companies had signed up by 2004 – including such well-known TNCs as Aventis, BASF, BP, Daimler

Chrysler, Nike, Novantis, Rio Tinto, Shell and Unilever – indicates that many major corporations perceive informational and reputational benefits from participating in the Global Compact. Corporate engagement is sustained through a web-based Learning Forum, regular multi-stakeholder policy dialogues (on topics such as conflict zones, least developed countries, HIV/AIDS, supply chain management and sustainable production/consumption) and the development of regional Global Compact networks. It is noteworthy that, unlike other global corporate responsibility initiatives, the Global Compact has achieved momentum in the global South (Kell, 2003: p45): over half of the participating companies are from developing countries.

Nevertheless, concerns have been raised about the much-vaunted inclusiveness of the Compact process. Even with the significant involvement of Southern companies, the strategic Compact dialogues have, it is claimed, been dominated by Northern-based TNCs and other companies that have imported uncritical attitudes on FDI as well as the apolitical technical take on corporate environmentalism (eco-efficiency) popularized by the WBCSD (Bendell, 2004: pp13–16). More problematic for the Global Compact has been its strained relations with civil society actors sceptical of its close relationship with big business. The US-based NGO Corpwatch, the secretariat of a global network of human rights, environment and development groups known as the Alliance for a Corporate-Free UN, has issued a number of articles and reports highly critical of the Global Compact, provoking a grating exchange of views with the Compact Office. One of Corpwatch's central criticisms is that the civil society stakeholders in the Global Compact have not played an important role, despite claims otherwise by Compact officials (Corpwatch, 2002; see also Utting, 2002). The Compact Office points to an Advisory Council containing such prominent transnational NGOs as Amnesty International and Oxfam International. But criticisms have also come from Advisory Council members (including Amnesty and Oxfam), who have expressed disquiet that the Global Compact has not engaged sufficiently with local and regional NGOs from Southern countries (Hobbs et al, 2003).

Another criticism from NGOs both outside and inside the Compact process is that there has been inadequate transparency and rigour in its monitoring of corporate participants. Corpwatch has publicized what it charges to be blatant violations of Compact principles by leading TNC partners: in the environmental domain alone (Principles 7–8), this has included allegations against Aventis (for contaminating US food supplies with genetically modified corn seeds), Bayer (for not taking due care over sales of its pesticides in Brazil) and Unilever (for the illegal dumping of toxic waste by its Indian subsidiary). In reply, the Global Compact Office has repeatedly stressed that it neither regulates nor monitors a company's submissions and initiatives (Kell, 2003: p38). Yet prominent NGOs on the Compact's Advisory Council have noted with concern that there are no criteria or mechanisms for dealing with cases where companies are alleged to have breached Global Compact principles

(Hobbs et al, 2003; Bendell, 2004: p9). Discussions within the Advisory Council about the need for a complaint mechanism have recently made some headway with the Global Compact Office, and it has declared as a new strategic priority an increase in transparency and accountability in the Compact-related activities of corporate participants.

A related source of anxiety for critical NGOs, and some UN staff elsewhere in the organization, has centred on the internal accountability of the Global Compact within the UN system. As a strategic initiative of the Secretary-General's Office in New York, the Global Compact is unusual within the UN bureaucracy in that it is not directly controlled by an intergovernmental board. To be sure, it is required to coordinate Compact work with five core UN agencies (International Labour Organization, Office of the High Commissioner for Human Rights, UN Development Programme, UN Environment Programme and the UN Industrial Development Organization), but in 2004 none of these had mandates from their governing bodies to work proactively with the Compact (Bendell, 2004: pp21–3). The Compact Office has therefore been allowed significant organizational autonomy, which has facilitated an impressive range of collaborative activities around the world. However, as expressed most publicly within the UN by senior staff at its Geneva-based Research Institute for Social Development (Utting, 2002; Zammit, 2003), the Global Compact operates more or less cut free from established UN lines of accountability and it therefore lacks the legitimacy derived from representative state-based deliberation and decisions.

Transnational NGOs on the Global Compact Advisory Council have pressed the Compact office to demonstrate unequivocal support for initiatives underway elsewhere in the UN to strengthen private-sector accountability for universal principles and values (Hobbs et al, 2002). Of key relevance here are the UN Norms on the Responsibilities of Transnational Corporations and Other Business Enterprises with Regard to Human Rights, adopted in August 2003 by the UN Sub-Commission on the Promotion and Protection of Human Rights following a four-year period of consultation around the world with governments, businesses, NGOs and unions. Interestingly, these include the following explicit obligations with regard to environmental protection:

> *14. Transnational corporations and other business enterprises shall carry out their activities in accordance with national laws, regulations, administrative practices and policies relating to the preservation of the environment of the countries in which they operate, as well as in accordance with relevant international agreements, principles, objectives, responsibilities and standards with regard to the environment as well as human rights, public health and safety, bioethics and the precautionary principle, and shall generally conduct their activities in a manner contributing to the wider goals of sustainable development.*

The commentary to these obligations is more prescriptive and detailed than for the Global Compact's environment principles, as well as, in contrast, expressly recognizing a universal right to a clean and healthy environment (UN Sub-Commission on the Promotion and Protection of Human Rights, 2003: p12). While these are not binding legal obligations, they have been integrated more fully than the Global Compact principles into UN intergovernmental deliberations. In April 2004 the UN Commission on Human Rights adopted by consensus a request from twelve states (headed by the UK) to require the Office of the High Commissioner for Human Rights to report on the scope and legal status of existing institutions and standards relating to the human rights responsibility of TNCs and related businesses, having regard, *inter alia*, to the norms developed by its Sub-Commission. Unless the Global Compact Office registers more fully these political moves within the UN, it risks being sidelined in international norm development on corporate social and ecological responsibility.

Conclusion

In this chapter I have surveyed a number of emerging mechanisms by which TNCs are being obliged to answer for and justify the environmental impacts of their operations. *Corporate environmentalism* represents the clearest example of TNCs positively embracing ecological performance goals and, for all the variety of frameworks applied, it has led to significant transnational standardization of environmental practices within some major companies and industrial sectors. The contribution of this harmonization to ecological harm prevention and mitigation obviously merits systematic empirical investigation. Such research is not made easy by self-regulating structures not delivering full environmental performance and compliance information (e.g. ISO 14001), or not facilitating independent monitoring and verification (e.g. GRI). Commonalities in the voluntary scope and rapid uptake of business environmentalism support the thesis that social pressures are the key drivers of firms making substantive and/or symbolic commitments to improve their ecological footprint. While some of these pressures are registered through conventional contract-based business relationships (e.g. from consumers, unions, insurers), leading TNCs have also had to respond to environmental values expressed by, or on behalf of, third-party constituencies (e.g. from local communities affected by their operations, environmental NGOs). Normally articulated in political rather than market terms, the ecological claims coming from this latter group have exposed the environmental accountability shortfall of corporate voluntarism, notably the lack of means for effective redress by affected publics.

Civil regulation, as discussed above, entails sustained campaigns undertaken by civil society groups as a way of urging TNCs and related businesses to align themselves with new standards of business behaviour. While corporate environmentalism promises no more than fuller public answerability for the ecological performance of TNCs, which is a necessary condition for enhanced accountability to affected communities, civil regulation seeks to add a form of coercive power to ensure that public environmental interests cannot be easily dismissed. I briefly reviewed a number of civil regulation instruments – direct action, investor action, stewardship regimes and multi-stakeholder partnerships – commenting on their respective contributions to progressing corporate accountability for environmental impacts. In the absence of effective state-based rules, some form of civil redress is essential in order to empower environmental constituencies otherwise without leverage on the businesses damaging their well-being. What civil regulation can achieve is to realize these environmental concerns in a language resonant with corporations; that is, by directly influencing market conditions. If some of these actions can be seen as positive incentives (e.g. new sources of capital from ethical investment funds, consumer demand for green products), they ultimately rely on the capacity to impose sanctions against laggard corporations (e.g. consumer boycotts, reputational shaming). Yet public accountability gaps in civil regulation occur as a result of Northern-based NGOs possessing a greater power to disrupt corporate activities than civil society organizations from poorer countries.

Given the uncertain, unpredictable coverage of civil regulation with regard to foreign publics adversely affected by the activities of TNCs, *foreign direct liability* has been flagged up as potentially a more secure guarantor of their environmental interests. This accountability mechanism apportions legal responsibility to parent companies for physical harm caused by the conduct of their branches or subsidiaries outside the territory of the home state (country of legal incorporation of the TNC). Like civil regulation, its emergence is explained in part by the dearth of public international law governing the environmental impacts of TNCs. However, rather than generate standards for corporate behaviour outside existing rules, it invokes private-law remedies to empower affected parties: more precisely, it applies tort liability across borders to seek redress for significant harm. By definition, tort liability addresses wrongdoing outside contractual business relationships, thus unsettling the market liberal model of the firm where corporations have no legal responsibility for third-party social and environmental costs. In my discussion above, though, I noted that foreign direct liability is still very much of minor importance in advancing the environmental accountability of TNCs, being contingent on small windows of legal opportunity and adequate support being available for resource-poor plaintiffs.

As mechanisms of accountability, corporate environmentalism, civil regulation and foreign direct liability are, in their different ways, exposing TNCs to the ecological and social consequences of their decisions. They are appealing to norms which, by raising awareness about new standards for appropriate behaviour by businesses, are at least assisting those groups adversely affected by

TNC activities to recognize themselves as publics – as jointly experiencing threats to their well-being. Of course, a central element of the (Deweyan) notion of publics employed in this book is that affected parties are able themselves to exercise collective judgment about how the ill-effects they face should be addressed. I have raised concerns about how each of the three accountability forms has difficulties accommodating fully the needs of environmental publics for answerability and redress from TNCs.

Ultimately, systematic treatment of the negative ecological impacts of TNCs requires effective *national and international regulation*. The rise of corporate environmentalism across borders followed the failed attempts of the UNCTC to place environmental regulation on the agenda of the international community (notably at the UN Conference on Environment and Development in 1992). Since that time the neoliberal fixation with investment liberalization has relegated calls for binding environmental standards on FDI to the corporate accountability campaigns of environment and development NGOs. Civil regulation and foreign direct liability are responses to the growing power of TNCs not being matched by public responsibilities to affected communities in their host countries or beyond (e.g. as with their greenhouse gas emissions). There are signs, though, that even senior executives from TNCs are recognizing the risk of a popular backlash against FDI as stoked up by global anti-capitalist activists and networks. A desire for investment stability and security coming from the major Northern-hemisphere sources of FDI is therefore motivating the recent willingness of OECD states to concede that their corporate nationals may legitimately be subject to public-interest regulation in other countries. This is evident from the inclusion of a 'right to regulate' in various international investment and trade agreements (UNCTAD, 2003: pp145–7). In other words, the global ideological hold of the contractual model of corporate accountability is less secure now than in the past two decades.

The empowerment of affected publics is at the crux of an ecologically and socially just constitution of TNC accountability. In soft international codes of corporate responsibility, it is typical now to encounter provisions obliging companies to engage in adequate consultation with communities directly affected by their environmental policies and practices (e.g. Organization for Economic Cooperation and Development, 2000: p23). Yet by itself, this is insufficient to establish legal rights to enable individuals and communities impacted by corporate activities to protect their environmental well-being. Beyond voluntary codes, civil regulation and transnational tort claims, there is a need to enshrine minimum standards of corporate accountability to these publics. Suggested modalities for achieving this within an international treaty framework include rights of affected communities to consultation and judicial review over corporate decisions (Dine, 2000: pp176–82) and criminal sanctions for corporate environmental harm (Wells, 2001: pp140–5). Much remains to be done to realize these new accountability rights; more still to give them political and policy currency across the world.

Conclusion

In a world of greatly intensified connections across borders, featuring far-reaching transformations in social and ecological relations, it is no longer credible to pretend that the effects of our behaviour take place only locally or regionally. It also becomes less tenable, therefore, to limit our moral horizon to proximate individuals and groups impacted by our actions: scientific understanding is making clearer the ways in which many local actions have transboundary or global impacts, while modern telecommunications technologies can convey to us in real time scenes of human distress and ecological destruction taking place on the other side of the planet.

The central normative argument of this book is that actors causing significant environmental harm should be answerable to injured parties, whatever the nationality or residence of the victims. Moral obligations are established here on the basis of duties on those with decision-making authority to protect vital ecological conditions of life and to consider fairly the perspectives of affected parties. As set out in Chapter 1, I claim that three moral principles legitimize the political claims of these publics – harm prevention, democratic inclusion and impartiality. These are all articulated in established liberal democratic notions of democratic accountability, but are conventionally restricted in their application to territorial spaces of state sovereignty, which limits the extension of environmental accountability norms across borders. Where ecological damage is the result of transnational relationships of control, influence or authority, moral accountability nevertheless is owed directly to affected parties: its political expression depends on these publics acknowledging a common experience of harm and seeking answerability and redress from culpable actors.

Successive chapters of this study have explored the emergence of public accountability norms directed at sources of transboundary or global environmental harm: what is their nature and scope? In the first place, this entailed looking at the self-styled champions of the 'new accountability' – activist groups, networks and social movements. Chapter 2 considered the organizational forms and accountability demands animating these civil society actors, who invest substantial political capital in publicizing environmental abuses of authority and demanding justice for injuries suffered by vulnerable publics. A contrast was evident between, on the one hand, the efforts of environmental advocacy groups and networks to secure redress for *particular* instances of ecological damage and, on the other, the radical accountability challenges issuing from the anti-capitalist or global justice movement, targeting *systemic* processes of environmental harm production. While the reformist demands of the former have more currency in transnational civil society campaigning, the latter activists have opened space for essential questioning about the reasons for the unremitting incidence of many major pathways of environmental harm.

The next two chapters of the book moved to distinctive domains of international rule-making in order to gauge the adoption of environmental accountability obligations to affected publics. International environmental law is the obvious arena in which to look for such public entitlements. In Chapter 3 I observed that the progressive institutionalization of harm prevention norms in multilateral environmental treaties serves a critical role in protecting public interests but, by being realized in terms of sovereign state responsibilities, duties to prevent or mitigate harm usually preclude direct participation rights for affected individuals and groups. However, non-discriminatory opportunities for public access have become established in several international conventions on the environment, and are already being treated as legal precedents. Of course, environmental accountability issues arise in other areas of international rule-making: Chapter 4 focused on the crucial position of the World Trade Organization (WTO), examining the scope for public answerability and redress concerning the extra-territorial ecological impacts of global trade policy. There has been pressure both from transnational advocacy groups and some WTO member states to realign world trade rule-making expressly to respect norms embracing environmental protection and civil society accountability. The prospects for this are made possible, at least in principle, by a legal overlap in fairness standards between the trade and environmental governance regimes. In practice these prospects rest on the more challenging political task of convincing a majority of WTO member states that ecological protection norms are reconcilable with their economic development priorities.

Chapters 5 and 6 addressed the direct responsibility of economic actors for transboundary ecological harm. For reasons outlined in Chapter 5, private law obligations have become the favoured modality for apportioning financial responsibility when environmental damage has taken place. Above all, this has featured the international harmonization of civil liability rules, as applied to economic activities considered potentially hazardous in terms of their impacts. Civil liability standards realize an important accountability function and are spreading to cover new areas of transboundary environmental risk. I contended that the accountability gains being made here must be set against the constraints placed on civil liability by both its reliance on market-based entitlements and its restriction to damage occurring within national jurisdictions. As observed in the last chapter, civil liability claims are being made against major corporations for environmental harm in countries hosting their foreign direct investment. Parent company liability actions accompany various forms of civil society pressure on corporate behaviour, provoked by the absence of internationally binding rules of social and ecological responsibility on transnational enterprises. Chapter 6 surveyed in addition the voluntary subscription to environmental performance standards by corporations and a high-profile international initiative to facilitate such self-regulation. There are cogent arguments for encouraging this type of business engagement: I concluded, though, that it fails to displace an underlying contractual framework of corporate accountability – one that is unwilling to concede meaningful legitimacy or rights to affected publics.

It has not been my intention in this work to explain the evolution of new norms of public accountability for environmental harm: that would have required an in-depth, historical analysis of the subject matter of each chapter. Nevertheless, a recurrent thesis has emerged in accounting for the uptake of these norms – that, other things being equal, a necessary condition for their effective diffusion in global civil society and legal institutionalization is that they 'fit' with existing norms in their area of application (Finnemore and Sikkink, 1998; Bernstein, 2001). These path dependencies are themselves skewed by underlying political or economic opportunity structures. Thus, it was acknowledged in Chapter 2 that environmental groups have found that environmental accountability claims in transnational campaigns achieve more public salience when they correspond with widely shared values about harm prevention and fair treatment. This reflects a communicative realm in which persuasive appeals to the moral sentiments of large numbers of people are critical for success. Within institutional domains of action, where structures of power entrench core interests, public accountability norms advance or not in so far as they can adapt to these canonical ideas; notably, sovereign state norms (Chapter 3), trade liberalization principles (Chapter 4), property-based liability rules (Chapter 5) and contractual forms of corporate governance (Chapter 6). The relatively slow progress of non-territorial environmental accountability in each of these areas demonstrates how it runs against the grain of their foundational values.

That there has been the emergence of new accountability norms attests to the force of environmentalist claims as a challenge to prevailing political and economic institutions. For transnational capitalist elites in particular, the threat to the legitimacy of neoliberalism has been perceived as serious enough as to warrant some form of accommodation or co-option. Bernstein (2001) explains the development of 'liberal environmentalism' as such a political compromise, trying to render at least some ecological protection goals compatible with a free-market economic orthodoxy. More crucially here, he also suggests that broadening public accountability demands – fuelled by the spread of liberal democratic and human rights norms – could potentially destabilize this compromise (2001: p240). I agree: new accountability claims have found sympathetic symbolic and institutional contexts even in advanced capitalist states, highlighting the contested, often contradictory, way in which transnational environmental obligations are expressed.

According to Scheffler (2001: pp32–47), this is part and parcel of a wider unsettling of what liberal democracies have long taken to be the key 'normative responsibilities' of their citizens (their moral duties, that is, as individual agents). The ordinary conception of responsibility, rooted in Western countries, is portrayed as restrictive – prioritizing, for moral obligations, acts over emissions, near effects over far effects, and individual effects over group effects. What processes of globalization shake up is this simple moral world of small-scale interactions among individuals; no more so of course than for the transboundary and global environmental effects arising from unprecedented human modifications of the biosphere. The complex distribution of (often unintended) ecological impacts in space–time – with harmful consequences for individuals and communities – is merely one front of activity, Scheffler maintains (2001: p40), where the restrictive conception of responsibility is found to be wanting. But, he adds, the idea of transnational or global lines of responsibility, where causal connections may be difficult to discern, seems over-ambitious in response. I hope this book has shown that this challenge is not insurmountable. In conclusion I want, therefore, to outline some conditions that I take to be necessary for expanding our boundaries of moral and legal accountability for environmental harm.

Conditions for realizing transnational and global publics

In his prescient study, *The public and its problems* (first published in 1927), John Dewey had already anticipated Scheffler's anxiety about whether a more expansive conception of responsibility is plausible in a world of particularist loyalties. The global indirect consequences of what Dewey terms the 'machine age' are, he maintains, so expanded, multiplied and intensified that the resultant publics cannot identify and distinguish themselves – they seem too diffused and scattered in composition to articulate common interests (Dewey, 1954: pp126–31). In these circumstances, which hold even more in our twenty-first-century world, conditions allowing these publics both to map trajectories of harm and identify responsible agents are pivotal:

> *An inchoate public is capable of organization only when indirect consequences are perceived, and when it is possible to project agencies which order their occurrence. At present, many consequences are felt rather than perceived, they are suffered, but they cannot be said to be known,*

for they are not, by those who experience them, referred to their origins
(1954: p131).

From the preceding discussion in this book, it is possible, I contend, to pull out some key pointers on conditions conducive to the formation of democratically organized transnational and global publics. These pointers are schematic rather than exhaustive, but are presented as a contribution to an open discourse in which public themselves are the foremost interpreters of their political interests.

1   A public is constituted by the *collective exercise of practical judgment* concerning the harmful effects of material transactions. As set out in Chapter 1, this entails inclusive deliberation about pathways of harm and their distributive consequences. In so far as communication among victims fairly allows the expression of individual as well as shared grievances that would meet with the approval of all affected, the conclusions of the public have greater democratic legitimacy. In other words, the moral principle of equal respect for all that justifies taking into account the interests of affected publics in the first place by those with decision-making authority, also applies to the internal constitution of the publics themselves. Evidence from within of impaired communication or unequal communication opportunities for prospective members of an affected public would, if it were successfully organized, weaken the claim of its spokespersons to present a genuine community of interests.

2   In the exercise of collective judgment over the negative ecological consequences of human activities, individuals and groups potentially perceiving themselves as a public are best served by the *availability of multiple environmental valuation methods*. Several chapters above (notably Chapters 4, 5 and 6) have noted how environmental accountability claims issuing from civil society actors have clashed with sources of authority receptive only to market-based environmental evaluation. Ecological harms not susceptible to monetary quantification or not commensurate with marginal utility principles of resource allocation suggest the need to allow open-ended valuation methods for public communication on impacts and responsibilities. Martin O'Connor (2002: p42) captures well the condition of deliberation needed here when he refers to valuation simply as 'people's notion of what matters for the future, and why'. A public inquiring effectively into ecological harms typically deals with complex distributional issues (e.g. impacts on future generations) not reducible to a single metric of valuation.

3   Reliable information about the cross-border consequences of human activities is a precondition of the constitution of effective transnational and global publics. To recap from the discussion of sustainability science and adaptive management in the Introduction to this book, this calls for the

integration of plural methodologies and understandings in the investigation of the multi-scale effects of socio-ecological changes. Dewey reproaches the glorification of 'pure' science cut off from human concerns as a 'shirking of responsibility' (1954: p175). Both sustainability science and adaptive management promote the involvement of affected publics – and other communities – in social learning about specific ecological problems, Of course, there are frequently widely divergent assessments of the environmental consequences of human actions, particularly when these effects spin out widely through space–time. The development of mutual understanding in these circumstances is facilitated by open, inclusive discourse oriented to ecological problem-solving (see Norton, 2003).

4   The formation of transnational and global publics is facilitated by the *moral and legal protection of their vital interest in secure ecological conditions of existence.* Much of this book has been preoccupied with showing how territorial norms of environmental accountability are often ill-suited to acknowledging the collective concerns of publics receiving harm as a result of industrial activities or decisions taking place in other countries. Affected parties typically rely on obligations (if they exist) owed to them as national citizens as a result of international environmental agreements entered into by their home states. While this type of indirect consideration of their ecological interests obviously serves a crucial role, cosmopolitan (non-territorial) entitlements to protection are also needed. Human rights represent a clear case of legitimate standards for empowering the claims of persons, regardless of their nationality, to have their vital ecological conditions of existence safeguarded. Alongside existing human rights, there are uncertainties about the content and application of universal environmental entitlements: nevertheless, I argued in Chapters 1 and 3 that environmental rights are acquiring force in international law. They provide a growing source of direct entitlements for individuals and groups with which to project – as publics – overriding ecological interests.

5   Transnational and global publics are encouraged to locate and identify themselves through the *exercise of freedoms of association and communication.* I gave an indication in Chapter 2 of the rich variety of civil society organizations engaged in raising environmental accountability claims against states and private actors. Rights to association, expression and assembly – as enshrined in international human rights law and also many national constitutions – are the foundation of independent civic action oriented to public interest goals. Yet, as Fries (2003: p237) notes, there is the lack of a legal institutional framework for supporting civil society organizations to operate across national borders. These organizations are enabled or constrained by the national laws of the countries where they are legally constituted, though the growth of transnational environmental activism reported in Chapter 2 indicates the rise in favourable national contexts for popular mobilization over ecological issues (notably in the

new democracies of central and eastern Europe). Nongovernmental organizations and networks are efficient vehicles for relaying environmental concerns, but whether their claims to represent affected publics are legitimate rests both on the validity of their observations about relevant ecological damage and the credibility of their political arguments on behalf of these publics.

6   The organization of environmental publics for transboundary and global effects would be encouraged by *formal opportunities for public consultation and deliberation in political and administrative decision-making at multiple levels*. As well as the strengthening of existing environmental institutions (e.g. United Nations Environment Programme – UNEP), this is likely to require the creation of new global governance structures. Numerous suggestions have been put forward to foster institutional spaces whereby affected publics and civil society organizations can engage more directly with political authorities over global issues like environmental protection. These range from a reformed UN General Assembly, new regional parliamentary bodies and the staging of general referenda (Held, 2004: pp94–116) to, more modestly, the idea of global public policy partnerships, implementation councils (to support major multilateral agreements) and high-level policy entrepreneurs (Kaul and Le Goulven, 2003). There is the potential in all of these to facilitate the application of new accountability norms.

7   *Increased transparency and direct civil society access to key multilateral economic organizations* (International Monetary Fund, World Bank, WTO) is necessary to enable those negatively affected by the environmental impacts of their policies to hold them to account. Chapter 4 laid out the incremental institutional response of the WTO to recent accountability demands from environmental advocacy groups and networks. Some of the modest procedural innovations within the WTO have been mirrored in the International Monetary Fund and World Bank, with arguably the greatest reform in the Bank (Georgieva, 2002). Whatever their respective levels of environmental accountability, there is still ample scope for all three organizations further to develop mechanisms for civil society answerability. This may well also serve to enhance their democratic legitimacy.

8   As suggested by the Conclusion to Chapter 4, though, *institutionalizing direct public accountability in multilateral economic organizations must, in order to be politically feasible, supplement rather than displace the internal dynamics of state-based accountability*. Keohane (2003: pp153–4) warns that, in so far as civil society groupings are able to set and amend policy agendas, states may lose interest in these organizations, abandoning their commitment to rule-based multilateralism to revert to unrestrained power-based geopolitics. In other words, greater transparency and civil society access to international economic organizations rely on sufficient support from

influential states. The propensity of powerful democratic states to subscribe to such policy reforms might be heightened as a result of pressure from ecologically aware domestic publics and civil society organizations. What is highlighted here is a need to acknowledge the interplay within multilateral bodies of internal accountability to states and external accountability to affected publics and their civil society representatives.

9   Finally, an intellectual journey by affected parties to uncover common ecological and social interests is unlikely to be enough to generate cross-border public identities. Transnational and global publics are also sustained by, and in turn nurture, *cosmopolitan emotions among both environmental victims and background populations.* Cosmopolitan solidarities build on existing emotional dispositions to have regard for the well-being of others – dispositions prevalent in all societies but often restricted to local networks of loyalty and empathy. The development of cosmopolitan emotions is encouraged when actors causing transboundary environmental harm trigger such affective responses as shame, sorrow and compassion (Linklater, 2005). Even if those responsible for injuring others or the physical environment fail to demonstrate guilt or regret for their actions, wider emotional sentiments may work against them. Indeed, the absence on their part of any express moral indebtedness to affected parties may well energize these victims to organize themselves politically as publics. It certainly motivates the activities of advocacy groups in calling attention to accountability failings.

A new accountability in an unsafe world

There is now sufficient evidence – from global civil society and international environmental law – to assert that a distinctive set of obligations has emerged oriented to advancing public accountability for cross-border ecological harm. I have termed these obligations a 'new accountability' in order to capture their embrace of non-territorial modes of environmental responsibility, whereby culpable state and private actors are held directly answerable to affected publics. The legal institutionalization of new accountability norms remains some way behind their widespread articulation by civil society advocacy groups and networks, yet I would claim that they nevertheless have some significant currency in several domains of international rule-making. What are the prospects, though, for these nascent accountability norms in an unruly world?

In its last comprehensive appraisal of the state of the global environment, UNEP projects four possible futures over the next 30 years (United Nations Environment Programme, 2002: pp319–400). The most familiar to us, on the basis of the established hold of neoliberalism on leading industrialized states and international economic organizations, is the *Markets First* scenario, which anticipates economic liberalization continuing as the main driver of development paths around the world. Deference by states to market forces acknowledges their innate capacity for technological innovation and wealth creation, but not their failure to register, let alone address, the new risks and inequalities generated. With national economic interests harnessed to unimpeded market liberalization, systems of ecological governance are likely to remain poorly developed, for collective policy measures will be reactive rather then proactive. The environmental accountability gains of this market fundamentalist trajectory are marginal and indirect, at best entailing, where feasible, the (re)allocation of property rights to avoid external environmental costs.

An alternative *Policy First* scenario reflects the possible creation of an international political consensus that seeks to strengthen governance institutions at all scales in order to address ecological and social goals. This planetary future is broadly social democratic – support for continuing economic growth runs alongside policies to eradicate poverty and reverse environmental degradation across the globe. More attention is afforded to issues of responsibility for ecological harm than in the Markets First scenario, but at the reformist end of accountability politics. For example, trade and industry actors are encouraged to commit to improved ecological performance through self-regulatory measures. And citizens are treated as largely passive: they rely on (inter)governmental action to correct environmental injuries rather than organize themselves to express their collective interests.

Only what UNEP calls the *Sustainability First* scenario implies a deep-seated institutionalization of environmental accountability at the heart of centres of governmental and private authority. Concerted multilateral rule-making for accountability ensures that state and corporate actors are everywhere answerable for the ecological and social impacts of their decisions. This regulation, integrated across policy sectors as well as political borders, is systematically informed by the deliberations of local and transnational publics. It anticipates the ascription of rights protection for all planetary citizens to vital ecological conditions of existence, alongside other critical sustainability entitlements (e.g. economic security, social welfare provision). Indeed, the Sustainability First scenario would see the realization of more or less all the conditions for public empowerment listed above in this Conclusion. In this way local and regional experiences of environmental harm will feed straight into democratically constituted forms of governance.

However, the Sustainability First scenario demands a level of international cooperation and civil society engagement at odds with the prevailing geopolitical climate – one that approximates the *Security First* scenario in the UNEP appraisal. Recent geopolitical trends have signalled a worrying move away from multilateral rule-making and enforcement. In the Security First future, systemic economic inequality, driven by neoliberal globalization, feeds extremist political ideologies and transnational criminal networks. Yet the focus of Western democracies is more on defending their positions in the upper hierarchy of the international order than with addressing their complicity in the global production of ecological and social harm. Above all, the 'war against terrorism' initiated at the start of this century by the neoconservative Bush administration is the crucible from which the Security First scenario may assume global precedence. It is a geopolitical venture that has revived the Cold War notion of security through military strength and control of strategic resources, although one country, the United States, is internationally dominant. And, as evident from American opposition to multilateral rule-making in such areas as biological weapons monitoring, global climate change and international criminal justice, accountability to transnational and planetary publics is rejected as a constraint on the exercise of state power.

Of course, the rise to global pre-eminence of a Security First agenda is by no means inevitable: there remains political space to realize an alternative future. An important ideological counterweight to unilateralist state security policy has been generated by the Progressive Governance Network of countries, including Brazil, Canada, Chile, the Czech Republic, Hungary, New Zealand, Poland and South Africa. The Progressive Governance coalition acknowledges the gravity of current threats to global security (e.g. terrorism, weapons proliferation), but favours a multilateral response in accordance with universal norms of international law. Its organizing paradigm for achieving enduring peace encompasses global poverty reduction, the deepening of democratic governance and environmental protection (Solana, 2003). In contrast to Security First thinking, breaching state sovereignty to respond to grave threats must not deviate, it is claimed, from the principles of the United Nations Charter. And against the charge of United Nations impotence, it is argued that there is scope, within the terms of the Charter, legitimately to intervene with force in countries when human rights are jeopardized. For states have a 'responsibility to protect' which can apply across borders to non-domestic publics.

An environmental precedent in support of this stance is arguably the military intervention taken in August 2000 by NATO troops, under a United Nations mandate (United Nations Security Council 1999), to shut down a heavily polluting lead smelter (under Serb control) in the Kosovan city of Mitrovice. This example is a provocative one, as the generation of grave environmental damage would seem to fall outside the narrow set of conditions in which incursions into another state are accepted to be legally justifiable in international affairs. Furthermore, the controversial grounds of NATO's wider humanitarian intervention in Kosovo, spearheaded as it was by six months of air strikes in 1999, would seem to make the Mitrovice incident even more difficult to condone. And there is also the possible charge of environmental double standards, given the uncertainties remaining about the long-term effects of depleted uranium fragments and dust caused by weapons fired from

NATO aircraft in the conflict (United Nations Environment Programme, 2001).

However, I want to maintain that accepting a progressive security agenda, in which the responsibility to protect is a core element, pulls severe environmental abuses into the field of moral vision. If we accept, as argued in the Introduction to this book, that clean, healthy and stable ecological conditions of existence are part of the vital interests of all persons, any security strategy committed to the protection of universal human rights would need to acknowledge a central role for environmental security. Needless to say, military intervention for ecological protection purposes would be truly exceptional and subject to highly demanding thresholds of action (e.g. serious levels of harm suffered, the absence of democratic governance, the unavailability of non-military options for action). Why the Mitrovice intervention is noteworthy is that it demonstrated, according to the UN Interim Administration Mission in Kosovo, a measured, proportionate response (no casualties ensued) to the blatant disregard for the health of local publics by an authoritarian, incompetent city administration (Steele, 2000). The threat or use of force across borders to prevent severe, systematic environmental damage may well become more likely in a world where the proliferation of ever-more destructive weaponry threatens the conditions of life of potentially untold victims. It is the task of advocates of new accountability norms to exhaust all others means of public answerability and redress prior to that step and, should it prove to be unavoidable, to strive to ensure that such action adheres to the rules of international law.

References

Abaza H (2002) Personal communication: Executive Secretary, Secretariat of the United Nations Convention on Biological Diversity, Geneva, 12 November.

Agius E, S Busuttil, T-C Kim and K Yazaki (eds) (1998) *Future generations and international law*, Earthscan, London.

Albin C (2001) *Justice and fairness in international negotiation*, Cambridge University Press, Cambridge.

Amnesty International (2004) *The UN human rights norms for business: towards legal accountability*, Amnesty International, London. Accessed at: http://web. amnesty.org/aidoc/aidoc_pdf.nsf/Index/IOR420022004ENGLISH/$File/ IOR4200204.pdf.

Andersen S O and K Madhava Sarma (2002) *Protecting the ozone layer: the United Nations history*, Earthscan, London.

Anheier H, M Glasius and M Kaldor (eds) (2001) *Global civil society 2001*, Oxford University Press, Oxford.

Anheier H and N Themudo (2002) 'Organisational forms of global civil society: implications of going global', in M Glasius et al (eds), pp191–216.

Archer S B and S T Piper (2003) 'Voluntary governance or a contradiction in terms? Are voluntary codes accountable and transparent governance tools?' in R A Shah et al (eds), pp142–65.

Arsanjani M H and W M Reisman (1998) 'The quest for an international liability regime for the protection of the global commons' in K C Wellens (ed) *International law: theory and practice: essays in honour of Eric Suy*, Martinus Nijhoff, The Hague, pp469–92.

Arts B (1998) *The political influence of global NGOs: case studies on the climate and biodiversity conventions*, International Books, Utrecht.

Arts B and S Mack (2003) 'Environmental NGOs and the Biosafety Protocol: a case study of political influence', *European Environment*, Vol 13, No 1, pp19–33.

Barry B (1995) *Justice as impartiality*, Clarendon Press, Oxford.

Barry B (1999) 'Sustainability and intergenerational justice' in A Dobson (ed), pp93–117.

Barry J (1999) *Rethinking green politics*, Sage, London.

Beck U (1992) *Risk society: towards a new modernity*, Polity Press, Cambridge.

Beck U (1999) *World risk society*, Polity Press, Cambridge.

Beitz C (2001) 'Human rights as a common concern', *American Political Science Review*, Vol 95, No 2, pp269–82.

Bellmann C and R Gerster (1996) 'Accountability in the World Trade Organization', *Journal of World Trade*, Vol 30, No 6, pp31–74.

Bendell J (2004) 'Flags of inconvenience? The Global Compact and the future of the United Nations', *CCR Research Paper Series: No 22-2004*, International Centre for Corporate Social Responsibility, Nottingham University.

Bendell J and D F Murphy (2002) 'Towards civil regulation: NGOs and the politics of corporate environmentalism' in P Utting (ed), pp245–67.

Bennett P (2001) 'Mutual risk: P&I insurance clubs and maritime safety and environmental performance', *Marine Policy*, Vol 25, No 1, pp13–21.

Berkes F and C Folke (eds) (1998) *Linking social and ecological systems: management practices and social mechanisms for building resilience*, Cambridge University Press, Cambridge.

Bernstein S (2001) *The compromise of liberal environmentalism*, Columbia University Press, New York.

Bianchi A (1997) 'Harm to the environment in Italian practice: the interaction of international law and domestic law' in P Wetterstein (ed), pp83–100.

Biermann F (2001) 'Big science, small impacts – in the South? The influence of global environmental assessments on expert communities in India', *Global Environmental Change*, Vol 11, No 4, pp297–309.

Birnie P and A Boyle (2002) *International law and the environment*, second edition, Oxford University Press, Oxford.

Blaikie P, T Cannon, I Davis and B Wisner (1994) *At risk: natural hazards, people's vulnerability and disasters*, Routledge, London.

Boehmer-Christiansen S (2002) 'Investing against climate change: why failure remains possible', *Environmental Politics*, Vol 11, No 3, pp1–30.

Boele R, H Fabig and D Wheeler (2001) 'Shell, Nigeria and the Ogoni: a study in unsustainable development: I. The story of Shell, Nigeria and the Ogoni people – environment, economy, relationships: conflicts and prospects for resolution', *Sustainable Development*, Vol 9, No 2, pp74–86.

Boyle A E (1996) 'The role of international human rights law in the protection of the environment' in A E Boyle and M R Anderson (eds) *Human rights approaches to environmental protection*, Clarendon Press, Oxford, pp43–69.

Boyle A E (1997) 'Remedying harm to international common spaces and resources: compensation and other approaches' in P Wetterstein (ed), pp83–100.

Boyle A E (1999) 'Codification of international environmental law and the International Law Commission: injurious consequences revisited' in A Boyle and D Freestone (eds) *International law and sustainable development: past achievements and future challenges*, Oxford University Press, Oxford, pp61–85.

Breitmeyer H and V Rittberger (2000) 'Environmental NGOs in an emerging global civil society' in P S Chasek (ed), pp130–63.

Brown Weiss E (1999) 'Opening the door to the environment and to future generations' in L B de Chazournes and P Sands (eds) *International law, the International Court of Justice and nuclear weapons*, Cambridge University Press, Cambridge, pp338–53.

Brown Weiss E and H K Jacobson (eds) (1998) *Engaging countries: strengthening national compliance with international environmental accords*, MIT Press, Cambridge, Mass.

Brunkhorst H (2002) 'Globalising democracy without a state: weak public, strong public, global constitutionalism', *Millennium*, Vol 31, No 3, pp675–90.

Byron N (2001) 'Risk, the environment and MEAs' in D Robertson and A Kellow (eds) *Globalization and the environment: risk assessment and the WTO*, Edward Elgar, Cheltenham, pp27–40.

Cameron H (2003) 'Southern agenda on trade and environment enters second phase', *Bridges: Between Trade and Sustainable Development*, Vol 7, No 3, p19.

Cameron M A (2002) 'Global civil society and the Ottawa process: lessons from the movement to ban anti-personnel mines' in J English and R Thakur (eds) *Enhancing global governance: towards a new diplomacy*, United Nations University Press, Tokyo, pp69–89.

Cameron J and Abouchar J (1996) 'The status of the precautionary principle in international law' in D Freestone and E Hey (eds) *The precautionary principle and international law: the challenge of implementation*, Kluwer Law International, The Hague, pp29–52.

Cameron J and K R Gray (2001) 'Principles of international law in the WTO Dispute Settlement Body', *International and Comparative Law Quarterly*, Vol 50, pp248–98.

Cane P (2001) 'Are environmental harms special?', *Journal of Environmental Law*, Vol 13, No 1, pp3–20.

Carter A (2001) 'Can we harm future people?' *Environmental Values*, Vol 10, No 4, pp429–54.

Cash D W and S C Moser (2000) 'Linking global and local scales: designing dynamic assessment and management processes', *Global Environmental Change*, Vol 10, No 2, pp109–20.

Castells M (1996) *The rise of the network society*, Blackwell, Oxford.

Chandhoke N (2002) 'The limits of global civil society' in M Glasius et al (eds), pp35–53.

Charnovitz S (2002) 'WTO cosmopolitics', *Journal of International Law and Politics*, Vol 34, No 2, pp299–354.

Chasek P S (ed) (2000) *The global environment in the twenty-first century: prospects for international cooperation*, United Nations University Press, Tokyo.

Churchill R R and A V Lowe (1999) *The law of the sea*, third edition, Manchester University Press, Manchester.

Clapp J (1998) 'The privatization of global environmental governance: ISO 14000 and the developing world', *Global Governance*, Vol 4, No 3, pp295–316.

Clark J (2003) *Worlds apart: civil society and the battle for ethical globalization*, Earthscan, London.

Clark A M, E J Friedman and K Hochstetler (1998) 'The sovereign limits of global civil society: a comparison of NGO participation in UN world conferences on the environment, human rights and women', *World Politics*, Vol 51, No 1, pp1–35.

Cochran M (1999) *Normative theory in international relations: a pragmatic approach*, Cambridge University Press, Cambridge.

Cohen J (1998) 'Democracy and liberty' in J Elster (ed) *Deliberative democracy*, Cambridge University Press, Cambridge, pp185–231.

Colás A (2002) *International civil society*, Polity Press, Cambridge.

Commission of the European Communities (2002) *Proposal for a directive of the European Parliament and of the Council on environmental liability with regard to the prevention and remedying of environmental damage: COM (2002) 17 Final*.

Commission on Environmental Law of IUCN (2000) *Draft international covenant on environment and development*, second edition, World Conservation Union, Gland.

Commoner B, P W Bartlett, H Eisl and K Couchot (2000) *Long-range air transport of dioxin from North American sources to ecologically vulnerable receptors in Nunavut, Arctic Canada*, North American Commission for Environmental Cooperation, Montreal.

Conca K (2000) 'The WTO and the undermining of global environmental governance', *Review of International Political Economy*, Vol 7, No 3, pp484–94.

Corell E and M M Betsill (2001) 'A comparative look at NGO influence in international environmental negotiations: desertification and climate change', Global Environmental Politics, Vol 1, No 4, pp86–107.

Corpwatch (2002) *Greenwash + 10: the UN's Global Compact, corporate accountability and the Johannesburg Earth Summit*, Corpwatch, Oakland, California. Accessed at: http://www.corpwatch.org/campaigns/PCD.jsp?articleid=1348.

Council of Europe (1998) *Convention on the protection of the environment through criminal law: explanatory report*. Accessed at: http://conventions.coe.int/treaty/en/Reports/html/172.htm.

Covey J G (1998) 'Critical cooperation? Influencing the World Bank through policy dialogue and operational cooperation' in J A Fox and L David Brown (eds), pp. 81–119.

Crawford J (1999) *Second report on state responsibility UN General Assembly A/CN.4/498*, United Nations, New York.

Ddamilura D and H N Abdi (2003) *Civil society and the WTO: Participation in national trade policy design in Uganda and Kenya*, CAFOD, London.

Dean J (2001) 'Publicity's secret', *Political Theory*, Vol 29, No 5, pp624–50.

De La Fayette L (2001) 'The Marine Environment Protection Committee: the conjunction of the Law of the Sea and international environmental law', *International Journal of Marine and Coastal Law*, Vol 16, No 2, pp155–238.

De La Fayette L (2002) Personal communication (by email): IUCN Observer – International Maritime Organization, 7 April.

Deleuze G and F Guattari (1987) *A thousand plateaus*, University of Minnesota Press, Minneapolis.

Demeritt D (2001) 'The construction of global warming and the politics of science', *Annals of the Association of American Geographers*, Vol 91, No 2, pp307–37.

Desai M and Y Said (2001) 'The new anti-capitalist movement: money and global civil society' in H Anheier et al (eds), pp51–78.

Deudney D (1998) 'Global village sovereignty: intergenerational sovereign publics, federal-republican earth constitutions, and planetary identities' in K Litfin (ed), pp299–325.

Devetak R and R Higgott (1999) 'Justice unbound? Globalization, states and the transformation of the social bond', *International Affairs*, Vol 75, No 3, pp483–98.

Dewey J (1954) *The public and its problems*, Swallow Press/Ohio University Press, Athens, Ohio.

Dine J (2000) *The governance of corporate groups*, Cambridge University Press, Cambridge.

Dobson A (1998) *Justice and the environment*, Oxford University Press, Oxford.

Dobson A (ed) (1999) *Fairness and futurity: essays on environmental sustainability and social justice*, Oxford University Press, Oxford.

Dobson A (2003) *Citizenship and the environment*, Oxford University Press, Oxford.

Downs A (1998) *Political theory and public choice*, Edward Elgar, Cheltenham.

Drache D (ed) (2001) *The market or the public domain? Global governance and the asymmetry of power*, Routledge, New York.

Dryzek J (1990) *Discursive democracy: politics, policy and political science*, Cambridge University Press, Cambridge.

Dryzek J (1999) 'Transnational democracy', *Journal of Political Philosophy*, Vol 7, No 1, pp30–51.

Dunn J (1999) 'Situating democratic accountability' in A Przeworski, S C Stokes and B Manin (eds) *Democratic accountability and representation*, Cambridge University Press, Cambridge, pp329–44.

Duwe M (2001) 'The Climate Action Network: a glance behind the curtains of a transnational NGO network', *Review of European Community & International Environmental Law*, Vol 10, No 2, pp177–89.

Eckersley R (1999) 'The discourse principle and the problem of representing nature', *Environmental Politics*, Vol 8, No 2, pp24–49.

Economic Commission for Europe (2002) Report of the first Meeting of the Parties to the Convention on Access to Information, Public Participation in Decision-Making and Access to Justice in Environmental Matters: ECE/MP.PP/2, United Nations Economic and Social Council, New York. Accessed at: http://www.unece.org/env/documents/2002/pp/ece.mp.pp.2.e.pdf.

Economy E and M A Schreurs (1997) 'Domestic and international linkages in environmental politics' in M A Schreurs and E Economy (eds) *The internationalization of environmental protection*, Cambridge University Press, Cambridge, pp1–18.

ENDS (2004) 'Europe's EMAS scheme continues to slide', *ENDS Environment Daily*, Issue 1600, 2 February.

Esty D C (1999) 'Environmental governance at the WTO: outreach to civil society' in G P Sampson and W Bradnee Chambers (eds) *Trade, environment, and the millennium*, United Nations University Press, New York, pp97–117.

Falkner R (2003) 'Private environmental governance and international relations: exploring the links', *Global Environmental Politics*, Vol 3, No 2, pp72–85.

Featherstone D (2003) 'Spatialities of transnational resistance to globalization: the maps of grievance of the Inter-Continental Caravan', *Transactions of the Institute of British Geographers*, Vol 28, No 4, pp404–21.

Finnemore M and K Sikkink (1998) 'International norm dynamics and political change', *International Organization*, Vol 52, No 4, pp887–917.

Fitzmaurice M (1996) 'Liability for environmental damage caused to the global commons', *Review of European Community & International Environmental Law*, Vol 5, No 4, pp305–11.

Fitzmaurice M (2003) 'Public participation in the North American Agreement on Environmental Cooperation', *International and Comparative Law Quarterly*, Vol 52, No 2, pp333–68.

Flinders M (2001) *The politics of accountability in the modern state*, Ashgate, Aldershot.

Ford L (2003) 'Challenging global environmental governance: social movement agency and global civil society', *Global Environmental Politics*, Vol 3, No 2, pp120–34.

Forsyth T (2003) *Critical political ecology: the politics of environmental science*, Routledge, London.

Fox J A and L D Brown (eds) (1998) *The struggle for accountability: the World Bank, NGOs and grassroots movements*, MIT Press, Cambridge, Mass.

Fox G H and B R Roth (eds) (2000) *Democratic governance and international law*, Cambridge University Press, Cambridge.

Francioni F and T Scovazzi (eds) (1991) *International responsibility for environmental harm*, Graham & Trotman, London.

Franck T M (1995) *Fairness in international law and institutions*, Clarendon Press, Oxford.

French D A (2001) 'A reappraisal of sovereignty in the light of global environmental concerns', *Legal Studies*, Vol 21, No 3, pp376–99.

Friends of the Earth Europe (2003) 'North + South civil society statement on WTO Agreement on Agriculture talks', 24 February. Available at: http://www.foei.org/media/2003/0224.html.

Friends of the Earth International (2001) 'Trade case study: beef-hormone dispute'. Accessed at: http://www.foei.org/trade/activistguide/hormone.htm.

Friends of the Earth International (2002) Implications of WTO negotiations for biodiversity, FOE International, Amsterdam. Accessed at http://www.foei.org/publications/pdfs/wto_int.pdf.

Friends of the Earth International (2003) *Annual report 2002*, FOE International, Amsterdam. Accessed at: http://www.foei.org/publications/pdfs/ar2002.pdf.

Friends of the Earth International (2004) *Exxon's climate footprint: the contribution of Exxon Mobil to climate change since 1882*, FOE International, Amsterdam. Accessed at: http://www.foei.org/publications/pdfs/exxons_climate_footprint.pdf.

Fries R (2003) 'The legal environment of civil society' in M Kaldor et al (eds), pp221–38.

Garcia-Johnson R (2000) *Exporting environmentalism: US multinational corporations in Brazil and Mexico*, MIT Press, Cambridge, Mass.

Gauci G (1997) *Oil pollution at sea: civil liability and compensation for damage*, Wiley, Chichester.

Gauci G M (1999) 'Protection of the marine environment through the international ship-source oil pollution compensation regimes', *Review of European Community & International Environmental Law*, Vol 8, No 1, pp29–36.

Gaventa J (2001) 'Global citizen action: lessons and challenges' in M Edwards and J Gaventa (eds) *Global citizen action*, Earthscan, London, pp. 275–87.

Georgieva K (2002) 'Environment and development: the role of the World Bank', lecture delivered at Harvard University, Cambridge, Mass., 19 December.

Giddens A (2000) *The consequences of modernity*, Polity Press, Cambridge.

Glasius M, M Kaldor and H Anheier (eds) (2002) *Global civil society 2002*, Oxford University Press, Oxford.

Greenpeace International (2002) *Greenpeace comments and annotations on the WTO Doha Ministerial Declaration*, Greenpeace International, Amsterdam. Accessed at: http://archive.greenpeace.org/earthsummit/docs/Dohafinal.pdf.

Greenpeace International (2003) *Greenpeace annual report 2003*, Greenpeace International, Amsterdam. Accessed at: http://www.greenpeace.org/annualreport/.

Gunderson L, C S Holling and S Light (1995) *Barriers and bridges to the renewal of ecosystems and institutions*, Columbia University Press, New York.

Habermas J (1987) *The theory of communicative action. Volume 2: A critique of functionalist reason*, Polity Press, Cambridge.

Habermas J (1990) *Moral consciousness and communicative action*, Polity Press, Cambridge.

Habermas J (1996) *Between facts and norms: contributions to a discourse theory of law and democracy*, Polity Press, Cambridge.

Habermas J (1999a) *On the pragmatics of communication*, Polity Press, Cambridge.

Habermas J (1999b) *The inclusion of the other: studies in political theory*, Polity Press, Cambridge.

Habermas J (2001) *The postnational constellation: political essays*, Polity Press, Cambridge.

Hansen M (2002) 'Environmental regulation of transnational corporations' in P Utting (ed), pp159–86.

Hansenclever A, P Mayer and V Rittberger (1997) *Theories of international regimes*, Cambridge University Press, Cambridge.

Harmann R, N Acutt and P Kapelus (2003) 'Responsibility versus accountability? Interpreting the World Summit on Sustainable Development for a synthesis model of corporate citizenship', *Journal of Corporate Citizenship*, Issue 9, pp32–48.

Harvey D (2003) *The new imperialism*, Oxford University Press, Oxford.

Haufler V (2001) *A public role for the private sector: industry self-regulation in a global economy*, Carnegie Endowment for International Peace, Washington, DC.

Held D (1995) *Democracy and the global order: from the modern state to cosmopolitan governance*, Polity Press, Cambridge.

Held D (2004) *Global covenant: the social democratic alternative to the Washington Consensus*, Polity Press, Cambridge.

Hertz N (2001) *The silent takeover: global capitalism and the death of democracy*, William Heinemann, London.

Hilson C (2001) 'Greening citizenship: boundaries of membership and the environment', *Journal of Environmental Law*, Vol 13, No 3, pp335–48.

Hirschland M J (2003) 'Strange bedfellows makes for democratic deficits: the rise and challenges of corporate social responsibility engagement' in R A Shah et al (eds), pp79–97.

Hobbs, J, I Khan, M Posner and K Roth (2003) Letter to Louise Fréchette raising concerns on UN Global Compact. Accessed at: http://web.amnesty.org/web/web.nsf/print/ec-gcletter070403-eng.

Hoffman A J (2001) *From heresy to dogma: an institutional history of corporate environmentalism*, Stanford University Press, Stanford, California.

Holliday C O, S Schmidheiny and P Watts (2002) *Walking the talk: the business case for sustainable development*, Greenleaf Publishing, Sheffield.

Holling C S, F Berkes and C Folke (1998) 'Science, sustainability and resource management' in F Berkes and C Folke (eds), pp342–62.

Hovden E (1999) 'As if nature doesn't matter: ecology, regime theory and international relations', *Environmental Politics*, Vol 8, No 2, pp50–74.

Howlett L (2002) Personal communication: Legal Advisor – International Chamber of Shipping, London, 20 February.

Howse R (2002) 'From politics to technocracy and back: the fate of the multilateral trading regime', *American Journal of International Law*, Vol 96, No 1, pp94–117.

International Law Commission (1996) *Report of the International Law Commission on the work of its forty-eighth session, 6 May–26 July 1996: UN General Assembly A/51/10*, United Nations, New York.

International Law Commission (1999) *Report of the International Law Commission on the work of its fifty-first session, 3 May–23 July 1999: UN General Assembly A/54/10*, United Nations, New York.

International Law Commission (2000) *Report of the International Law Commission on the work of its fifty-second session, 23 April–1 June and 2 July–10 August 2000: UN General Assembly A/55/10*, United Nations, New York.

International Law Commission (2001) *Report of the International Law Commission on the work of its fifty-third session, 23 April–1 June and 2 July–10 August 2001: UN General Assembly A/56/10*, United Nations, New York.

International Law Commission (2002) *Report of the International Law Commission on the work of its fifty-fourth session, 29 April–7 June and 22 July–16 August 2002: UN General Assembly A/57/10*, United Nations, New York.

International Law Commission (2003) *Report of the International Law Commission on the work of its fifty-fifth session, 5 May–6 June and 7 July–8 August 2003: UN General Assembly A/58/10*, United Nations, New York.

International Maritime Organization (1993a) *Official records of the International Conference on Liability and Compensation for Damage in Connexion with the Carriage of Certain Substances by Sea, 1984: Volume 1*, IMO, London.

International Maritime Organization (1993b) *Official records of the International Conference on Liability and Compensation for Damage in Connexion with the Carriage of Certain Substances by Sea, 1984: Volume 2*, IMO, London.

International Maritime Organization (1993c) *Official records of the International Conference on Liability and Compensation for Damage in Connexion with the Carriage of Certain Substances by Sea, 1984: Volume 3*, IMO, London.

International Maritime Organization (1993d) *Official records of the International Conference on the Revision of the 1969 Civil Liability Convention and the 1971 Fund Convention, 1992*, IMO, London.

International Oil Pollution Compensation Fund (1980) *Resolution No. 3 – pollution damage: FUND/A/ES1/13*, IOPC Fund, London.

International Oil Pollution Compensation Fund (1994) *Criteria for the admissibility of claims for compensation: FUND/WGR.7/4*, IOPC Fund, London.

International Oil Pollution Compensation Fund 1992 (1996) *Guidelines on relations between the International Oil Pollution Compensation Fund 1992 (1992 Fund) and intergovernmental organizations and international non-governmental organizations: 92FUND/A.1/34/1*, IOPC Fund 1992, London.

International Oil Pollution Compensation Fund 1992 (2000) *Claims manual*, IOPC Fund 1992, London.

International Oil Pollution Compensation Fund 1992 (2001) *Record of decisions of the sixth session of the Assembly: 92FUND/A.6/28*, IOPC Fund 1992, London.

International Oil Pollution Compensation Funds (2001) *Annual report 2000*, IOPC Funds, London.

International Oil Pollution Compensation Funds (2002) *Annual report 2001*, IOPC Funds, London.

Jawara F and A Kwa (2003) *Behind the scenes at the WTO: the real world of international trade negotiations*, Zed Books, London.

Jenkins H (2002) Interview: Programme Officer, United Nations Non-Governmental Liaison Service, Geneva, 3 December.

Jenkins R (2002) 'Environmental regulation, trade and investment in a global economy', in R Jenkins et al (eds) *Environmental regulation in a global economy: the impact on industry and competitiveness*, Edward Elgar, Cheltenham, pp293–314.

Jones C (1999) *Global justice: defending cosmopolitanism*, Oxford University Press, Oxford.

Jones T (1998) 'Economic globalisation and the environment: an overview of the linkages' in Organisation for Economic Cooperation and Development, *Globalisation and the environment*, OECD, Paris, pp17–28.

Kaldor M (2003) 'Civil society and accountability', *Journal of Human Development*, Vol 4, No 1, pp5–27.

Kaldor M, H Anheier and M Glasius (eds) (2003) *Global civil society 2003*, Oxford University Press, Oxford.

Kasperson J X and R E Kasperson (2001a) 'Border crossings' in J Linnerooth-Bayer et al (eds), pp207–43.

Kasperson J X and R E Kasperson (eds) (2001b) *Global environmental risk*, Earthscan, London.

Kasperson R E, J X Kasperson and K Dow (2001) 'Vulnerability, equity and global environmental change' in J X Kasperson and R E Kasperson (eds) (2001b), pp247–72.

Kates R W et al (2001) 'Sustainability science', *Science*, Vol 292, pp641–42.

Kaul I and K Le Goulven (2003) 'Institutional options for protecting global public goods' in I Kaul, P Conceição, K Le Goulven and R U Mendoza (eds) *Providing public goods: managing globalization*, Oxford University Press, New York, pp371–409.

Keane J (2001) 'Global civil society?' in H Anheier et al (eds), pp23–47.

Keck M and K Sikkink (1998) *Activists beyond borders: advocacy networks in international politics*, Cornell University Press, Ithaca.

Kell G (2003) 'The Global Compact: origins, operations, progress, challenges', *Journal of Corporate Citizenship*, Issue 11, pp35–49.

Kellow A (1999) *International toxic risk management: ideals, interests and implementation*, Cambridge University Press, Cambridge.

Kellow A (2000) 'Norms, interests and environment NGOs: the limits of cosmopolitanism', *Environmental Politics*, Vol 9, No 3, pp1–22.

Keohane R (2003) 'Global governance and democratic accountability' in D Held and M Koenig-Archibugi (eds) *Taming globalization: frontiers of governance*, Polity Press, Cambridge, pp130–59.

Keohane R, A Moravcsik and A-M Slaughter (2000) 'Legalized dispute resolution: interstate and transnational', *International Organization*, Vol 54, No 3, pp457–88.

Keselj T (1999) 'Port state jurisdiction in respect of pollution from ships: the 1992 United Nations Convention on the Law of the Sea and the Memoranda of Understanding', *Ocean Development and International Law*, Vol 30, No 1, pp 127–60.

Kim I (2002) 'Ten years after the enactment of the Oil Pollution Act of 1990: a success or failure?' *Marine Policy*, Vol 26, No 3, pp97–207.

Knox J H (2002) 'The myth and reality of transboundary environmental impact assessment', *American Journal of International Law*, Vol 96, No 2, pp291–319.

Kohn M (2000) 'Language, power and persuasion: toward a critique of deliberative democracy', *Constellations* Vol 7, No 3, pp408–29.

Kollman K and A Prakash (2001) 'Green by choice? Cross-national variations in firms' responses to EMS-based environmental regimes', *World Politics*, Vol 53, No 3, pp399–430.

Korten D (1995) *When corporations rule the world*, Kumarian Press, West Hartford, Connecticut.

Kovach H, C Neligan and S Burrall (2003) *Power without accountability*, Sage, London.

Krasner S D (1999) *Sovereignty: organized hypocrisy*, Princeton University Press, Princeton, NJ.

Krasner S D (2000) 'Rethinking the sovereign state model', *Review of International Studies*, Vol 27, No 1, pp17–42.

Kratochwil F V (1989) *Rules, norms, and decisions: on the conditions of practical and legal reasoning in international relations and domestic affairs*, Cambridge University Press, Cambridge.

Krut R and H Gleckman (1998) *ISO 14001: a missed opportunity for sustainable global industrial development*, Earthscan, London.

Kuehls T (1996) *Beyond sovereign territory: the space of ecopolitics*, University of Minnesota Press, Minneapolis.

Kuehls T (1998) 'Between sovereignty and environment: an exploration of the discourse of governmentality' in K Litfin (ed), pp31–53.

Lee M and C Abbot (2003) 'The usual suspects? Public participation under the Aarhus Convention', *Modern Law Review*, Vol 66, No 1, pp80–108.

Linklater A (1998) *The transformation of political community: ethical foundations of the post-Westphalian era*, Polity Press, Cambridge.

Linklater A (1999) 'The evolving spheres of international justice', *International Affairs* Vol 75, No 3, pp473–82.

Linklater A (2001) 'Citizenship, humanity, and cosmopolitan harm conventions', *International Political Science Review*, Vol 22, No 3, pp261–77.

Linklater A (2005) 'Cosmopolitanism' in A Dobson and R Eckersley (eds) *Political theory and the ecological challenge*, Cambridge University Press, Cambridge.

Linnerooth-Bayer J, R E Löfstedt and G Sjöstedt (eds) (2001) *Transboundary risk management*, Earthscan, London.

Lipschutz R D with J Mayer (1996) *Global civil society and global environmental governance*, State University of New York Press, Albany.

Litfin K (ed) (1998) *The greening of sovereignty in world politics*, MIT Press, Cambridge, Mass.

Little G and J Hamilton (1997) 'Compensation for catastrophic oil spills: a transatlantic comparison', *Lloyd's Maritime and Commercial Law Quarterly*, Part 3, pp391–405.

Loy F (2001) 'Public participation in the World Trade Organization' in G Sampson (ed), pp113–35.

Luke T W (1997) *Ecocritique: contesting the politics of nature, economy, and culture*, University of Minnesota Press, Minneapolis.

Luke T W (1999) 'Environmentality as open governmentality' in E Darier (ed) *Discourses of the environment*, Blackwell, Oxford, pp125–51.

Macnaghten P and J Urry (1998) *Contested natures*, Sage, London.

Malhotra A (1998) 'A commentary on the status of future generations as a subject of international law' in E Agius et al (eds), pp39–49.

Marceau G and P N Pedersen (1999) 'Is the WTO open and transparent? A discussion of the relationship of the WTO with non-governmental organisations and civil society's claims for more transparency and participation', *Journal of World Trade*, Vol 33, No 1, pp5–49.

Martinez-Alier J (2002) *The environmentalism of the poor: a study of ecological conflicts and valuation*, Edward Elgar, Cheltenham.

Mason M (1999) *Environmental democracy*, Earthscan, London.

Mattoo A and P C Mavroidis (1997) 'Trade, environment and the WTO: the dispute settlement practice relating to Article XX of GATT' in E-U Petersmann (ed) *International Trade Law and the GATT/WTO Dispute Settlement System*, Kluwer, London, pp325–43.

McIntyre O and T Mosedale (1997) 'The precautionary principle as a norm of customary international law', *Journal of Environmental Law*, Vol 9, No 2, pp221–41.

Miller D (1999) *Principles of social justice*, Harvard University Press, Cambridge, Mass.

Minteer B A and R E Manning (1999) 'Pragmatism in environmental ethics: democracy, pluralism, and the management of nature', *Environmental Ethics*, Vol 21, No 2, pp191–207.

Mitchell R, M L McConnell, A Roginko and A Barrett (1999) 'International vessel-source pollution' in O R Young (ed) *The effectiveness of international regimes: causal connections and behavioral mechanisms*, MIT Press, Cambridge, Mass., pp33–90.

Mol A P J (2001) *Globalization and environmental reform: the ecological modernization of the global economy*, MIT Press, Cambridge, Mass.

Muchlinski P (2001) 'Corporations in international litigation: problems of jurisdiction and the United Kingdom asbestos case', *International and Comparative Law Quarterly*, Vol 50, No 1, pp1–25.

National Research Council (2002) *Oil in the Sea III: Inputs, Fates and Effects*, National Research Council, Washington.

Neumayer E (2001) *Greening trade and investment: environmental protection without protectionism*, Earthscan, London.

Newell P (2001) 'Managing multinationals: the governance of investment for the environment', *Journal of International Development*, Vol 13, No 7, pp907–19.

Newell P and S Bellour (2002) 'Mapping accountability: origins, contexts and implications for development', *IDS Working Paper* 168, Institute of Development Studies, Brighton.

Nollkaemper A (2003) 'Concurrence between individual responsibility and state responsibility in international law', *International and Comparative Law Quarterly*, Vol 52, No 3, pp615–40.

Nordström H and S Vaughan (1999) *Trade and environment: WTO special studies series: No. 4*, WTO, Geneva.

Norton B (1996) 'Integration or reduction; two approaches to environmental values' in A Light and E Katz (eds) *Environmental pragmatism*, Routledge, London, pp105–38.

Norton B (1999) 'Pragmatism, adaptive management and sustainability', *Environmental Values*, Vol 8, No 4, pp451–66.

Norton B (2003) *Searching for sustainability*, Cambridge University Press, Cambridge.

Norton B and A C Steinemann (2001) 'Environmental values and adaptive management', *Environmental Values*, Vol 10, No 4, pp473–506.

O'Brien R, A-M Goetz, J A Scholte and M Williams (1999) *Contesting global governance: multilateral economic institutions and global social movements*, Cambridge University Press, Cambridge.

O'Connor M (2002) 'Reframing environmental valuation: reasoning about resource use and the redistribution of sustainability' in H Abaza and A Baranzini (eds) *Implementing sustainable development: integrated assessment and participatory decision-making processes*, Edward Elgar, Cheltenham, pp32–52.

Ohmae K (1995) *The end of the nation state: the rise of regional economies*, Harper Collins, London.

Okowa P N (2000) *State responsibility for transboundary air pollution in international law*, Oxford University Press, Oxford.

Oliviero M B and A Simmons (2002) 'Who's minding the store? Global civil society and corporate responsibility' in M Glasius et al (eds), pp77–107.

Olsen J M F, J M Salazar-Xirinachs and M Araya (2001) 'Trade and environment at the World Trade Organization: the need for constructive dialogue' in G Sampson (ed), pp137–54.

O'Neill O (1996) *Towards justice and virtue: a constructivist account of practical reasoning*, Cambridge University Press, Cambridge.

O'Neill O (2000) *Bounds of justice*, Cambridge University Press, Cambridge.

Organization for Economic Cooperation and Development (2000) *The OECD guidelines for multinational enterprises*, OECD, Paris. Accessed at: http://www.oecd.org/dataoecd/56/36/1922428.pdf.

Osgood D (2001) 'Dig it up: global civil society's response to plant biotechnology' in H Anheier et al (eds), pp79–107.

Ostrom E (1990) *Governing the commons: the evolution of institutions for collective action*, Cambridge University Press, Cambridge.

Ó Tuathail G (1996) *Critical geopolitics: the politics of writing global space*, Routledge, London.

Oxfam (2002) *Rigged rules and double standards: trade, globalisation and the fight against poverty*, Oxfam International, Geneva. Accessed at: http://www.maketradefair.com/assets/english/Report_English.pdf.

Paehlke R (2003) *Democracy's dilemma: environment, social equity and the global economy*, MIT Press, Cambridge, Mass.

Paterson M (2000) *Understanding global environmental politics: domination, accumulation, resistance*, Macmillan, Basingstoke.

Patomäki H (2001) *Democratising globalisation: the leverage of the Tobin tax*, Zed Books, London.

Peel J (2001) 'New state responsibility rules and compliance with multilateral environmental obligations: some case studies of how the new rules might apply in the international environmental context', *Review of European Community and International Environmental Law*, Vol 10, No 1, pp82–97.

Pevato P M (1999) 'A right to environment in international law: current status and future outlook', *Review of European Community & International Environmental Law*, Vol 8, No 3, pp309–21.

Pianta M (2001) 'Parallel summits of global civil society' in H Anheier et al (eds), pp169–94.

Pianta M and F Silva (2003) 'Parallel summits of global civil society: an update' in M Kaldor et al (eds), pp387–94.

Pisillio-Mazzeschi R (1991) 'Forms of international responsibility for environmental harm' in F Francioni and T Scovazzi (eds), pp185–205.

Pogge T (2002) *World poverty and human rights: cosmopolitan responsibilities and reforms*, Polity Press, Cambridge.

Poncelet E C (2003) 'Resisting corporate citizenship: business–NGO relationships in multi-stakeholder environmental partnerships', *Journal of Corporate Citizenship*, Issue 9, pp97–115.

Porter M E and C van der Linde (1995) 'Green and competitive: ending the stalemate', *Harvard Business Review*, Vol 73, No 5, pp120–33.

Price R (1998) 'Reversing the gun sights: transnational civil society targets land mines', *International Organization*, Vol 52, No 3, pp613–44.

Princen T (1994) 'NGOs: creating a niche in environmental diplomacy' in T Princen and M Finger (eds), pp29–47.

Princen T (1995) 'Ivory conservation and environmental transnational coalitions' in T Risse-Kappen (ed), pp227–53.

Princen T and M Finger (eds) (1994) *Environmental NGOs in world politics: linking the local and the global*, Routledge, London.

Ragazzi M (1997) *The concept of international obligations erga omnes*, Clarendon Press, Oxford.

Rao P S (1998a) 'First report on prevention of transboundary damage from hazardous activities', *UN General Assembly A/CN.4/487*, United Nations, New York.

Rao P S (1998b) 'First report on prevention of transboundary damage from hazardous activities: addendum 1', *UN General Assembly A/CN.4/487/Add.1*, United Nations, New York.

Rao P S (1999) 'Second report on international liability for injurious consequences arising out of acts not prohibited by international law (prevention of transboundary damage from hazardous activities)', *UN General Assembly A/CN.4/501*, United Nations, New York.

Rao P S (2000) 'Third report on international liability for injurious consequences arising out of acts not prohibited by international law (prevention of transboundary damage from hazardous activities)', *UN General Assembly A/CN.4/510*, United Nations, New York.

Rao P S (2003) 'First report on the legal regime for allocation of loss in case of transboundary harm arising out of hazardous activities', *UN General Assembly A/CN.4/531*, United Nations, New York.

Ratner S R (2000) 'Democracy and accountability: the criss-crossing paths of two emerging norms' in G H Fox and B R Roth (eds) *Democratic governance and international law*, Cambridge University Press, Cambridge, pp449–90.

Ratner S R and J S Abrams (2001) *Accountability for human rights atrocities in international law*, second edition, Oxford University Press, Oxford.

Raustiala K (1997) 'States, NGOs and international environmental institutions', *International Studies Quarterly*, Vol 41, No 4, pp719–40.

Raustiala K and D G Victor (1998) 'Conclusions' in D G Victor, K Raustiala and E B Skolnikoff (eds) *The implementation and effectiveness of international environmental commitments*, MIT Press, Cambridge, Mass., pp659–707.

Rawls J (1999) *The law of peoples*, Harvard University Press, Cambridge, Mass.

Renn O and A Klinke (2001) 'Public participation across borders' in J Linnerooth-Bayer et al (eds), pp245–78.

Retallack S (2001) 'The environmental costs of economic globalization' in E Goldsmith and J Mander (eds) *The case against the global economy and for a turn towards localization*, Earthscan, London, pp189–202.

Ringbom H (2001) 'The Erika accident and its effects on EU maritime regulation', Maritime Safety Unit, Directorate General for Energy and Transport, European Commission, Brussels.

Risse T (2000) 'Let's argue! Communicative action in world politics', *International Organization*, Vol 54, No 1, pp1–39.

Risse-Kappen T (ed) (1995) *Bringing transnational relations back in: non-state actors, domestic structures and international institutions*, Cambridge University Press, Cambridge.

Roberts S M (1998) 'Geo-governance in trade and finance and political geographies of dissent' in A Herod, G Ó Tuathail and S M Roberts (eds) *An unruly world? Globalization, governance and geography*, Routledge, London, pp116–35.

Rosenau J N (1997) *Along the domestic-foreign frontier: exploring governance in a turbulent world*, Cambridge University Press, Cambridge.

Routledge P (2003) 'Convergence space: process geographies of grassroots globalization networks', *Transactions of the Institute of British Geographers*, Vol 28, No 3, pp333–49.

Ruggie J G (2002) 'The theory and practice of learning networks: corporate social responsibility and the Global Compact', *Journal of Corporate Citizenship*, Issue 5, pp27–36.

Ruiz-Marrero C (2003) 'The troubled marriage of environmentalists and oil companies', Corpwatch, 22 December. Accessed at: http://www.corpwatch.org/issues/PID.jsp?articleid = 9448.

Rutherford K (2000) 'The evolving arms control agenda: implications of the role of NGOs in banning antipersonnel mines', *World Politics*, Vol 53, No 1, pp74–114.

Sampson G (ed) (2001) *The role of the World Trade Organization in global governance*, United Nations University Press, Tokyo.

Sand P (1999) *Transnational environmental law: lessons in global change*, Kluwer Law International, The Hague.

Sands P (1995) *Principles of international environmental law I: frameworks, standards and implementation*, Manchester University Press, Manchester.

Sands P (1998) 'Protecting future generations: precedents and practicalities' in E Agius et al (eds), pp83–91.

Sands P (1999) 'Environmental protection in the twenty-first century: sustainable development and international law' in N J Vig and R S Axelrod (eds), pp116–37.

Sandvik B and S Suikkari (1997) 'Harm and reparation in international treaty regimes: an overview' in P Wetterstein (ed), pp57–71.

Sassen S (1996) *Losing control: sovereignty in an age of globalization*, Columbia University Press, New York.

Scheffler S (2001) *Boundaries and allegiances: problems of justice and responsibility in liberal thought*, Oxford University Press, Oxford.

Schoenbaum T J (2002) 'International trade and environmental protection' in P Birnie and A Boyle, pp697–756.

Scholte J A (2001) 'The IMF and civil society: an interim progress report' in M Edwards and J Gaventa (eds) *Global citizen action*, Earthscan, London, pp87–103.

Scholte J A with R O'Brien and M Williams (1999) 'The WTO and civil society', *Journal of World Trade*, Vol 33, No 1, pp107–23.

Schönleitner G (2003) 'World Social Forum: making another world possible?' in J Clark (ed) *Globalizing civil engagement: civil society and transnational action*, Earthscan, London, pp127–49.

Schweitz M L (2001) 'NGO network codes of conduct: accountability, principles and voice'. Paper presented to International Studies Association Annual Convention, February, Chicago.

Scott C (ed) (2001) *Torture as tort: comparative perspectives on the development of transnational human rights litigation*, Hart Publishing, Oxford.

Scott C (2001) 'Translating torture into transnational tort: conceptual divides in the debate on corporate accountability for human rights harms' in C Scott (ed), pp45–63.

Shaffer G C (2001) 'The World Trade Organization under challenge: democracy and the law and politics of the WTO's treatment of trade and environment matters', *Harvard Environmental Law Review*, Vol 25, No 1, pp1–93.

Shah R A, D F Murphy and M McIntosh (eds) (2003) *Something to believe in: creating trust in organisations: stories of transparency, accountability and governance*, Greenleaf, Sheffield.

Shapiro M J and H R Alker (eds) (1996) *Challenging boundaries: global flows, territorial identities*, University of Minnesota Press, Minneapolis.

Shell International Limited (2002) *People, planet and profits*, Shell Centre, London.

Singh O (1999) Personal communication: Deputy Attaché, Jamaican High Commission, London, 26 July.

Skirbekk G (1997) 'The discourse principle and those affected', *Inquiry*, Vol 40, No 1, pp63–72.

Sklair L (1994) 'Global sociology and global environmental change' in M Redclift and T Benton (eds) *Social theory and the global environment*, Routledge, London, pp205–22.

Sklair L (2000) *The transnational capitalist class*, Blackwell, Oxford.

Skogly S and M Gibney (2001) 'Transnational human rights obligations'. Paper presented to the International Studies Association Annual Meeting, Chicago, 21–24 February.

Smith B D (1988) *State responsibility and the marine environment*, Clarendon Press, Oxford.

Smith J, C Chatfield and R Pagnucco R (eds) (1997) *Transnational social movements and global politics: solidarity beyond the state*, Syracuse University Press, New York.

Social Investment Forum (2003) *2003 report on socially responsible investing trends in the United States*, Social Investment Forum, New York. Accessed at: http://www.socialinvest.org/areas/research/trends/sri_trends_report_2003.pdf.

Solana J (2003) 'Global governance working group report', Progressive Governance Summit, London, July 13–14. Accessed at: http://www.policy-network.net/php/article.php?sid=5&aid=196.

Sornarajah M (2001) 'Linking state responsibility for certain harms caused by corporate nationals abroad to civil recourse in the legal systems of home states' in C Scott (ed), pp491–512.

Steele J (2000) 'NATO troops move into Serb-held city', *Guardian*, 14 August. Accessed at: http://www.guardian.co.uk/Kosovo/Story/0,2763,354079,00.html.

Steinberg R H (2002) 'In the shadow of law or power? Consensus-based bargaining and outcomes in the GATT/WTO', *International Organization*, Vol 56, No 2, pp339–74.

Strong M (2001) *Where on earth are we going?* Vintage Canada, Toronto.

SustainAbility (2003) *The 21st century NGO: in the market for change*, SustainAbility, London.

Tarrow S (2001) 'Transnational politics: contention and institutions in international politics', *Annual Review of Political Science*, Vol 4, No 1, pp1–20.

Taylor P (1998) *An ecological approach to international law: responding to challenges of climate change*, Routledge, London.

Third Intersessional Working Group (2001a) Admissibility for claims under environmental damage under the 1992 Civil Liability and Fund Conventions: Submission by the International Tanker Owners Pollution Federation Limited: 92FUND/WGR.3/5/2. IOPC Fund 1992, London.

Third Intersessional Working Group (2001b) Review of the international compensation regime: Submission by the United States: 92FUND/WGR.3/8/7. IOPC Fund 1992, London.

Third Intersessional Working Group (2001c) Compensation for environmental damage under the auspices of the CLC Fund Conventions: documents submitted by the French Delegation: 92FUND/WGR.3/8/8. IOPC Fund 1992, London.

Third Intersessional Working Group (2001d) Report on the second and third meetings of the Third Intersessional Working Group: 92FUND/WGR.3/9. IOPC Fund 1992, London.

Tolentino P E (1999) 'Transnational rules for transnational corporations: what next?' in J Michie and J Grive (eds) *Global instability: the political economy of world economic governance*, Routledge, London, pp171–97.

Townsend M (2002) 'Seasickness', *The Ecologist*, Vol 32, No 5, pp20–3.

Trzyna T and J Didion (eds) *World directory of environmental organizations*, sixth edition, Earthscan, London.

Udall L (1998) 'The World Bank and public accountability: has anything changed?' in J A Fox and L D Brown (eds), pp391–436.

Ulph A (ed) (2001) *Environmental policy, international agreements and international trade*, Oxford University Press, Oxford.

UNCTAD (2003) *World investment report 2003: FDI policies for development: national and international perspectives*, UNCTAD/WIR/2003, United Nations, New York and Geneva.

Underhill G (2001) 'The public good versus private interests and the global financial and monetary system' in D Drache (ed), pp274–95.

United Nations (1993) *Agenda 21: the United Nations Programme of Action from Rio*, United Nations, New York.

United Nations Environment Programme (2001) *Depleted uranium in Kosovo: post-conflict environmental assessment*, UNEP, Nairobi.

United Nations Environment Programme (2002) *Global environment outlook 3: past, present and future perspectives*, Earthscan, London.

United Nations Environment Programme and Center for Clouds, Chemistry and Climate (2002) *The Asian brown cloud: climate and other environmental impacts*, UNEP Regional Resource Centre for Asia and the Pacific, Pathumthani, Thailand. Accessed at: http://www.rrcap.unep.org/abc/impactstudies/.

United Nations Security Council (1999) *Resolution 1244: S/RES/1244 (1999)*, United Nations, New York.

UN Sub-Commission on the Promotion and Protection of Human Rights (2003) *Commentary on the Norms on the Responsibilities of Transnational Corporations and Other Business Enterprises with Regard to Human Rights: UN Doc E/CN.4/Sub.2/2003038/Rev2*, UN Commission on Human Rights, Geneva.

Utting P (2002) 'The Global Compact and civil society: averting a collision course', *Development in Practice*, Vol 12, No 5, pp644–7.

Utting P (ed) (2002) *The greening of business in developing countries: rhetoric, reality and prospects*, Zed Books, London.

Van Dyke J M (2002) 'The legal regime governing sea transport of ultrahazardous radioactive materials', *Ocean Development and International Law*, Vol 33, No 1, pp77–108.

Vig N J and R S Axelrod (eds) (1999) *The global environment: institutions, law and policy*, Earthscan, London.

Vogler J (2000) *The global commons: a regime analysis*, second edition, John Wiley, Chichester.

Von Bar C (1997) 'Environmental damage in private international law', *Recueil des Cours*, Vol 268, pp303–411.

Walker R B J (1993) *Inside/outside: international relations as political theory*, Cambridge University Press, Cambridge.

Wall D (2003) 'Environmental citizenship and the political'. Paper presented to ESRC seminar series on 'Citizenship and the environment', Newcastle, 27 October 2003.

Wapner P (1996) *Environmental activism and world civic politics*, State University of New York Press, Albany.

Wapner P (2000) 'The transnational politics of environmental NGOs: governmental, economic, and social activism' in P S Chasek (ed), pp87–108.

Wapner P (2002) 'Horizontal politics: transnational activism and global cultural change', *Global Environmental Politics*, Vol 2, No 2, pp37–62.

Ward H (2001) Governing multinationals: the role of foreign direct liability, *Royal Institute of International Affairs Briefing Paper, New Series* No 18, RIIA, London.

Ward H (2002) 'Corporate accountability in search of a treaty? Some insights from foreign direct liability', *Royal Institute of International Affairs Sustainable Development Programme Briefing Paper* No 4, RIIA, London.

Ward V (1998) 'Sovereignty and ecosystem management: clash of concepts and boundaries?' in K Litfin (ed), pp79–108.

Warren R C (2000) *Corporate governance and accountability*, Liverpool Academic Press, Liverpool.

Wates J (2003) Personal communication: Secretary to the Aarhus Convention, Newcastle, 28 October.

Weber M (2001) 'Competing political visions: WTO governance and green politics', *Global Environmental Politics*, Vol 33, No 1, pp92–113.

Wells C (2001) *Corporations and criminal responsibility*, second edition, Oxford University Press, Oxford.

Werner H-P (2002) Interview: Public Affairs Officer, World Trade Organization, Geneva, 11 October.

Wetterstein P (1994) 'Trends in maritime environmental impairment liability', *Lloyd's Maritime and Commercial Law Quarterly*, Part 2, pp230–47.

Wetterstein P (ed) (1997) *Harm to the environment: The right to compensation and the assessment of damages*, Clarendon Press, Oxford.

Wettestad J (2000) 'The ECE Convention on Long-Range Transboundary Air Pollution: from common cuts to critical loads' in A Andresen, T Skodvin, A Underdal and J Wettestad, *Science and politics in international environmental regimes: between integrity and involvement*, Manchester University Press, Manchester, pp95–121.

Wicks E (2000) 'State sovereignty – towards a refined legal conceptualization', *Anglo-American Law Review*, Vol 29, No 3, pp282–314.

White I (2002) Interview: Managing Director – International Tanker Owners Pollution Federation. London, 17 January.

Wilde M (2002) *Civil liability for environmental damage: a comparative analysis of law and policy in Europe and the United States*, Kluwer Law International, The Hague.

Willetts P (1996) 'From Stockholm to Rio and beyond: the impact of the environmental movement on the United Nations consultative arrangements for NGOs', *Review of International Studies*, Vol 22, No 1 pp57–80.

Williams M and L Ford (1999) 'The World Trade Organisation, social movements and global environmental management', *Environmental Politics*, Vol 8, No 1, pp268–89.

Wissenburg M L J (1999) 'An extension of the Rawlsian savings principle to liberal theories of justice in general' in A Dobson (ed), pp173–98.

Wonham J (1998) 'Agenda 21 and sea-based pollution: opportunity or apathy?', *Marine Policy*, Vol 22, Nos 4/5, pp375–91.

World Commission on Environment and Development (1987) *Our common future*, Oxford University Press, Oxford.

World Trade Organization (1996) 'Guidelines for arrangements on relations with non-governmental organizations', WTO/L/162, WTO, Geneva.

World Trade Organization (2001) 'Ministerial Declaration: Ministerial Conference – fourth session, Doha, 9–14 November 2001', WTO/MIN(01)/DEC/1, WTO, Geneva.

World Trade Organization (2002) *Annual report 2002*, WTO, Geneva.

World Trade Organization Committee on Trade and Environment (2002) 'Enhancing synergies and mutual supportiveness of MEAs and WTO: a synthesis report', WT/CTE/W/213, WTO, Geneva.

WTO Appellate Body (1998a) 'EC Measures concerning meat and meat products (hormones)', WT/DS26/AB/R; WT/DS48/AB/R, 16 January, WTO, Geneva.

WTO Appellate Body (1998b) 'United States – import prohibition of certain shrimp and shrimp products', WT/DS58/AB/R, 12 October, WTO, Geneva.

WTO Appellate Body (2001a) 'European Communities – measures affecting asbestos and asbestos-containing products', WT/DS135/AB/R, 12 March, WTO, Geneva.

WTO Appellate Body (2001b) 'United States – import prohibition of certain shrimp and shrimp products', WT/DS58/AB/RW, 22 October, WTO, Geneva.

Wu C (2001) *Liability and compensation for bunker pollution*, Thomas Miller P&I Ltd., New Jersey.

WWF (2003) WWF annual report 2002. Accessed at: http://www.panda.org/news_facts/publications/general/annual_report/2002.

Yeung H W C (1998) 'Capital, state and space: contesting the borderless world', *Transactions of the Institute of British Geographers*, Vol 23, No 3, pp291–309.

Zadek S (2001) *The civil corporation: the new economy of corporate citizenship*, Earthscan, London.

Zammit A (2003) *Development at risk: reconsidering UN-business relations*, United Nations Research Institute for Social Development, Geneva.

Zedan H (2002) Personal communication: Chief, Economics and Trade Branch, United Nations Environment Programme, Geneva, 12 November.

Index